Diversity Intelligence

Claretha Hughes

Diversity Intelligence

Reimagining and Changing Perspectives

Second Edition

Claretha Hughes
University of Arkansas
Fayetteville, AR, USA

ISBN 978-3-031-33249-4   ISBN 978-3-031-33250-0   (eBook)
https://doi.org/10.1007/978-3-031-33250-0

This Palgrave Macmillan imprint is published by the registered company Springer Nature Switzerland AG
The registered company address is: Gewerbestrasse 11, 6330 Cham, Switzerland

To the memory of my brother Eugene Hughes, Jr. and my father Eugene Hughes, Sr. who ensured that I was able to function in a world and workplace that is not always accepting of differences, especially those of American Black Females.

PREFACE

Worldwide changes were made to diversity acceptance in organizations after the murder of George Floyd and subsequent protests. However, there is still a lot of work to do for meaningful and sustainable changes inside organizations that want to improve their diversity efforts. Most of the language around the diversity changes have been centered around anti-racism. Racism had been ignored and is still being ignored along with many of the other protected class groups and categories, so it is good to see at least a concerted effort toward improvement. The plight of American Black women, for example, requires that organizations extend their efforts beyond anti-racism to include intersectionality as defined by Crenshaw (1989) and extended by Collins (1990).

Intersectionality is interlocking oppressions of race, sex, and class. Race, sex, and class discrimination are simultaneously by Black women and cannot be separated. Crenshaw noticed Black women's exclusion from employment in industrial plants through intersectional discrimination based on gender and race. The courts did not recognize these overlapping, discriminating systems and made Black women choose between racial and sex discrimination in lawsuits. Black women experience intersectional failures of the white feminist movement because they did not include questions of racism, and the anti-racism movement did not include questions of patriarchy. "The failure to interrogate patriarchy in anti-racism and racism within feminism continues to shape modern politics...they undermine our collective capacity to create a more robust coalition around social justice." (Crenshaw, 2016, Youtube Video, 30:46).

Diversity intelligence® DQ is "the capability of individuals to recognize the value of workplace diversity and to use this information to guide thinking and behavior" (Hughes & Brown, 2018, p. 264). The value of workplace diversity is found in all its people, not a select few. If individuals, especially leaders, are incapable of recognizing the value of each employee, they are not yet diversity intelligent.

This book fits in the literature in areas of leadership and business value. It is not written to be pigeon-holed as a marginalized diversity book. Diversity by itself only means different. DQ defines diversity in the context of manifest destiny (see Chapter 1) and workplace laws and mandates that have been required since 1964 in the United States and similarly in the United Kingdom and other developed nations. Multinational corporations throughout the world must follow protected class laws, mandates, and policies as applicable.

The debate that this book engages continues to be how do we reimagine diversity? How do we align diversity alongside intellectual, cultural, and emotional intelligence in the workplace? How do we truly have compliance when we see limited and measured changes in behavior toward protected class employees in the workplace? How do organizations continue to market themselves as Equal Employment Opportunity (EEO) compliant organizations when the evidence (i.e., Department of Labor settlements, EEOC filings, and settlements, Class Action lawsuits, etc...) shows otherwise?

This book aims to satisfy the need for solutions to why diversity training and management efforts continue to fall short of stated goals within organizations. With leaders who are not yet diversity intelligent, it is difficult for organizations to accomplish many goals—not just diversity goals. When leaders are incapable of utilizing all the talented employees within their organization because they lack the DQ to properly engage and interact with all their employees, the organization loses. They lose productivity, employee creativity, investment in developed employees who choose to leave the organization, credibility of being an EEO employer, potential of hiring diverse employees, contracts, and stock market price reductions because of their reputation toward diversity.

The benefits of DQ are different ways to see diversity as a positive for the organization; an end to the misinformation and confusion around why organizations must adhere to protected class groups and category laws, mandates, and policies; an understanding of the historical and moral link to diversity; and why it is more of a moral and ethical issue versus a legal issue.

One research question that is guiding this book is: How can something that is morally and ethically wrong be legally right? How can racism, agism, ableism, colorism, sexism, etc., ever be treated as if they are legally right in the workplace? In essence that is what this is all about. The laws exist to protect against these moral and ethical concerns; yet they are not followed and very few violators are held accountable.

DQ should be developed and integrated into leadership and career development plans. Organization leaders are not fully equipped to enhance organization goals through all employees without DQ. This updated book emphasizes the need for greater astuteness and strategic approaches toward diversity as it relates to leadership and career development.

DQ should be taught through both education and training. Leaders are missing the information somewhere throughout their leadership development journey. There are many books and research articles available that have covered the topic of diversity. However, diversity needs to be reimagined and DQ offers that opportunity. Some articles have suggested that global organizations integrate motivational CQ programs with diversity management (Christiansen & Sezerel, 2013). The diversity publications are often marginalized and isolated within the field of diversity as opposed to integrated into the leadership and career development literature.

As the global economy expands and the demographics within US society become more diverse, DQ is essential. There has been little evidence of diversity training success, and as organizations continue to adapt to global changes; diversity continues to be a buzz word without extensive tangible evidence of success in the workplace. This book suggests that DQ is a competency or skill that can be developed by organization leaders and integrated into leadership and career development plans and career management systems. Without effective DQ, organization leaders are creating and/or perpetuating adverse relationships between and among employees and reducing the effectiveness and productivity of employees within organizations.

This book seeks to offer changing perspectives to help leaders of a protected class employees lead all their employees ethically and fairly in the workplace. Racism is but one protected class category and Whites are not the only ones mistreating employees within the workplace nor are they the only group that lacks DQ. Having DQ and the proper tools and resources to apply it may reduce EEOC complaints, labor disputes, and lawsuits associated with diversity and other unfair practices in the workplace (D'Netto & Sohal, 1999; Fulkerson & Schuler, 1992; Jayne & Dipboye, 2004; Loden & Rosener, 1991; Morrison, 1992; Powell & Butterfield, 1994; Schreiber et al., 1993; Schuler et al., 1992).

Fayetteville, USA   Claretha Hughes

Acknowledgments Thank you to my daughter Karla R. Banks. I hope that she will face a better workplace than some that I have experienced. Thank you to Teuta Lokaj-Azemi for all her assistance with the reference list. Thank you to DeVaugh Stephens for specific feedback.

References

Christiansen, B., & Sezerel, H. (2013). Diversity Management in Transcultural Organizations. *Global Business Perspectives, 1*(2), 132–143.

Collins, P. H. (1990). *Black Feminist Thought: Knowledge, Consciousness, and the Politics of Empowerment*. Routledge.

Crenshaw, K. (1989). Demarginalizing the Intersection of Race and Sex: A Black Feminist Critique of Antidiscrimination Doctrine, Feminist Theory and Antiracist Politics. *University of Chicago Legal Forum, 1989*, 139–167.

Crenshaw, K. W. (2016, March 14). *On Intersectionality*. Youtube Video, 30:46. https://Www.Youtube.Com/Watch?V=-Dw4hlgypla

D'Netto, B., & Sohal, A. S. (1999). Human Resource Practices and Workforce Diversity: An Empirical Assessment. *International Journal of Manpower, 20*(8), 530–547.

Fulkerson, J. R., & Schuler, R. S. (1992). Managing Worldwide Diversity at Pepsi-Cola International. In S. E. Jackson (Ed.), *Diversity in the Workplace: Human Resources Initiatives, Society for Industrial and Organisational Psychology* (The Professional Practice Series). Guildford Press.

Hughes, C., & Brown, L. M. (2018). Exploring Leaders' Discriminatory, Passive-Aggressive Behavior Toward Protected Class Employees Using Diversity Intelligence. *Advances in Developing Human Resources, 20*(3), 263–284.

Jayne, M. E. A., & Dipboye, R. L. (2004). Leveraging Diversity to Improve Business Performance: Research Findings and Recommendations for Organizations. *Human Resource Management, 43*(4), 409–424.

Loden, M., & Rosener, J. B. (1991). *Workforce America! Managing Employee Diversity as a Vital Resource*. Business One Irwin.

Morrison, A. M. (1992). *The New Leaders: Guidelines on Leadership Diversity in America*. Jossey-Bass Publishers.

Powell, G. N., & Butterfield, D. A. (1994). Race, Gender and the Glass Ceiling: Empirical Study of Actual Promotions to Top Management. In *Annual Meeting of the Academy of Management*, Dallas, TX.

Schreiber, C. T., Price, K. F., & Morrison, A. (1993). Workplace Diversity and the Glass Ceiling: Practices, Barriers, Possibilities. *Human Resource Planning*, *16*(2), 51–69.

Schuler, R. S., Dowling, P. J., Smart, J. P., & Huber, V. L. (1992). *Human Resource Management in Australia* (2nd ed.). Harper Educational Publishers.

CONTENTS

1   Diversity Intelligence   1

2   Diversity Theories and Diversity Intelligent Perspectives   35

3   Diversity in Practice   45

4   Diversity Intelligence and Leadership Development:
    How Allyship, Anti-Racism, and Inclusive Language
    Hinder Diversity Efforts   73

5   Diversity Intelligence, Career Development,
    and Digital/Virtual Work   107

6   Diversity Intelligence and the Need for Diversity
    Expertise   135

7   Current Issues and Evolving Trends   153

Bibliography   169

Index   233

ABOUT THE AUTHOR

Claretha Hughes, Ph.D. Professor, teaches Human Resource Development at the University of Arkansas in Fayetteville, Arkansas. She has over 31 years of extensive professional experience in business and industry and continues to serve as a consultant to international, national, and state organizations. Her research interests include valuing people and technology in the workplace, technology development, diversity intelligence, learning technologies, and ethical and legal issues. She has published numerous articles in peer-reviewed journals and books and has authored or co-authored 16 books. She is a book proposal reviewer for SAGE, Emerald, IGI Global, and Palgrave Macmillan. She has completed a National Science Foundation Research in Formation of Engineers grant as a Co-PI. She is the 2022 recipient of the University of Arkansas Provost's Office Outstanding Mentor Award, 2021 recipient of the Academy of Human Resource Development's FORWARD Award, 2012 recipient of the Academy of Human Resource Development's R. Wayne Pace Book of the Year Award, and the 2009 University Council of Workforce and Human Resource Education Outstanding Assistant Professor Award. Dr. Hughes has a Ph.D. in Career and Technical Education from Virginia Tech specializing in training and development, an MT degree in Textile Technology Management from NC State University, a B.A. in Chemistry from Clemson University, and an M.B.A. from the Sam M. Walton College of Business at the University of Arkansas. She has publications in journals such as *Human Resource Development Review, Advances in Developing Human Resources, New Horizons in Adult Education and Human Resource Development, Human Resource Development International,* the *International Journal of Human Resource Development and Management,* and the *Journal of the North American Management Society.*

LIST OF FIGURES

Fig. 1.1   Hughes's Human Resource Development (HRD)
Value Creation Model (*Note* Hughes's HRD Value
Creation Model is printed with permission from Diversity
Intelligence® [DQ], LLC ©2022)   3
Fig. 1.2   Hughes' Diversity Intelligence (DQ) Conceptual Model   23

LIST OF TABLES

Table 1.1   The five values and DQ implications   5
Table 4.1   Eight drivers of execution and DQ implications   81
Table 4.2   High EQ versus DQ implications and propositions   90
Table 7.1   2015–2023 News headlines related to protected class
groups   160

CHAPTER 1

Diversity Intelligence

Diversity intelligence (DQ) evokes the question—why should anyone need it? To answer this question, diversity management has not been as successful as it could be because we have seen very little change in the workplace since the introduction of diversity management (Avery et al., 2023; Byrd & Hughes, 2021; Yadav & Lenka, 2020). DQ will not be embedded with diversity management or diversity and inclusion failure efforts. DQ looks at leadership development and why leaders are not following protected class laws, mandates, and policies while leading all their employees. If diversity management and diversity and inclusion efforts were being successfully implemented by workplace leaders, there would be no need for DQ. Leaders have shown themselves incapable of leading all their employees despite EQ (emotional), CQ (cultural), and IQ (intellectual) intelligence efforts.

To further respond to the question, the origin DQ as used in the context of this book, was derived from Dr. Hughes's (2010, 2012, in press) research on valuing people and technology in the workplace. Central to the valuing people and technology research are five common values of people and technology. The five common values are location, use, maintenance, modification, and time. When seeking to develop measures for leaders to measure the five values, it became evident that leaders could not measure the five values of people because leaders were missing a leadership component or competency to value all employees. How can leaders value all employees when they marginalize some protected class employees because they are different? At this point, there needed to be a way to ensure that leaders saw all employees. DQ became the competency and tool needed to ensure that leaders see and value all employees.

A Brief Description of Hughes's HRD Value Creation Model

DQ is centrally located in *Hughes's Human Resource Development (HRD) Value Creation Model* © 2022 (see Fig. 1.1). *Hughes's HRD Value Creation Model* is a seven-point model derived from Hughes's high-performance manufacturing industry experiences and extends Hughes's (2010) PT conceptual model. *Hughes's HRD Value Creation Model* provides a theoretical framework for further research and practical applications of management practices, training practices (Cascio, 2019), and HRD philosophy and strategies within organizations. The model will hopefully inspire the transformation of thinking and examination of ways to develop measures for the five values.

The Seven Points

1. The first point shows the three (cognitive, behavioral, and cultural) philosophical perspectives within which all organizations operate. The cognitive, behavioral, and cultural philosophical perspectives can be categorized as:

   - Cognitive: *Thinking.*
   - Behavioral: *Doing.*
   - Cultural: *Cultural Context.*

   Organizations typically operate within one dominant philosophical perspective that supports organizational strategies for performance but can include a combination of the philosophical perspectives.
2. The second point is the People as Technology (PT) conceptual model (Hughes, 2010) which contains the five values that explain how people and technology relate to each other within the workplace. PT suggests that managers and leaders should think of people positively and similarly to how they positively view technology within the workplace.

The Hughes HRD Value Creation Model

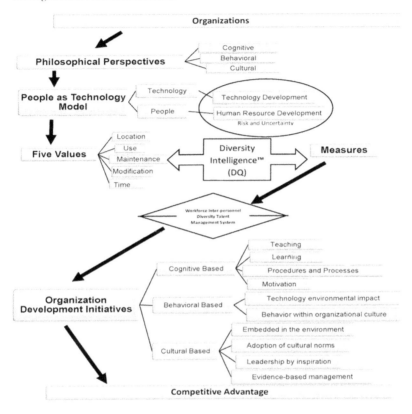

Fig. 1.1 Hughes's Human Resource Development (HRD) Value Creation Model (*Note* Hughes's HRD Value Creation Model is printed with permission from Diversity Intelligence® [DQ], LLC ©2022)

3. Point three involves the five values. The values are distinct and represent the multidimensionality of technology and people. Quantifying the values is important so that leaders can see their people's value as clearly as they see their technology value.

4. Point four describes DQ (Hughes, 2016) and how it can be used by leaders to better understand all employees. Diversity intelligent leaders will have the knowledge, workforce education and

training, and an understanding of their own perception of their behavior toward all employees. DQ will have the capability to lead all employees. Integrating DQ within organizational systems provides a reimagining diversity, equity, inclusion, and belonging efforts within organizations.

5. Point five describes ways that measurable five values can be integrated into the organization. The five values can be measured individually or collectively. There is no specified formula for the measures because the values are represented differently within organizations. Researchers, professionals, and practitioners can develop new measures.

6. Point six is the workforce inter-personnel diversity talent management system (Hughes, 2018) which includes employee potential (Cascio & Collings, 2022). Diversity intelligent leaders should be able to see the potential of all employees and manage all talent. Hughes (2012) introduced the concept of inter-personnel diversity and suggested that organizations resolve constraints related to workplace diversity to remain competitive. Inter-personnel means that there is diversity among all the employees—each individual employee is different and provides different values to the organization, and the difference can be assessed based on the individual characteristics of the location, use, maintenance, modification, and time value. She suggested that organization leaders determine diverse employees' benefit from career development opportunities; learn to recognize the inter-personnel diversity among employees who are perceived to be the same; and determine ways to avoid discriminating against employees by leveraging their understanding of the five values to achieve workforce diversity goals (Hughes, 2018). Organizations must educate their leaders to recognize and value the diversity of their workforce.

7. Point seven of the model addresses organization development (OD) initiatives that are used to develop technology and people and are aligned with the organizations' philosophical perspective.

Using DQ and the Five Values

The five values from *Hughes's HRD Value Creation Model* (Hughes, in press) can be used to help integrate DQ into leadership and career development processes within organizations (Table 1.1).

Table 1.1 The five values and DQ implications

Five values	DQ implications
Location value	
Location value is synonymous with power. It represents power of position, power to generate revenue, power to leverage resources, and power to serve as a catalyst for change	Protected class employees must have positions of power to achieve organization goals
Use value	
Use value (Hughes, 2010, 2012) can be described as a created value (Wenstop & Myrmel, 2006) as leaders learn to create more value through the effective use of employee skills and abilities within the workplace. Use value relates to the quality factor in a worker's productivity and requires integrity and a relationship of positive, mutual respect between the organization and the employee	Organizations leaders must end the mistreatment of protected class employees based on personal characteristics and value their contributions
Maintenance value	
Maintenance value is the alignment of employee KSAs with organization needs expressed by job analysis and job description. Organization must see growth potential for employee growth during the hiring process that can be enhanced through organization-provided training and development. Employee maintenance value is expressed through training and development and motivation. Maintenance value requires that the organization and the employee understand the formal knowledge needed by the employee to perform his job	For DQ to be achieved through maintenance value, protected class employees may need to teach others how to treat them. Leaders must recognize that they need DQ training to understand why protected class employees may not need training to solve problems presented to them by others who lack DQ
Modification value	

(continued)

Table 1.1 (continued)

Five values	DQ implications
Modification value is recognized through observation of the drive and ambition that the employee shows when wanting to personally enhance their job performance through self-developed growth and change. Employees use their intrinsic motivation to self-develop. Modification value examines how the individual grows and changes not only through activities provided by the organization but also activities that individuals use for self-development including education that may or may not align with their current jobs (Hughes, 2012). The key for the organization is to understand that some employees want to grow and change (Hughes, 2010, 2012; Kotter & Cohen, 2002)	Organization leaders must also understand how to adjust to protected class employees' need or convince the employees to adapt their new knowledge to the goals of the organization if feasible. Organization leaders must stop treating protected class group members' interpersonal leadership styles as wrong as opposed to recognizing the difference. Mutual, positive trust must be established between the organization and protected class group members. Protected class employees should continue to self-develop and recognize their strengths. They should not apologize for who are and strengthen their use of strategies to enhance leadership skills
Time value	
Time is measured in a continuum despite efforts to segregate its value in the workplace (Taylor, 1911). Protected class employees must determine if the organization is appropriate for their KSAs and whether organization leaders value their inputs	Continuous turnover of protected class employees is not cost-effective or valuable for the organization. Underpaying protected class employees for their time does not reflect DQ

DIVERSITY HISTORY AS A FOUNDATION OF DQ

Understanding the history of the topic of diversity and exploring the influence that has on the current reality is the foundation of DQ. Anand and Winters (2008) found that although "rooted in social justice philosophy, civil rights legislation, and more recently, business strategy, diversity has evolved into a rather amorphous field where the very word itself invokes a variety of meanings and emotional responses" (p. 356). Why is there such controversy when the word diversity is mentioned in the US society and the workplace? Many organizations and individuals say that they value diversity, but they have simply corrupted the term diversity. Some people are also corrupting the term woke (Thomason et al., 2023; Zavattaro & Bearfield, 2022) to create confusion while others appreciate the benefits of being woke (Okpokiri, 2022) or aware of racial prejudice and discrimination. Both terms are being corrupted because it works for the agenda of those individuals who fear change to their comfortable status quo.

DQ is not a shorthand to imply diversity and inclusion (D&I); diversity, equity, and inclusion (DEI); belongingness; or diversity management because those practices have not involved the history of manifest destiny or defined diversity within the context or protected class groups and categories. DQ defines diversity specifically in a context and is measurable using the Hughes and Liang DQ scale© 2020.

WHITE MALES INTRODUCED THE TERM DIVERSITY INTO THE WORKPLACE

The term diversity was introduced into the workplace by White males to replace Affirmative Action (AA) (Peterson, 1999) and create an environment of confusion. Diversity, in some ways, has reduced the progress that could have been made by those who have been and continue to be discriminated against because of their race. Those who continue to create confusion misusing the term diversity cannot be allowed to win because of the chaos and misunderstandings that have been stimulated. DQ is the answer to resolve the abundance of ignorance, confusion, and chaos in the US society and the workplace. DQ requires the creation of a knowledge structure that supports differences and eliminates ignorance, confusion, and chaos.

Langston Hughes (1936) in his great poem "*Let America Be America Again*" suggests that we, the people, must redeem our nation together. When did the need to redeem our nation begin? When the United States' Black citizens are excluded, marginalized, ignored, and prevented from achieving their full potential, a nation, and subsequently, the nation's organizations suffer. However, the damage can be repaired. It can be repaired by ending accusations against Black citizens of race-card playing, being too sensitive, and being paranoid. Gaslighting employees on the job must end.

SOME HUMANS HAVE NOT VALUED DIVERSITY

Historically, some humans have, consistently, not valued diversity (e.g., Holocaust, Slavery, Colonialism, Apartheid, and Southern United States' Segregation Laws). DNA evidence reveals that the entire human race originated in Africa. Yet, human beings appear stoically dedicated to segregating themselves based on personal characteristics. The primary characteristic has been race, but gender, ethnicity, religion, and other characteristics are also used for discrimination. Racism has been an ugly part of human history from centuries. The root of diversity began with racism. The best leaders have role clarity and are cognizant of personal biases and mitigate their effect, while wise organizations actively promote cultures that assist in avoiding biases. Manifest destiny is an example of the negative and unabated outcome of biases.

Manifest Destiny

Although slavery in North America can be traced back to 1619, the concept of diversity within the diversity movement away from AA can be traced to the idea of Manifest Destiny which originated in the eighteenth century (Gates & Curran, 2022; Gómez, 2007; Horsman, 1981; Pratt, 1927; Schlesinger, 2005; Stefancic, 2011). America's imperial age focused on a two-part political ideology of American Exceptionalism and Manifest Destiny. American Exceptionalism meant that the people who discovered America believed that they were God's chosen people, and Manifest Destiny meant that they were supposed to control the North American continent from and spread American citizens over the North American continent (Pratt, 1927; Stefancic, 2011; Woodard, 2011). Manifest Destiny was used to perpetuate the idea that Americans were superior to all other people (Gómez, 2007; Horsman, 1981; Mehan, 1996; Stefancic, 2011). Individuals who spread and continue to spread the idea of Manifest Destiny believed that they must convert others to the American way of life. The manifest destiny quest is founded upon and rooted in a White, colonial mindset whose aim was and is to neutralize differences among the people represented in North America, and primarily in the United States (US). Manifest destiny is a quest for an all-White male leadership, forever, that diminishes all other races of people despite them being a people of the global minority. Some life activities, including activities in the workplace, are based on racial distinctions, and have led to the unsubstantiated, marginalization of many people. Manifest destiny was used to say that all Blacks, for example, had inferior intellectual/mental intelligence (IQ) (Stern, 1912). While many manifest destiny proponents' premises have been debunked (Chua & Rubenfeld, 2014), some of the remnants still proliferate throughout US society and workplaces. Some US citizens still seek to maintain homogeneity in executive leadership roles.

Manifest destiny is relevant to the theory of DQ because of the US's role in the globalization efforts. Manifest destiny has been suggested as too specific for this theory because of the suggestion that US citizens who support manifest destiny feel that they must convert others to the US way of doing things. The transhistorical and global phenomenon called "imperial instinct" that insists on colonizing, occupying, and othering other people may provide a better explanation of the conversion process, but manifest destiny is the root concept for creating difference.

MANMADE DESIGNATION OF DIVERSE PEOPLES

According to Schlesinger (2005)

> "Imperialism" did not appear as a word until the nineteenth century. Its first application was not to overseas expansion but to the domestic pretensions of Napoleon III, emperor of France. As late as 1874, when Walter Bagehot wrote "Why an English Liberal May Look Without Disapproval on the Progress of Imperialism in France," he referred to France's internal polity, not to its foreign policy. The contemporary meaning of imperialism as the domination of distant peoples appeared toward the end of the nineteenth century. (p. 43)

Manifest destiny and imperialism during the Enlightenment era (Gates & Curran, 2022) both helped to create diverse populations and are obviously the source of intercultural misunderstandings in world history and the workplace. Many diverse Americans such as Native Americans, African Americans, Cuban Americans, Marshallese Americans, Vietnamese Americans, Hawaiians, Alaskans, Puerto Ricans, European Americans, Mexican Americans, and others came into existence because of the White Americans' quest for manifest destiny (Gómez, 2007; Horsman, 1981). These Americans' identities are not simply a result of the mixing of two peoples (for example, Mexican Americans) under the colonial conquest of Hispanic territories. White men, using manifest destiny, created entirely new non-hybrid identities and some mixing of peoples including Mexican Americans, Marshallese Americans, and others. Their expansion of manifest destiny within and beyond North America to spread democracy across the world created diversity. When the US military polluted the Marshall Islands with nuclear waste during atomic bomb testing, some of the Marshallese people were forced to leave their islands for health reasons and become Americans. The results of wars started by America's quest also forced many other populations including the Vietnamese, Syrians, Cubans, Iraqis, and others to become ethnic minorities in this country and protected class groups when they enter the workforce. A societal, generalizable definition of diversity is: "The product of one's origin and White men's quest for manifest destiny" (Hughes, 2016).

In addition to all the subcultures in America, Woodard (2011, 2013) suggested that there are 11 different American Nations within the United States. Why is it that we have all these types or subcultures of Americans and 11 identifiable American Nations as opposed to everyone just being American? If this question were not needed, there would be little need for the many definitions of diversity that exist. Every group, including families, has their own definition of diversity—they are diverse because everyone is a different age; however, for workplace purposes, the federal government provided protected class groups and categories of employees. These are groups and categories of people the government has deemed at risk for discrimination and marginalization based on some aspect(s) of who they are. In this book, the protected class groups and categories will be used to frame the readers' understanding of diversity in the workplace. Workplace leaders should have DQ to effectively lead people from protected class groups and categories.

Some leaders manipulate classifications of people to perpetuate their personal desires.

"The federal government officially categorizes people with origins in Lebanon, Iran, Egypt and other countries in the MENA region as White" (Wang, 2022). The US government designates what are considered to be the "good" African nations and classifies their citizens as white (Maghbouleh et al., 2022) even when those citizens do not agree with the white designation (Resnicow et al., 2022; Wang, 2022). There will always be individuals telling you how you should act, what you should think and do; but there is nothing better for you than being who you are. Everyone is different and should be appreciated for that difference.

DQ Theory and Model Concept

DQ Theory is built upon manifest destiny and American pragmatism. Manifest destiny is a US version of the global problem that creates diversity among people and pragmatism seeks to understand why and how this DQ theory will be put into practice. Pragmatism is also the philosophical approach and justification of DQ solutions. Manifest destiny describes and situates a broader global phenomenon—that large nations tend to seek to expand their borders (e.g., continentalism plus nationalism)—in the context of this book's engagement with US workplace culture and the global reach of its professional norms. DQ theory situates diversity in the workplace girded by the federal government's definition of protected class groups and categories along with other mandates including AA.

Hughes (2014) is defined within the context of the US workplace because there is currently not a consistently accepted and generalizable definition of diversity (Banks, 2009; Hughes, 2015; Jones, 1999; Peterson, 1999; Qin et al., 2014; Roberson, 2019; Van Ewijk, 2011; Wellner, 2000). DQ is defined by Hughes as "the capability of individuals to recognize the value of workplace diversity and to use this information to guide thinking and behavior" (Hughes & Brown, 2018, p. 264). Hughes (2016) described DQ as "valuing the differences in people without trying to make everyone alike" (p. 5). Banks et al. (2010) noted that over 66 percent of participants did not agree with their own workplace definition of diversity. Thus, DQ is based on the federal government's definition of protected class groups and categories of laws and mandates that contribute to the diversity and are used within US organizations. After leaders have received the federally required training on the laws and mandates, they should begin to be able to apply some concepts of DQ.

NEGATIVE INTENTIONAL BEHAVIORS OF LEADERS

Intentional behaviors from leadership as expressed through their mistreatment of protected class employees have not been extensively explored (Mackey et al., 2021). Laws were created based on some egregious action and evidence of that action cannot be overlooked. However, not enough leaders know what has happened because of gag orders and non-disclosure agreements when legal cases are settled. We know that compliance and legal training has been provided to leaders, and after that training the mistreatment of protected class employees has increased (Dobbin & Kalev, 2022).

LEADERS' LACK OF INTERPERSONAL SKILLS

The ability to influence and communicate among several groups, which should include protected class employees, are two leadership competencies that are drivers of promotion and advancement (Ireland & Hitt, 1999; Tarique & Schuler, 2010). Human resource development organizations have identified interpersonal skills as a highly valued, critical competency for leaders in the workplace (Arneson et al., 2013; Davis et al., 2004; Greer & Peters, 2022; Hogan & Kaiser, 2005). Laud and Johnson (2013) found that interpersonal skills which included people interaction, social communications, and emotional intelligence was ranked first by both men and women and considered a foundational skill used to advance professional careers. Regardless of being ranked first by the leaders, interpersonal skills are not one-person-dependent competencies (Hughes, 2014). American Black females are often treated as if they are the only determinants of the success of their interpersonal relationships in the workplace because they are confident about their self-management (Hughes, 2014). Others use their confidence against them by downgrading their interpersonal skills to prevent them from achieving strategic, introspective, and thoughtful work that is worthy of promotion and advancement.

As workforce demographics continue to change to include more protected class employees, so must the interpersonal skills of leaders (Byrd, 2007; Doverspike et al., 2000; Helgesen, 1990). Leaders pride themselves on having appropriate interpersonal skills and consistently degrade others whom they perceive to be lacking in interpersonal skills when they do not communicate in ways that are comfortable to and for the leader. This does not mean that the person, necessarily, has poor interpersonal skills. It means that the leader has chosen to present the person to others as having poor interpersonal skills to keep the person from progressing within the organization. This has been notoriously perpetrated against American Black females within the workplace by leaders who profess to them that they respect their difference in communication style. Yet, it is used against them mercilessly to keep them from moving into leadership positions for which they are qualified. It is not what you said, it is how you said it is the constant refrain. Right does not become wrong because you did not like the way it was presented to you. However, right most often becomes wrong when it is the American Black woman who makes the first mention of something new that someone else wants to take credit for. American Black women have benefitted the least from AA and other diversity-related policies. White women have benefitted the most, followed by Black males, from AA.

Workplace environments have evolved and require increased inter-personal skills (Hogan & Kaiser, 2005; Laud & Johnson, 2013), but leaders are often given a pass when their interpersonal skills are inappropriate. Leaders, in many organizations, are allowed to self-manage their performance and expectations (Vroom, 1964). Self-management strategies would be fine if leaders could be trusted to treat protected class employees fairly and if they were to objectively assess their own needed personal and behavioral changes (Abele & Wiese, 2008; Kouzes & Posner, 1995; Manz, 1986; Murphy & Ensher, 2001; Pfeffer, 1994) which would include the lack of DQ.

Some protected class employees perceive that leaders who lack DQ are disrespecting them, are insensitive to their needs, stereotyping their behaviors, and showing ignorance of their protected class status. Protected class employees are compelled to suffer and endure poor inter-personal treatment in the workplace because of leaders' lack of DQ. Protected class employees' interpersonal skills are supposed to help them handle situations in a professional manner within workplace settings despite leaders' lack of the appropriate interpersonal skills to treat them fairly.

RELATIONSHIP MANAGEMENT AND DIVERSITY

The work environment is almost singularly dependent on relationship management, and it is difficult to build relationships with others when there is a lack of understanding regarding differences. As a key compo-nent in the leadership development of executives in an organization, relationship management has been avoided or has not been used to hold leaders accountable for the lack of diversity in executive positions. Nothing has compelled executives to build relationships with protected class employees to the extent that they are appropriately represented in leadership positions within many organizations.

LEADERS' NEED FOR DQ

Leaders can no longer feign ignorance or purposely ignore their responsibility to protected class employees and lead successfully. Leaders must be able to objectively distinguish personal culture from organization culture without creating tension within the workplace. They cannot marginalize employees who are not like them or who do not assimilate to their standards. "The more you know about an individual, the less it makes sense to rely on general findings about a group of which he or she is a part" (Benko & Pelster, 2013, p. 81). Leaders must respect everyone in the workplace and not make assumptions about anyone based solely on identity groups (Hughes, 2012).

Appreciation and understanding of diversity by leaders need to be a permanent part of organizational culture. Diversity needs to be ingrained within the entire organization system. Executive leaders have the power (Pfeffer, 1994) to influence the diversity culture of the organization and provide justice to protected class employees. There is ignorance displayed by some leaders when it relates to diversity. Some leaders make the cognitive choice to discriminate against some protected class employees. Some leaders' ignorance is revealed by their actions and leads to questions such as: Are leaders' actions and behaviors negative toward protected class employees because there are few or no consequences for their behaviors? Are leaders' behaviors and actions against protected class employees accepted because the culture within the workplace supports this type of behavior? Do leaders not know better? Are leaders truly ignorant or are they doing this intentionally? How can leaders be this unconscious about their personal actions and how those actions are perceived by others?

CASE SCENARIO: HOW LEADERS' WORDS DIMINISH BLACK FEMALES AS HUMAN BEINGS

The University of South Carolina's women's basketball team finished the 2022–2023 basketball season 36–1. The team is a predominantly Black team with a Black female head coach who won the National Championship for the 2021–2022 season. They were seeking to defend their National Title. The team height averages around 6'2" tall, and they were the best rebounding and defensive team in the nation. However, when they defeated the University of Connecticut for the first time ever in Connecticut, the UCONN Head coach stated in the

National media "It's just appalling what teams do to her now," he said. "It's not basketball anymore. I don't know what it is, but it's not basketball" Forcing Coach Staley of SC to defend her team (see South Carolina's Staley defends team after Auriemma comments—ABC News (go.com) https://abcnews.go.com/Sports/wireStory/south-car olinas-staley-defends-team-after-auriemma-comments-96976101.

Auriemma later stated that his comments were aimed at the referees (see UConn's Auriemma says criticism aimed at refs, not Gamecocks https://www.espn.com/womens-college-basketball/story/_/id/356 20030/uconn-auriemma-says-criticism-aimed-refs-not-gamecocks). However, some damage had been done. After his comments, national news media writers wrote articles calling two of the team's inside players bruisers: "South Carolina's bruisers Aliyah Boston and Kamilla Cardoso established the paint as their protected domain. The Tigers ventured near the rim at a risk and were fortunate to emerge with their ego intact" (see Kim Mulkey is right about South Carolina. Good luck stopping Gamecocks (theadvertiser.com) https://www.theadvertiser.com/story/ sports/college/lsu/2023/02/13/south-carolina-womens-basketball-gamecocks-kim-mulkey-lsu-score/69892729007/). Bruisers is a male term not a female term to be used to describe young college-aged women.

When the team made it to the final four, their opposing team's head coach stated to the national media that "I mean, they're an amazing offensive rebounding team," Bluder said. "Somebody kind of just described it to me as you're going to a bar fight when you try to go rebound against them, they're just so good." She later stated: "There was absolutely no ill intent," Bluder said in the news conference setting up the Hawkeyes' meeting Sunday with LSU in the national championship game. "I know coaches will take things and spin it to try to motivate their team," the Iowa coach said. "I've done that, I'm sure. So be it with that. I really meant it as a compliment, like you are going to have to fight harder than you've ever fought in your life to get a defensive rebound against this team because they are so good. That's what my intent was."

Coach Staley stated: "We're not bar fighters. We're not thugs. We're not monkeys. We're not street fighters." Staley said comments relayed to her after the event Thursday night were hurtful to her players. "If you really knew them, if you really knew them, like you really want to know other players that represent this game, you would think differently," Staley said Friday. "So don't judge us by the color of our skin. Judge us by how we approach the game" (see Staley defends players again; Iowa coach says no ill intent https://apnews.com/article/iowa-south-carolina-staley-blu der-bar-fight-ce250bbe1ff45e99d84964b50cebf616).

The concern is not that the team lost in the semifinal game, the concern is how the words of leaders and national media writers who should know better, choose not to know and do better. They verbalized many of the negative stereotypes against Black women. They only saw their Blackness and chose to ignore the intersectionality of Gender and Class that these young women represent for themselves, their team, their university, and young Black women throughout the world. Questions to consider:

1. Why should a Black female head coach have to defend her and her players' Blackness when White coaches do not have to defend their and their players' Whiteness?
2. To what extent should head coaches who are representing their institutions be held accountable to protected class status policies of their institution as it relates to students and peers both on and off campus?

The opposite of ignorance is intelligence. DQ was missing from many leaders' core competencies when dealing with others who are different than themselves. This missing competency in and of itself would not be a problem if the leader realized their lack of knowledge and genuinely tried to learn the information. However, many leaders do not invest the time necessary to learn what they do not know nor communicate with the offended employee to find out more about why the behavior was offensive. The superiority complex and ego tripping (Lawrence, 1987, 2002) displayed by some leaders do not allow much room for vulnerability and genuine caring behavior. The many workplace problems from leaders without DQ continue. There are many employees, representing protected class groups and categories receiving mistreatment from leaders who were supposed to be protecting them using federal, state, and local laws, mandates, and policies designed for such purposes. EEOC becomes irrelevant when the law violations are not reported.

The main question that this book seeks to answer is: With all the forms of leadership that have been researched and adopted within organizations (Burke et al., 2006; Chandler et al., 2022; Fischer & Sitkin, 2023;

Legood et al., 2021; Mackey et al., 2021; Vogel et al., 2021), why has diversity not been integrated into organizations effectively? How can this be when there is diversity training available to leaders in many workplaces? Billions of dollars have been spent on diversity training; yet there are still numerous diversity-related lawsuits, EEOC complaints, and Department of Labor settlements, so the training cannot be working effectively. Or the training is working, and leaders choose not to use what they have learned during training when they return to their jobs.

How is it acceptable that leaders are routinely allowed to ignore federal laws and organization policies that leaders were trained to uphold? Leaders are still discriminating against protected class employees ethically and illegally. In some cases, diversity training is not mandated, so many leaders are not attending and are not being taught the required laws and policies. The laws and policies are also not often taught within k-12, undergraduate, graduate, and professional schools, so the ignorance is perpetuated until it becomes a problem within workplaces as is evidenced by the many EEOC complaints and legal cases brought forth and settled which proves that there exists a lack of DQ among leaders.

Resistance to DQ

In practice, diversity has been difficult to quantify and achieve. Opposition to diversity is always swift when diversity is mentioned in the workplace. Why the continued opposition to diversity? The answer includes leaders' lack of DQ, and the insecurity shown, by leaders with power, toward those who seek equal treatment, and procedural and organizational justice (Quillian et al., 2017; Sonnemaker, 2021). Many protected class employees do not receive procedural or organizational justice in the workplace (Areheart, 2019; Cropanzano et al., 2007; Hoang et al., 2022). Without DQ, leaders cannot provide procedural justice.

There are numerous areas of resistance from individuals who believe that DQ is not needed and/or should not be a theory because there is already CQ. My argument is that there is diversity within cultures which further supports my assertion that there is a lack of DQ among individuals who believe CQ addresses all diversity issues. There is also resistance to the idea of diversity being an intelligence. It is an intelligence because it can be taught the same way that IQ, EQ, and CQ are taught.

AA has provided some opportunities for minorities and women. American Blacks are often not employed because of their skin color (Sims,

2010; Sissoko et al., 2023), and when they are hired and display their natural, cultural differences, they are viewed as difficult to manage when in fact they are not understood. Leaders have not done enough to educate themselves on the difference between difficult to manage and their lack of understanding that each individual American Black person is different. The use of stereotypes is inappropriate when attempting to manage American Black persons. Some diversity efforts have failed (Dobbin & Kalev, 2016, 2022; Hemphill & Haines, 1997; Tallarigo, 1998) and these failures occur and will continue without DQ in the workplace. DQ is needed so that leaders can channel its use throughout the workplace like IQ, EQ, and CQ.

EQUITY THEORY AND RESISTANCE TO DIVERSITY

Equity theory (Adams, 1963) offered the belief that employees weigh their input against their outcome from their jobs and compare their perceived input-outcome ratio with the perceived input-outcome ratio to that of relevant others. Equity theory may be the motivational theory that some individuals are using to oppose diversity in the workplace. Equity theory "suggests that motivation is strongly influenced by the desire to be treated fairly and be people's perceptions about whether they have been treated fairly" (Werner & DeSimone, 2012, p. 53). Those in opposition to protected class employees' treatment in the workplace may perceive that they, personally, are not being treated fairly because they, personally, did no harm to protected class employees and the treatment that protected class employees receive is unwarranted. They fail to understand systemic discrimination as described by critical race theory (CRT) that has existed for centuries with the lingering effects remaining as described by Bell (1980, 1995, 2003) and Crenshaw (2010). The damage must be rectified by those who remain. Their lack of DQ knowledge fuels their unsubstantiated behavior toward protected class group individuals.

COGNITIVE-BASED THEORY
AND RESISTANCE TO DIVERSITY

Cognitive-based Theory explains that a person will behave based on their thoughts and beliefs (Werner & DeSimone, 2012) and may also be another theory that could explain the negative behavior that is displayed by individuals opposed to protected class employees. Employees harbor learned thoughts and beliefs from their childhood that effect their adult behavior. Discrimination including prejudices and biases are taught and are valid examples of cognitive-based behaviors. Discriminatory actions and behaviors are moral and ethical judgments made by individuals in society and the workplace.

DQ and Leadership Responsibility

Organizations expect effective leadership techniques and characteristics to be always used and displayed by their leaders. The characteristics and techniques of leaders vary depending upon who the leader is and the organization's expectations. There are continuous debates regarding who is and what makes an effective leader. Bruce (2001) provided the following characteristics and techniques of effective leaders: Leaders are authentic; express their humanity; understand key competencies; plan for success; involve everyone in strategic planning; plan for succession; manage human capital; possess integrity, values, and intuition; build strong teams; are competent coaches; manage performance through communications; exercise influence; manage and build hope and trust in others; manage knowledge effectively; have vision; and create better ways to measure performance. There is no mention of diversity within these techniques and characteristics. It is assumed that effective leaders will use these techniques and characteristics to benefit all employees including protected class employees. If they do not use their effectiveness to benefit all employees, how can they be considered effective leaders?

Zenger and Folkman (2012), after more than 30 years of research, identified 16 traits most exemplified by top leaders who were deemed to be displaying effectiveness. The traits are taken initiative; practice self-development; display high integrity and honesty; drive for results; develop others; inspire and motivate others; build relationships; collaboration and teamwork; establish stretch goals; champion change; solve problems and analyze issues; communicate powerfully and prolifically; connect the group to the outside world; innovate; technical or professional expertise; and develop strategic perspective. Again, none of the traits include diversity suggesting that the researchers assume that diversity is encompassed within the traits. Taking it for granted that leaders will treat protected class group members fairly to achieve organizational diversity goals has proven to not be an effective decision.

According to Bossidy et al. (2002), organizations cannot deliver on its commitments or adapt well to change unless all leaders practice the discipline of execution at all levels. Execution is the missing link between aspirations and results and must be a part of the organization's strategy so that it can meet its goals. Strategies and goals fail because essential execution steps that are supposed to happen do not happen. Diversity goals often fail in organizations because of a lack of execution. Execution of diversity fails because of leaders' lack of DQ. Bossidy et al. further suggested that the leader institutes a culture and processes for executing goals. Thus, leaders must develop and institute a culture and processes for executing DQ. Proper execution of diversity-intelligent initiatives suggests that leaders are proficient in their knowledge regarding what needs to be done and do not mind championing diversity efforts.

Leaders with DQ can navigate broad social, cultural, racial, and other human differences. They are also able to comprehend and appropriately use their extensive knowledge of protected class employees in the workplace. DQ requires leaders to obtain and exemplify the knowledge to understand protected class employees, the legal mandates, and the executive orders that were established for protected class employees' protection in the workplace (Hughes, 2016). DQ is established through an understanding of manifest destiny, the history and reasoning for the existence of the Civil Rights Act of 1964, the Equal Employment Opportunity Commission (EEOC), Affirmative Action (Thomas, 1990), and other policies to protect diverse individuals from discriminatory practices in the workplace. DQ requires both cognitive and behavioral actions on the part of the individual to be effective. Knowing what to do and not doing it is not an excuse (Buckley et al., 2001).

To exemplify DQ leaders should be able to appreciate and leverage diversity by doing the following:

1. DQ requires persons in leadership to show that they can influence the motivation of others who are different than themselves.
2. To be able to motivate diverse individuals the leader must first be able to recognize the difference between himself and others without it being an obstacle to performance (the leader and the diverse individual).
3. DQ requires leaders to show that they understand the difference between themselves and others through their actions and behaviors. It cannot be all talk and no action (Ng & Sears, 2020).

4. DQ requires leaders to demonstrate accepting of others' perceived differences as strengths and not weaknesses.

Leaders and managers must always display their DQ. DQ means knowing how to behave in the presence of diverse identity categories, including knowing when not to change one's behavior. Pretending, through verbal communication, that one has DQ when your actions reflect otherwise can be very destructive to workplace relationships.

Unless DQ is understood and taken seriously by all organization leaders, it is futile to expect change to occur. Leaders think that they know what diversity is and how to implement diversity initiatives, but there is a gap between what leaders perceive that they know and what they communicate, verbally and through their behavior, to diverse employees. The behavior subscale within the Hughes and Liang DQ scale© 2020 supports this statement. An example of feedback from someone who took the assessment:

> I think the questionnaire was helpful and it forced me to recognize that there were several areas where I thought I knew the answer, but [I] didn't always have a lot of confidence. In those areas, I know I need to improve, so the questions helped shine light on some blind spots of mine.

DQ can be used to bridge this gap by clearly assessing what leaders truly know and what they are consistently doing that is working to enhance diversity efforts. DQ can be used to improve leadership efforts, including communication style, work processes, training, education, and career development, toward employees.

DQ is knowledge which can be acquired and developed by organization leaders and integrated into organization leadership and talent development plans (Hughes, 2016). Without DQ, organization leaders struggle to maintain positive relationships with protected class employees and reduce their ability to inspire employees to increase productivity for organizations. Despite being taught to be intellectually intelligent (IQ), emotionally intelligent (EQ), and culturally intelligent (CQ), organization leaders are routinely failing at achieving diversity goals. The failures are often reflected in high turnover among protected class employees, lawsuits, and EEOC cases filed and/or won by protected class employees.

DQ Model Development

Dubin's (1976) theory building model was used to develop the DQ model (see Fig. 1.2) and theory. Two units of the DQ model are leaders and employees. The laws of interaction within the model are among IQ, EQ, CQ, and DQ. The primary boundary of the model is the organization, and the secondary boundary of the model is a global society. The system states are primarily the leaders' cognitive and behavioral perspectives (Burkhardt & Brass, 1990; Cappelli & Singh, 1992; Huselid, 1995; Latham et al., 1979; Lawler, 1986; Sternberg & Vroom, 2002; Vroom, 2003; Walton, 1985) but secondarily those of the stakeholders as well (March & Simon, 1958; Vroom & Maier, 1961). The propositions of the model are:

> Proposition 1: When leaders use DQ, their and their employees' thoughts and actions about protected class employees will broaden and improve.
>
> Proposition 2: When the organization supports the use of DQ, protected class employees' integration and inclusion in organization activities will improve.
>
> Proposition 3: When leaders improve their DQ behavior, employee productivity will increase.
>
> Proposition 4: As leaders apply DQ, they will integrate DQ with other intelligences including IQ, EQ, and CQ and create value for the organization by reducing adverse situations with protected class employees.
>
> Proposition 5: As leaders improve their DQ, diversity training initiatives may result in tangible change for the organization as evidenced by increased intellectual capital and financial success.
>
> Proposition 6: When leaders use DQ organizations' goals and efforts are achieved and/or improved.
>
> Proposition 7: When leaders promote DQ within the organization, all employees become aware of DQ and confusion, ignorance, and chaos lessen.
>
> Proposition 8: When leaders use DQ organizations' diversity goals and efforts are achieved and/or improved.

Organization leaders are critical to the success of DQ because they lead other employees and manage the organization's diversity efforts including

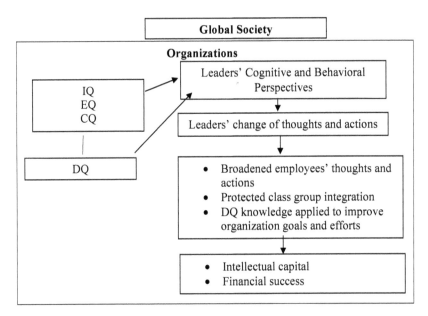

Fig. 1.2 Hughes' Diversity Intelligence (DQ) Conceptual Model

diversity training seminars and workshops, administering policies and laws that are designed to ensure protected class employees' welfare, and maintaining preventative measures such as whistleblowing protections (Gotanda, 1996; Kulik & Roberson, 2008; Milem et al., 2005).

Nahapiet and Ghoshal (1998) defined intellectual capital as "the knowledge and knowing capability of a social collectivity, such as an organization, intellectual community, or professional practice" (p. 245). To achieve and/or enhance intellectual capital, leaders are required to be intellectually capable (Swart, 2006) of using their IQ, EQ, CQ, and DQ to succeed. They must understand that all their actions affect the financial success of the organization, and that financial success is influenced by the social conscious efforts of stockholders and the public. Appropriate treatment of protected class employees using DQ benefits all stakeholders.

CONCLUSION

Mahatma Gandhi (2016) once said that "[t]he difference between what we are doing and what we're capable of doing would solve most of the world's problems." Capability is essential to leaders being able to apply the training and education that they receive in the workplace. Leaders may be capable, but do not always do what they need to do with regard to diversity. DQ gives leaders the capability to enhance the diversity efforts of their organizations and eliminates their excuses regarding with they are personally willing to do to improve their actions and behaviors toward all employees. Organization leaders are not showing that they have DQ and behave with DQ. There is clearly a place and a need for DQ within the leadership and career development competencies of organization leaders. If organizations can hire for EQ (Bielaszka-DuVernay, 2014), IQ, and CQ, they can also hire for DQ and not assume that it is a part of the other intelligences, particularly CQ. DQ is just as important as IQ, EQ, and CQ and the ability to appreciate and leverage diversity is an "intelligence" that is separate and apart from the other intelligences. DQ holds its own value in organizations and society. Diversity is a moral decision and an ethical issue.

Without an accepted and applied definition of diversity in the workplace, there is confusion, chaos, and ignorance among individuals who are tasked to implement diversity management and other diversity initiatives. Inequity in the workplace remains a problem, and I will not attempt to say that there is a broad solution to it. If each leader decides that discrimination of any kind will not occur because of any negative action on his part, the situation will become better. It has been 69 years since the Supreme Court's Brown vs. Board of Education decision and the country is still making progress at "all deliberate speed." All deliberate speed is like the word diversity, it is empty without any specific classification or categorization of meaning.

It doesn't seem to be a requirement for leaders to declare if they can be fair to all their employees within the workplace. They don't have to, to my knowledge, sign an oath against discrimination. If they do, then there needs to be better enforcement of the policy. I truly believe that employees should be provided an anonymous hotline to call, within their organization, and complain about discriminatory teachers and leaders. The caller need not be the person directly affected. Third-party notification is acceptable within sexual harassment policies and could be effective within all protected class group policies. When protected class group problem complaints are reported outside the organization to the EEOC, lawyers, or Department of Labor, and other entities, it is often too late to be resolved internally and amicably. All protected class discrimination, especially racism, should be treated the same way or more stringently than sexual harassment. There are few protected class categories as broad as sexual harassment, but somehow it is dealt with, and racism is almost always overlooked. This is beginning to change since the murder of George Floyd in 2020 (Barrie, 2020; Tedam & Cane, 2022).

DQ requires that one reflects upon one's own perception of others who are different than oneself. What understanding do you have of those who are different than you? What can you do to clarify any misunderstanding that you have of others who are different than you? The Human Resource Development literature will benefit from DQ theorization because it can impact how leaders can better engage with employees who are in protected class groups and categories. Often leaders assume that they have made appropriate engagement with protected class employees when they have not, and their actions are such that the protected class employees will not tell them that they have missed an opportunity. DQ will allow them to know the appropriate behaviors.

DQ has the potential to benefit the HR literature by allowing the HR literature to lean less heavily toward the viewpoint of the leaders and the protected class groups and categories of employees as well. The protected class groups and categories of employees will have a voice (Morrison, 2023) within the workplace and truly believe that they have been heard. It will also contribute to the National HRD (NHRD) literature as it attempts to achieve its humanistic goal of creating well-being of people in more under-developed nations. Its researchers may want to examine the effect of manifest destiny and similar concepts around the world including Slavophilism (the nineteenth-century Russian type), pan-Africanism (the late twentieth-century African type) and others. McLean and McLean (2001) proposed the following definition of NHRD:

> Human resource development is any process or activity that, either initially or over the long term, has the potential to develop … work-based knowledge, expertise, productivity and satisfaction, whether for personal or group/team gain, or for the benefit of an organization, community, nation, or, ultimately, the whole of humanity. (p. 322)

DQ awareness and instruction will help leaders and managers realize and tap into the positive potential that exists in relationships among workers who understand and appreciate the real differences that unite them in organizations. DQ training will attune leaders to recognize protected class subtleties. DQ theorization will make scholars aware of the multiplicity of intelligences and how those intelligences benefit HRD. The meaning of DQ theory cannot be fully understood until its consequences have also been understood like Wittgenstein's suggestion that the meaning of a word is its use in the language (Feyerabend, 1955). The importance of DQ for leaders is critical. There are many problems that can be solved, and organizational pitfalls avoided through an increase in leader and organizational DQ as defined and described within this book.

References

Abele, A. E., & Wiese, B. S. (2008). The Nomological Network of Self-Management Strategies and Career Success. *Journal of Occupational and Organizational Psychology, 81*(4), 733–749.

Adams, J. S. (1963). Toward an Understanding of Inequity. *Journal of Abnormal and Social Psychology, 67*(5), 422–436.

Anand, R., & Winters, M. F. (2008). A Retrospective View of Corporate Diversity Training from 1964 to the Present. *Academy of Management Learning & Education, 7*(3), 356–372.

Areheart, B. A. (2019). Organizational Justice and Antidiscrimination. *Minnesota Law Review, 104*, 1921–1986.

Arneson, J., Rothwell, W., & Naughton, J. (2013). Training and Development Competencies Redefined to Create Competitive Advantage. *Training & Development, 67*(1), 42–47.

Avery, D. R., Hall, A. V., Preston, M., Ruggs, E. N., & Washington, E. (2023). Is Justice Colorblind? A Review of Workplace Racioethnic Differences Through the Lens of Organizational Justice. *Annual Review of Organizational Psychology and Organizational Behavior, 10*, 389–412. https://www.annualreviews.org/doi/abs/10.1146/annurev-orgpsych-120920-052627

Banks, C. H., Collier, M. M., & Preyan, L. M. (2010). Leveraging Diversity Through Faculty Perception of Their Power to Influence Diversity. *International Journal of Human Resource Development and Management, 10*(3), 208–223.

Banks, K. H. (2009). A Qualitative Investigation of White Students' Perceptions of Diversity. *Journal of Diversity in Higher Education, 2*(3), 149–155.

Barrie, C. (2020). Searching Racism After George Floyd. *Socius, 6*. https://doi.org/10.1177/2378023120971507

Bell, D. (1980). Brown v. Board of Education and the Interest-Convergence Dilemma. *Harvard Law Review, 93*, 518–533.

Bell, D. (2003). Diversity's Distractions. *Columbia Law Review, 103*, 1622–1633.

Bell, D. A. (1995). Who's Afraid of Critical Race Theory. *University of Illinois Law Review*, 893–910.

Benko, C., & Pelster, B. (2013). How Women Decide. In B2B Selling, It Matters If Your Buyer Is Female. *Harvard Business Review, 91*(9), 78–84.

Bielaszka-DuVernay, C. (2014). Hiring for Emotional Intelligence. *Harvard Business Review Onpoint* (Summer), 12–16.

Bossidy, L., Charan, R., & Burck, C. (2002). *Execution: The Discipline of Getting Things Done*. Crown Publishing.

Bruce, A. (2001). *Leaders Start to Finish: A Road Map for Developing Top Performers*. American Society for Training and Development.

Buckley, M. R., Beu, D. S., Frink, D. D., Howard, J. L., Berkson, H., Mobbs, T. A., & Ferris, G. R. (2001). Ethical Issues in Human Resources Systems. *Human Resource Management Review, 11*(1), 11–29.

Burke, C. S., Stagl, K. C., Klein, C., Goodwin, G. F., Salas, E., & Halpin, S. M. (2006). What Type of Leadership Behaviors Are Functional in Teams? A Meta-Analysis. *The Leadership Quarterly, 17*(3), 288–307.

Burkhardt, M. E., & Brass, D. J. (1990). Changing Patterns or Patterns of Change: The Effects of a Change in Technology on Social Network Structure and Power. *Administrative Science Quarterly, 35*(1), 104–127.

Byrd, M. (2007). Educating and Developing Leaders of Racially Diverse Organizations. *Human Resource Development Quarterly, 18*(2), 275–279.

Byrd, M. Y., & Hughes, C. (2021). Re-conceptualizing Diversity Management: Organization-Serving, Justice-Oriented, or Both? In *Implementation Strategies for Improving Diversity in Organizations* (pp. 39–74). IGI Global.

Cappelli, P., & Singh, H. (1992). Integrating Strategic Human Resources and Strategic Management. In D. Lewin, O. S. Mitchell, & P. D. Sherer (Eds.), *Research Frontiers in Industrial Relations and Human Resources* (pp. 165–192). Industrial Relations Research Association.

Cascio, W. F. (2019). Training Trends: Macro, Micro, and Policy Issues. *Human Resource Management Review, 29*(2), 284–297. https://doi.org/10.1016/j.hrmr.2017.11.001

Cascio, W. F., & Collings, D. G. (2022). Potential: The Forgotten Factor in Talent Management Research. In D. Collings, V. Vaiman, & H. Scullion (Eds.), *Talent Management: A Decade of Developments (Talent Management)* (pp. 65–84). Emerald Publishing Limited. https://doi.org/10.1108/978-1-80117-834-120221004

Chandler, J. A., Johnson, N. E., Jordan, S. L., & Short, J. C. (2022). A Meta-Analysis of Humble Leadership: Reviewing Individual, Team, and Organizational Outcomes of Leader Humility. *The Leadership Quarterly*, 101660. https://doi.org/10.1016/j.leaqua.2022.101660

Chua, A., & Rubenfeld, J. (2014). *The Triple Package: How Three Unlikely Traits Explain the Rise and Fall of Cultural Groups in America*. The Penguin Press.

Crenshaw, K. W. (2010). Twenty Years of Critical Race Theory: Looking Back to Move Forward. *Connecticut Law Review, 43*, 1253–1353.

Cropanzano, R., Bowen, D. E., & Gilliland, S. W. (2007). The Management of Organizational Justice. *Academy of Management Perspectives, 21*(4), 34–48.

Davis, P., Naughton, J., & Rothwell, W. (2004). New Roles and New Competencies for the Profession. *Training and Development Journal, 58*(4), 26–36.

Dobbin, F., & Kalev, A. (2016). Why Diversity Programs Fail. *Harvard Business Review, 94*(7), 14.

Dobbin, F., & Kalev, A. (2022). *Getting to Diversity: What Works and What Doesn't*. Harvard University Press.

Doverspike, D., Taylor, M. A., Shultz, K. S., & McKay, P. F. (2000). Responding to the Challenge of a Changing Workforce: Recruiting Nontraditional Demographic Groups. *Public Personnel Management, 29*(4), 445–459.

Dubin, R. (1976). Theory Building in Applied Areas. In M. Dunnette (Ed.), *Handbook of Industrial and Organizational Psychology* (pp. 17–26). Rand McNally.

Feyerabend, P. (1955). Wittgenstein's Philosophical Investigations. *The Philosophical Review, 64*, 449–483.

Fischer, T., & Sitkin, S. B. (2023). Leadership Styles: A Comprehensive Assessment and Way Forward. *Academy of Management Annals, 17*(1), 331–372.

Gandhi, M. (2016). BrainyQuote.com, Xplore Inc. http://www.brainyquote.com/quotes/quotes/m/mahatmagan150718.html. Accessed 21 Feb 2016.

Gates, H. L., Jr, & Curran, A. S. (Eds.). (2022). *Who's Black and Why? A Hidden Chapter from the Eighteenth-Century Invention of Race*. Harvard University Press.

Gómez, L. E. (2007). *Manifest Destinies: The Making of the Mexican American Race*. New York University Press.

Gotanda, N. (1996). Failure of the Color-Blind Vision: Race, Ethnicity, and the California Civil Rights Initiative. *Ethnicity, and the California Civil Rights Initiative, 23*, 1135–1151.

Greer, T. W., & Peters, A. L. (2022). Understanding and Reducing Negative Interpersonal Behaviors: A Critical HRD Approach to Improve Workplace Inclusion. *The Palgrave Handbook of Critical Human Resource Development* (pp. 325–345). Springer International Publishing.

Helgesen, S. (1990). *The Female Advantage: Women's Ways of Leadership*. Doubleday Currency.

Hemphill, H., & Haines, R. (1997). *Discrimination, Harassment, and the Failure of Diversity Training: What to Do Now*. Greenwood Publishing Group.

Hoang, T., Suh, J., & Sabharwal, M. (2022). Beyond a Numbers Game? Impact of Diversity and Inclusion on the Perception of Organizational Justice. *Public Administration Review, 82*(3), 537–555.

Hogan, R., & Kaiser, R. B. (2005). What We Know About Leadership. *Review of General Psychology, 9*(2), 169–180.

Horsman, R. (1981). *Race and Manifest Destiny*. Harvard University Press.

Hughes, C. (2010). People as Technology Conceptual Model: Towards a New Value Creation Paradigm for Strategic Human Resource Development. *Human Resource Development Review, 9*(1), 48–71. https://doi.org/10.1177/1534484309353561

Hughes, C. (2012). *Valuing People and Technology in the Workplace: A Competitive Advantage Framework*. IGI Global.

Hughes, C. (2014). *American Black Women and Interpersonal Leadership Styles*. Sense Publishers.

Hughes, C. (Ed.). (2015). *The Impact of Diversity on Organization and Career Development*. IGI Global.

Hughes, C. (2016). *Diversity Intelligence: Integrating Diversity Intelligence Alongside Intellectual, Emotional, and Cultural Intelligence for Leadership and Career Development*. Palgrave Macmillan.

Hughes, C. (2018). *Workforce Inter-Personnel Diversity: The Power to Influence Human Productivity and Career Development*. Springer International Publishing.

Hughes, C. (in press). *Valuing People and Technology in the Workplace: Ethical Implications and Imperatives for Success*. IGI Global.

Hughes, C., & Brown, L. M. (2018). Exploring Leaders' Discriminatory, Passive-Aggressive Behavior Toward Protected Class Employees Using Diversity Intelligence. *Advances in Developing Human Resources, 20*(3), 263–284.

Hughes, J. L. (1936, July). Let America Be America Again. In *Esquire* (p. 92). https://classic.esquire.com/article/1936/7/1/let-america-be-america-again

Huselid, M. A. (1995). The Impact of Human Resource Management Practices on Turnover, Productivity, and Corporate Financial Performance. *Academy of Management Journal, 38*(3), 635–872.

Ireland, R. D., & Hitt, M. A. (1999). Achieving and Maintaining Strategic Competitiveness in the 21st Century: The Role of Strategic Leadership. *The Academy of Management Executive, 13*(1), 43–57.

Jones, D. (1999). The Definition of Diversity: Two Views: A More Inclusive Definition. *Journal of Library Administration, 27*(1–2), 5–15.

Kotter, J. P., & Cohen, D. S. (2002). *The Heart of Change: Real-Life Stories of How People Change Their Organizations*. Harvard University Press.

Kouzes, J. M., & Posner, B. Z. (1995). *The Leadership Challenge: How to Keep Getting Extraordinary Things Done in Organizations*. Jossey-Bass.

Kulik, C. T., & Roberson, L. (2008). 8 Diversity Initiative Effectiveness: What Organizations Can (and Cannot) Expect from Diversity Recruitment, Diversity Training, and Formal Mentoring Programs. In A. Brief (Ed.), *Diversity at Work* (pp. 265–317). Cambridge University Press.

Latham, G. P., Fay, C. H., & Saari, L. M. (1979). The Development of Behavioral Observation Scales for Appraising the Performance of Foremen. *Personnel Psychology, 32*(2), 299–311.

Laud, R. L., & Johnson, M. (2013). Journey to the Top: Are There Really Gender Differences in the Selection and Utilization of Career Tactics? *Journal of Organizational Culture, Communications and Conflict, 17*(1), 51–68.

Lawler III, E. E. (1986). *High Involvement Management*. Jossey-Bass.

Lawrence, C. R. (1987). The Id, the Ego, and Equal Protection: Reckoning with Unconscious Racism. *Stanford Law Review, 39*, 317–388.

Legood, A., van der Werff, L., Lee, A., & Den Hartog, D. (2021). A Meta-Analysis of the Role of Trust in the Leadership-Performance Relationship. *European Journal of Work and Organizational Psychology, 30*(1), 1–22.

Mackey, J. D., Ellen III, B. P., McAllister, C. P., & Alexander, K. C. (2021). The Dark Side of Leadership: A Systematic Literature Review and Meta-Analysis of Destructive Leadership Research. *Journal of Business Research, 132*, 705–718.

Maghbouleh, N., Schachter, A., & Flores, R. D. (2022). Middle Eastern and North African Americans May Not Be Perceived, Nor Perceive Themselves, to Be White. *Proceedings of the National Academy of Sciences, 119*(7). https://doi.org/10.1073/pnas.2117940119

Manz, C. C. (1986). Self-Leadership: Toward an Expanded Theory of Self-Influence Processes in Organizations. *The Academy of Management Review, 11*(3), 585–600.

March, J. G., & Simon, H. A. (1958). *Organizations*. Wiley.

McLean, G. N., & McLean, L. (2001). If We Can't Define HRD in One Country, How Can We Define It in an International Context? *Human Resource Development International, 4*(3), 313–326.

Mehan, H. (1996). Constitutive Processes of Race and Exclusion. *Anthropology & Education Quarterly, 27*(2), 270–278.

Milem, J. F., Chang, M. J., & Antonio, A. L. (2005). *Making Diversity Work on Campus: A Research-Based Perspective*. Association American Colleges and Universities.

Morrison, E. W. (2023). Employee Voice and Silence: Taking Stock a Decade Later. *Annual Review of Organizational Psychology and Organizational Behavior, 10*(1), 79–107. https://doi.org/10.1146/annurev-orgpsych-120920-054654

Murphy, S. E., & Ensher, E. A. (2001). The Role of Mentoring Support and Self-Management Strategies on Reported Career Outcomes. *Journal of Career Development, 27*(4), 229–246.

Nahapiet, J., & Ghoshal, S. (1998). Social Capital, Intellectual Capital, and the Organizational Advantage. *Academy of Management Review, 23*(2), 242–266.

Ng, E. S., & Sears, G. J. (2020). Walking the Talk on Diversity: CEO Beliefs, Moral Values, and the Implementation of Workplace Diversity Practices. *Journal of Business Ethics, 164*(3), 437–450. https://doi.org/10.1007/s10 551-018-4051-7

Okpokiri, C. (2022). We Are Never Going Back—Social Workers Should Be Proud 'Woke Champions.' *British Journal of Social Work, 52*(7), 3777–3782.

Peterson, L. (1999). The Definition of Diversity: Two Views. A More Specific Definition. *Journal of Library Administration, 27*(1–2), 17–26. https://doi.org/10.1300/J111v27n01_03

Pfeffer, J. (1994). *Competitive Advantage Through People: Unleashing the Power of the Work Force*. Harvard Business School Press.

Pratt, J. W. (1927). The Origin of "Manifest Destiny". *The American Historical Review, 32*(4), 795–798.

Qin, J., Muenjohn, N., & Chhetri, P. (2014). A Review of Diversity Conceptualizations: Variety, Trends, and a Framework. *Human Resource Development Review, 13*(2), 133–157.

Quillian, L., Pager, D., Hexel, O., & Midtbøen, A. H. (2017). Meta-Analysis of Field Experiments Shows No Change in Racial Discrimination in Hiring Over Time. *Proceedings of the National Academy of Sciences, 114*(41), 10870–10875. https://doi.org/10.1073/pnas.1706255114

Resnicow, K., Stiffler, M. J., & Ajrouch, K. J. (2022). Looking Back: The Contested Whiteness of Arab Identity. *American Journal of Public Health, 112*(8), 1092–1096.

Roberson, Q. M. (2019). Diversity in the Workplace: A Review, Synthesis, and Future Research Agenda. *Annual Review of Organizational Psychology and Organizational Behavior, 6*, 69–88.

Schlesinger, A. J. (2005). The American Empire? Not so Fast. *World Policy Journal, 22*(1), 43–46.

Sims, C. (2010). The Impact of African American Skin Tone Bias in the Workplace: Implications for Critical Human Resource Development. *Online Journal for Workforce Education and Development, 3*(4), 1–17.

Sissoko, D. R. G., Lewis, J. A., & Nadal, K. L. (2023). It's More Than Skin-Deep: Gendered Racial Microaggressions, Skin Tone Satisfaction, and Traumatic Stress Symptoms Among Black Women. *Journal of Black Psychology, 49*(2), 127–152.

Sonnemaker, T. (2021). 2020 Brought a Wave of Discrimination and Harassment Allegations Against Major Companies Like Amazon, McDonald's, and

Pinterest. These Are Some of the Year's High-Profile Legal Battles. *Business Insider*. https://www.businessinsider.com/every-company-that-was-sued-discrimination-and-harassment-lawsuits-2020-2021-1

Stefancic, J. (2011). Terrace v. Thompson and the Legacy of Manifest Destiny. *Nevada Law Journal, 12*, 532–548.

Stern, W. (1912). *The Psychological Methods of Intelligence Testing* (G. Whipple, Trans.). Warwick and York.

Sternberg, R. J., & Vroom, V. H. (2002). The Person Versus the Situation in Leadership. *The Leadership Quarterly, 13*(3), 301–323.

Swart, J. (2006). Intellectual Capital: Disentangling an Enigmatic Concept. *Journal of Intellectual Capital, 7*(2), 136–159.

Tallarigo, R. (1998). Discrimination, Harassment, and the Failure of Diversity Training: What to Do Now. *Personnel Psychology, 51*(3), 749–752.

Tarique, I., & Schuler, R. S. (2010). Global Talent Management: Literature Review, Integrative Framework, and Suggestions for Further Research. *Journal of World Business, 45*(2), 122–133.

Taylor, F. W. (1911). *The Principles of Scientific Management*. Harper & Row.

Tedam, P., & Cane, T. (2022). "We Started Talking About Race and Racism After George Floyd": Insights from Research into Practitioner Preparedness for Anti-Racist Social Work Practice in England. *Critical and Radical Social Work, 10*(2), 260–279.

Thomas, R. R., Jr. (1990, March/April). From Affirmative Action to Affirming Diversity. *Harvard Business Review, 68*(2), 107–117.

Thomason, B., Opie, T., Livingston, B., & Sitzmann, T. (2023). "Woke" Diversity Strategies: Science or Sensationalism? *Academy of Management Perspectives*.

Van Ewijk, A. R. (2011). Diversity and Diversity Policy: Diving into Fundamental Differences. *Journal of Organizational Change Management, 24*(5), 680–694.

Vogel, B., Reichard, R. J., Batistič, S., & Černe, M. (2021). A Bibliometric Review of the Leadership Development Field: How We Got Here, Where We Are, and Where We Are Headed. *The Leadership Quarterly, 32*(5), 101381.

Vroom, V. H. (1964). *Work and Motivation*. Wiley.

Vroom, V. H. (2003). Educating Managers for Decision Making and Leadership. *Management Decision, 41*(10), 968–978.

Vroom, V. H., & Maier, N. R. F. (1961). Industrial Social Psychology. *Annual Review of Psychology, 12*(1), 413–446.

Walton, R. E. (1985). From Control to Commitment in the Workplace. *Harvard Business Review, 63*(2), 77–84.

Wang, H. L. (2022). *The U.S. Census Sees Middle Eastern and North African People as White: Many don't*. https://www.npr.org/2022/02/17/1079181478/us-census-middle-eastern-white-north-african-mena

Wellner, A. (2000). How Do YOU Spell Diversity? *Training, 37*(4), 34–38.

Wenstop, F., & Myrmel, A. (2006). Structuring Organizational Value Statements. *Management Research News, 29*(11), 673–683.

Werner, J. M., & DeSimone, R. L. (2012). *Human Resource Development* (6th ed.). South-Western.

Woodard, C. (2011). *American Nations: A History of the Eleven Rival Regional Cultures of North America*. Penguin.

Woodard, C. (2013). Up in Arms: The Battle Lines of Today's Debates over Gun Control, Stand-Your-Ground Laws, and Other Violence-Related Issues Were Drawn Centuries Ago by America's Early Settlers. *Tufts University Alumni Magazine*, A91.

Yadav, S., & Lenka, U. (2020). Diversity management: A systematic review. *Equality, Diversity and Inclusion: An International Journal, 39*(8), 901–929.

Zavattaro, S. M., & Bearfield, D. (2022). Weaponization of Wokeness: The Theater of Management and Implications for Public Administration. *Public Administration Review, 82*(3), 585–593. https://doi.org/10.1111/puar.13484

Zenger, J., & Folkman, J. (2012). *A Study in Leadership—Women Do It Better Than Men*. Zenger Folkman.

CHAPTER 2

Diversity Theories and Diversity Intelligent Perspectives

Some concepts and theories such as cognitive diversity, theory of diversity management, and value-in-diversity hypothesis all reveal a gap in diversity theory that can be filled by DQ theory. There is a need for the DQ theory perspective because of its direct focus on leaders' role in diversity initiatives. The Hughes and Liang DQ scale©2020 adds support to the diversity intelligent perspectives for leaders across industries. Different theories and practices related to diversity (Brennan, 2023; Nkomo et al., 2019; Ray, 2019) have shaped the need for DQ. There are lots of theories that concern race such as critical race theory (Bell, 1980, 1995); however, there are few that deal directly with diversity. This is part of the confusion in the workplace caused by the introduction of the term diversity.

Diversity Terms

When most individuals hear the term diversity, they think that it means race, but it does not mean race in many organizations. There are no definitions and interpretations of diversity that all organizations and individuals agree to (Hughes & DeVaughn, 2012). The word diversity by itself has been insignificant to sustainable change. Protected class employees are clearly defined with enforceable laws, mandates, and policies. A consequence of the lack of clarity is that diversity is often mistaken for EEOC and AA. Diversity extends beyond the legal requirements of

C. Hughes, *Diversity Intelligence*, https://doi.org/10.1007/978-3-031-33250-0_2

EEOC and AA (Kelly & Dobbin, 1998). "[F]or many organizations, the definition of diversity has evolved from a focus on legally protected attributes such as race, gender, and age to a much broader definition that includes the entire spectrum of human differences" (Jayne & Dipboye, 2004, p. 410). The entire spectrum of human difference is the ideal of what diversity should be but stating it without ending discrimination and marginalization of employees who are different has created chaos in the workplace.

Despite the term diversity's extensive use within media publications and HR and workplace literature, little conceptual and theoretical research has been conducted on diversity theory. Diversity terms are varied and complex without any clear-cut generalizable application (Harrison & Klein, 2007). The complexity of diversity terms makes diversity theory development difficult without being situated in a specific environmental context. Some of the terms used interchangeably with diversity are heterogeneity, dissimilarity, and dispersion (Harrison & Klein, 2007). The variety of diversity terms and phrases helps to explain the difficulty in understanding the meaning of diversity. Carter et al. (1982) defined diversity as "people with different ethnic backgrounds, nationalities, age, religion and social class" (p. 49).

The Model Minority Viewpoint

Foster (1993) suggested that the diversity movement is "empty" because anything can be diverse; it advances essentialism by advocating that "different" viewpoints can only come from within the group designated as different; it was intended and introduced to suggest that White males may be individuals with individual views, but other individuals represent a monolithic, essential belief system; when one individual from the monolithic group is hired, the organization will get that entire group's viewpoint; and that diversity marginalizes protected class group and category differences and does not advance the goal of equality. Foster's viewpoint aligns with the concept of manifest destiny which has not often been used within the diversity debate. Manifest destiny's intent was for White males to marginalize all others.

Prasad (2022) all so discussed the fallacy of the model minority—the only one minority who is supposed to represent and entire group of people. Diverse employees must continuously fight against those who try to generalize everything about them (Prasad, 2022). DQ requires leaders to focus on the specifics of each employee. Protected class employees spend too much time asking leaders who have no DQ, or choose to ignore their DQ, to include them. They are seeking inclusion, acceptance, and belonging from leaders who have no DQ frame of reference for including and accepting anyone different than themselves. Baumeister and Leary (1995) defined belonging as the "pervasive drive to form and maintain at least a minimum quantity of lasting, positive and significant interpersonal relationships" (p. 497). The onus should not be on the protected class employee to develop the interpersonal relationship with a bad leader. Leaders behave this way because they can do so without any significant adverse consequences for their behavior.

Diversity continues to face opposition because discrimination is being taught to children and young people and allowed to persist throughout society and the workplace. Clement (2015) found that White millennials are as racially prejudiced as past generations. Clement used data from five measures of racial prejudice from the General Social Survey conducted by NORC's 2010, 2012, and 2014 and found that when examining explicit prejudice against blacks, non-Hispanic, White millennials are not much different than whites belonging to Generation X (born 1965–1980) or Baby Boomers (born 1946–1964).

> White millennials (using a definition of being born after 1980) express the least prejudice but not by a meaningful difference. Thirty-one percent of millennials rate blacks as lazier than whites on work ethic compared to 32 percent of Generation X whites and 35 percent of Baby Boomers. (Clement, 2015, ¶4)

These results provide ample evidence of the need for DQ because millennials are the largest group currently in the workplace representing 35 percent of all employees. If they are expressing discriminatory tendencies in society, how can they avoid expressing it through their behavior toward protected class groups and category employees in the workplace? Many believe that their beliefs are not transferred to others through their actions. It has been studied through the microaggression literature and believed by some individuals that recognizing microaggression is enough to influence change (Kossek et al., 2022; Pierce, 1970, 1995; Smith & Griffiths, 2022; Sue et al., 2007; Williams et al., 2021; Wong et al.,

2014). Simply recognizing microaggressions has not proven to be effective because there are seldom behavior changes. Microaggression is not truly micro in its impact on those who are affected by it (King et al., 2022; Pierce, 1970, 1995). Protected class group and category employees do not perceive their mistreatment as a micro problem. It is a macro problem for the employees affected. Some results have included trauma, Post-Traumatic Stress Disorder (PTSD), violence, and sometimes death (Hughes et al., 2016; Pierce, 1970, 1995).

DIVERSITY THEORIES

Jackson (2000) noticed that there were very few distinct diversity theories identified in the literature. A theory "tries to make sense out of the observable world by ordering the relationships among elements that constitute the theorist's focus of attention in the real world" (Dubin, 1976, p. 26). Diversity theory should try to make sense out of the relationships in the real world related to diversity; however, the broadness of the term restricts the desire to develop a diversity theory (Nkomo et al., 2019; Post et al., 2021; Ray, 2019; Waldman & Sparr, 2022).

Value-In-Diversity Hypothesis

Cox et al. (1991) created the "value-in-diversity hypothesis" and argued that diversity, when properly used from the economic perspective, can be beneficial for organizations and ultimately improve performance (Copeland, 1988; Cox, 1991; Cox & Blake, 1991; Etsy, 1988; Jackson, 1992; McLeod et al., 1996; Sodano & Baler, 1983; Thomas, 1990a; Walker & Hanson, 1992; Watson et al., 1993). The value-in-diversity hypothesis situates diversity within the workplace context. Some organizations' diversity efforts are often measured by simply counting the number of employees in each protected class group (Dass & Parker, 1999). This oversimplifies diversity to headcount and appeases those who oppose diversity by allowing it to remain a surface-level issue that requires minimal effort and attention. The headcount method of diversity is used to limit the number of protected class employees in the workplace. Once a certain number is reached, the organization believes that they have enough of a particular group to say that they are diverse.

Theory of Diversity Management

Dr. R. Roosevelt Thomas, Jr. introduced and developed a theory of diversity management in 1985. Thomas' theory was based on observations of the changing attitudes of college students. His theory focused on talent management. The tenets of his theory are that: managers and leaders must have the skills to manage a changing workforce; better business results are the goal of diversity management; diversity management must allow everyone to contribute naturally to organization goal; and diversity management cannot privilege one group to the disadvantage of other groups and be successful. His theory assumed that the managers and leaders had the DQ to achieve diversity management success. Organizations accepted this theory and have worked hard to manage diversity and had some success. However, diversity management cannot be sustained without leaders who value DQ. Some leaders may have DQ but do not value it enough to use it to benefit the organization. Their ego (Hughes in press; Jones & Carter, 1996; Lawrence, 1987, 2008; Winnubst, 2004) and adverse positions against change prevent them from acting to include others who are different.

Dr. Scott Page expanded the theory of diversity management from his work on problem-solving and prediction. Page's (2007) diversity-prediction and diversity-trumps-ability theorems are based on the dynamic behaviors of groups in the process of problem-solving, predicting, innovating, decision-making, and managing complexity. Page suggested that increased problem complexity requires more diversity within problem-solving groups; diversity must go beyond superficial characteristics and examine diverse perspectives, heuristics, categories, and models; that diversity management must rely on math, science, and empiricism, not anecdote and metaphor; that more diverse groups outperform less diverse groups; and that diversity supersedes ability. Page's perspective could be valuable to DQ if there are protected class group members appropriately represented within each group whose contributions are valued and accepted. Their contributions to the group must not be marginalized.

Cognitive Diversity Hypothesis

There are variations in the definition of cognitive diversity. It examines the multiple perspectives of beliefs regarding organizational goals (Glick et al., 1993; Miller, 1990; Miller et al., 1998, 2022). These different beliefs can be attributed to cultural differences and cause–effect relationship perceptions of team members. Cognitive diversity is believed to lead to more creative problem-solving and innovation within teams (Hong & Page, 2004). Earley and Ang (2003) to explore cognitive processes of intelligence including declarative and procedural knowledge, analogical reasoning, pattern recognition, external scanning, and self-awareness.

Cognitive diversity does not have to be separate from demographic diversity unless an organization's leaders choose to separate the two (Brennan, 2023; Miller et al., 2022; Talat et al., 2023). There are pros and cons of combining the two, but the biggest concerns are the leaders who assemble the teams have DQ and the capability of applying it to select protected class employees who have the cognitive ability to contribute to the team's success. Protected class employees cannot display their cognitive ability if they are never allowed on the team or better yet allowed to assemble the team.

CONCLUSION

Many of the leaders in organizations are not yet diversity intelligent. Defining diversity is not enough when employees do not feel that they have the power to enforce diversity goals (Banks et al., 2010). It has been said that knowledge is power. DQ knowledge is DQ power. DQ would let leaders know that many protected class employees do not want to spend their time defending their protected class status. They come to work to do their jobs and want to do so peacefully, productively, within teams, and individually.

REFERENCES

Banks, C. H., Collier, M. M., & Preyan, L. M. (2010). Leveraging Diversity Through Faculty Perception of Their Power to Influence Diversity. *International Journal of Human Resource Development and Management, 10*(3), 208–223.

Baumeister, R. F., & Leary, M. R. (1995). The Need to Belong: Desire for Interpersonal Attachments as a Fundamental Human Motivation. *Psychological Bulletin, 117*(3), 497–529. https://doi.org/10.1037/0033-2909.117.3.497

Bell, D. A. (1995). Who's Afraid of Critical Race Theory. *University of Illinois Law Review, 1995*, 893–910.

Bell, D. (1980). Brown v. Board of Education and the Interest-Convergence Dilemma. *Harvard Law Review, 93*, 518–533.

Brennan, J. (2023). *The Diversity, Equity and Inclusion Dilemma: The Wrong Reasons or the Wrong Kind?* (Occasional Paper). Bridwell Institute. https://www.smu.edu/-/media/Site/Cox/CentersAndInstitutes/BridwellInstitute/SMU-Bridwell-Occasional-Paper_Final-web.pdf

Carter, E., Kepner, E., Shaw, M., & Woodson, W. B. (1982). The Effective Management of Diversity. *Advanced Management Journal, 47*, 49–53.

Clement, S. (2015). *Millennials are Just about as Racist as Their Parents.* Retrieved July 28, 2015, from https://www.washingtonpost.com/blogs/wonkblog/wp/2015/04/07/white-millennials-are-just-about-as-racist-as-their-parents/

Copeland, L. (1988). Valuing Diversity: Part 1; Making the Most of Cultural Differences in the Workplace. *Personnel, 65*(6), 52–60.

Cox, T., Jr. (1991). The Multicultural Organization. *The Academy of Management Executive, 5*(2), 43–47.

Cox, T. H., & Blake, S. (1991). Managing Cultural Diversity: Implications for Organizational Competitiveness. *Academy of Management Executive, 5*(3), 45–56.

Cox, T. H., Lobel, S. A., & McLeod, P. L. (1991). Effects of Ethnic Group Cultural Differences on Cooperative and Competitive Behavior on a Group Task. *Academy of Management Journal, 34*(4), 827–847.

Dass, P., & Parker, B. (1999). Strategies for Managing Human Resource Diversity: From Resistance to Learning. *Academy of Management Executive, 13*(2), 68–80.

Dubin, R. (1976). Theory Building in Applied Areas. In M. Dunnette (Ed.), *Handbook of Industrial and Organizational Psychology* (pp. 17–26). Rand McNally.

Earley, P. C., & Ang, S. (2003). *Cultural Intelligence: Individual Interactions Across Cultures.* Stanford University Press.

Etsy, K. (1988). Diversity Is Good for Business. *Executive Excellence, 5*(1), 5–6.

Foster, S. (1993). Difference and Equality: A Critical Assessment of the Concept of Diversity. *Wisconsin Law Review, 93*, 105–161.

Glick, W. H., Miller, C. C., & Huber, G. P. (1993). The Impact of Upper-Echelon Diversity on Organizational Performance. In G. P. Huber & W. H. Glick (Eds.), *Organizational Change and Redesign: Ideas and Insights for Improving Performance* (pp. 176–214). Oxford University Press.

Harrison, D. A., & Klein, K. J. (2007). What's the Difference? Diversity Constructs as Separation, Variety, or Disparity in Organizations. *Academy of Management Review, 32*(4), 1199–1228.

Hong, L., & Page, S. E. (2004). Groups of Diverse Problem Solvers Can Outperform Groups of High-Ability Problem Solvers. *Proceedings of the National Academy of Sciences, 101*(46), 16385–16389.

Hughes, C. (2023). *Valuing People and Technology in the Workplace: Ethical Implications and Imperatives for Success.* IGI Global.

Hughes, C. (2023, in press). The Intersection of Diversity, Equity, and Inclusion (DEI), Diversity Intelligence, and Ethics with the Role of HRD Scholars, Professionals, and Practitioners. In D. Russ-Eft & A. Alizadeh (Eds.), *Ethics in Human Resource Development.* Palgrave Macmillan.

Hughes, C., & DeVaughn, S. (2012). Leveraging Workforce Diversity Through a Career Development Paradigm Shift. In C. L. Scott & M. Y. Byrd (Eds.), *Handbook of Research on Workforce Diversity in a Global Society: Technologies and Concepts* (pp. 262–272). IGI Global.

Hughes, C., Lusk, S., & Strause, S. (2016). Recognizing and Accommodating Employees with PTSD: Intersection of Human Resource Development, Rehabilitation, and Psychology. *New Horizons in Adult Education and Human Resource Development.*

Jackson, R. L. (2000). So Real Illusions of Black Intellectualism: Exploring Race, Roles, and Gender in the Academy. *Communication Theory, 10*(1), 48–63.

Jackson, S. E. (1992). Team Composition in Organizational Settings: Issues in Managing an Increasingly Diverse Workforce. In S. Worchel, W. Wood, & J. Simpson (Eds.), *Group Process and Productivity* (pp. 138–173). Sage.

Jayne, M. E. A., & Dipboye, R. L. (2004). Leveraging Diversity to Improve Business Performance: Research Findings and Recommendations for Organizations. *Human Resource Management, 43*(4), 409–424.

Jones, J. M., & Carter, R. T. (1996). Racism and White Racial Identity: Merging Realities. In B. P. Bowser & R. G. Hunt (Eds.), *Impacts of Racism on White Americans* (pp. 1–23). Sage.

Kelly, E., & Dobbin, F. (1998). How Affirmative Action Became Diversity Management: Employer Response to Antidiscrimination Laws, 1961 to 1996. *American Behavioral Scientist, 41*(7), 960–984.

King, D. D., Fattoracci, E. S. M., Hollingsworth, D. W., Stahr, E., & Nelson, M. (2022). When Thriving Requires Effortful Surviving: Delineating Manifestations and Resource Expenditure Outcomes of Microaggressions for Black Employees. *Journal of Applied Psychology, 108*(2), 183–207.

Kossek, E. E., Buzzanell, P. M., Wright, B. J., Batz-Barbarich, C., Moors, A. C., Sullivan, C., Kokini, K., Hirsch, A. S., Maxey, K., & Nikalje, A. (2022). Implementing Diversity Training Targeting Faculty Microaggressions and Inclusion: Practical Insights and Initial Findings. *The Journal of Applied Behavioral Science*, 1–27. https://doi.org/10.1177/00218863221132321

Lawrence, C. R. (1987). The Id, the Ego, and Equal Protection: Reckoning with Unconscious Racism. *Stanford Law Review, 39*, 317–388.

McLeod, P. L., Lobel, S. A., & Cox, T. H. (1996). Ethnic Diversity and Creativity in Small Groups. *Small Group Research, 27*(2), 248–264.

Miller, C. C. (1990). *Cognitive Diversity Within Management Teams: Implications for Strategic Decision Processes and Organizational Performance.* Unpublished doctoral dissertation, Graduate School of Business, University of Texas.

Miller, C. C., Burke, L. M., & Glick, W. H. (1998). Cognitive Diversity Among Upper-Echelon Executives: Implications for Strategic Decision Processes. *Strategic Management Journal, 19*(1), 39–58.

Miller, C. C., Chiu, S., Wesley II, C. L., Vera, D., & Avery, D. R. (2022). Cognitive Diversity at the Strategic Apex: Assessing Evidence on the Value of Different Perspectives and Ideas Among Senior Leaders. *Academy of Management Annals, 16*(2), 806–852.

Nkomo, S. M., Bell, M. P., Roberts, L. M., Joshi, A., & Thatcher, S. M. (2019). Diversity at a Critical Juncture: New Theories for a Complex Phenomenon. *Academy of Management Review, 44*(3), 498–517.

Page, S. E. (2007). *The Difference: How the Power of Diversity Creates Better Groups, Firms, Schools, and Societies.* Princeton University Press.

Pierce, C. (1995). Stress Analogs of Racism and Sexism: Terrorism, Torture, and Disaster. *Mental Health, Racism, and Sexism, 33*, 277–293.

Pierce, C. M. (1970, November). Black Psychiatry One Year After Miami. *Journal of the National Medical Association, 62*(6), 471–473. PMID: 5493608; PMCID: PMC2611929.

Post, C., Muzio, D., Sarala, R., Wei, L., & Faems, D. (2021). Theorizing Diversity in Management Studies: New Perspectives and Future Directions. *Journal of Management Studies, 58*(8), 2003–2023.

Prasad, A. (2022). The Model Minority and the Limits of Workplace Inclusion. *Academy of Management Review.* https://doi.org/10.5465/amr.2021.0352

Ray, V. (2019). A Theory of Racialized Organizations. *American Sociological Review, 84*(1), 26–53.

Smith, I. A., & Griffiths, A. (2022). Microaggressions, Everyday Discrimination, Workplace Incivilities, and Other Subtle Slights at Work: A Meta-Synthesis. *Human Resource Development Review, 21*(3), 275–299.

Sodano, A. G., & Baler, S. G. (1983). Accommodation to Contrast: Being Different in the Organization. *New Directions for Mental Health Services, 20*(December), 25–36.

44   C. HUGHES

Sue, D. W., Capodilupo, C. M., Torino, G. C., Bucceri, J. M., Holder, A., Nadal, K. L., & Esquilin, M. (2007). Racial Microaggressions in Everyday Life: Implications for Clinical Practice. *American Psychologist, 62*(4), 271–286.

Talat, A., Khan, S. N., Chaudary, S., & Neale, N. R. (2023). Investigating the ICT for Team Creativity: A Team Sensemaking Perspective. *IIMB Management Review*, 1–31. https://doi.org/10.1016/j.iimb.2023.03.004

Thomas, D. A. (1990a). *Strategies for Managing Racial Differences in Work-Centered Develop-Mental Relationships* (Working paper). Wharton School of Business, University of Pennsylvania.

Thomas, R. R., Jr. (1990b, March/April). From Affirmative Action to Affirming Diversity. *Harvard Business Review, 68*(2), 107–117.

Waldman, D. A., & Sparr, J. L. (2022). Rethinking Diversity Strategies: An Application of Paradox and Positive Organization Behavior Theories. *Academy of Management Perspectives*. https://doi.org/10.5465/amp.2021.0183

Walker, B. A., & Hanson, W. C. (1992). Valuing Differences at Digital Equipment Corporation. In S. E. Jackson (Ed.), *Diversity in the Workplace: Human Resources Initiatives* (pp. 119–137). Guilford.

Watson, W. E., Kumar, K., & Michaelsen, L. K. (1993). Cultural Diversity's Impact on Interaction Process and Performance: Comparing Homogeneous and Diverse Task Groups. *Academy of Management Journal, 36*(3), 590–602.

Williams, M. T., Skinta, M. D., & Martin-Willett, R. (2021). After Pierce and Sue: A Revised Racial Microaggressions Taxonomy. *Perspectives on Psychological Science, 16*(5), 991–1007.

Winnubst, S. (2004). Is the Mirror Racist? Interrogating the Space of Whiteness. *Philosophy & Social Criticism, 30*(1), 25–50.

Wong, G., Derthick, A. O., David, E. J. R., Saw, A., & Okazaki, S. (2014). The What, the Why, and the How: A Review of Racial Microaggressions Research in Psychology. *Race and Social Problems, 6*, 181–200.

CHAPTER 3

Diversity in Practice

The content of this chapter explores the questions: How does one truly apply diversity in practice? How does one talk about diversity exclusive of the actual application of diversity in practice? What is the applicable evidence of diversity success? According to Thomas and Ely (1996),

> Two perspectives have guided most diversity initiatives to date: the discrimination-and fairness paradigm and the access-and-legitimacy paradigm. But we have identified a new, emerging approach to this complex management issue. This approach, which we call the learning-and-effectiveness paradigm, incorporates aspects of the first two paradigms but goes beyond them by concretely connecting diversity to approaches to work. Our goal is to help business leaders see what their own approach to diversity currently is and how it may already have influenced their companies' diversity efforts. Managers can learn to assess whether they need to change their diversity initiatives and, if so, how to accomplish that change. (p. 2)

THE DQ PARADIGM

DQ is another paradigm to help resolve the diversity management issue, and it involves leaders assessing whether they need to change themselves, through knowledge, education and training, and behavior so that they are capable of changing diversity initiatives. Leaders have been trained on

© The Author(s), under exclusive license to Springer Nature Switzerland AG 2023
C. Hughes, *Diversity Intelligence*,
https://doi.org/10.1007/978-3-031-33250-0_3

the law in diversity training, and it has been the least effective type of training for diversity management (Anand & Winters, 2008; Dobbin & Kalev, 2022; Thomas & Ely, 1996) because leaders choose not to follow the law. Some leaders choose not to follow the law because there is no or weak accountability (Hirsh, 2009; Yang & Liu, 2021) and not enough evidence that the law in diversity training content was received by the leaders during training and transferred back to the job (Holladay et al., 2003). The knowledge subscale within the Hughes and Liang DQ scale ©2020 is designed to measure the leaders' knowledge of the protected class group and category law. The compliance training itself is usually not the problem. The problem is the leaders who attend the training are resistant to the legal requirements covered in the training (Anand & Winters, 2008; Chow et al., 2021; Holladay et al., 2003; Kidder et al., 2004; Livingston, 2020). Holladay et al. (2003) found that men were least receptive of diversity training and Dobbin and Kalev (2022) found that "legalistic training led to declines in managerial diversity" (p. 24) with the most effect on American Black women.

Three types of intelligence are currently accepted as mainstream among organization leaders. They are intellectual (IQ), emotional (EQ) (Salovey & Mayer, 1990), and cultural (CQ) (Konyu-Fogel, 2011). IQ, EQ, and CQ are typically assessed when examining organization leaders' effectiveness. These assessments have included aspects of diversity but address peripheral problems and not the core problems that protected class employees experience within many workplaces.

US Workplaces Under Employ Protected Class Employees

US workplaces are not representative of the diversity of the US because the unemployment rate of American Blacks and American Hispanics is continuously lower than White Americans (Chua & Rubenfeld, 2014; Dias, 2023; Farley, 1987; Sum & Khatiwada, 2010; Taylor et al., 2011). The disabled, women, and veterans are also disproportionately underrepresented in the US workplaces (Brault, 2012; Hoynes et al., 2012; Mattingly & Smith, 2010). American Blacks, Hispanic Americans, White Americans, disabled Americans, American women, and American veterans are all protected in the workplace under federal laws (Gutman et al., 2011; U. S. EEOC Performance and Accountability Report, 2013), but White American males are often the last to be dismissed from their jobs during layoffs, recessions, and general workplace layoffs. In many instances making the most vulnerable in society unemployed is inhumane. It is inhumane especially when no severance pay or unemployment benefits are available.

Protected Class Employees Do Not Feel Protected at Work

A problem that many organizations can resolve with DQ is the problem that many protected class employees do not feel protected when they encounter discrimination and incivility in the workplace (Amis et al., 2020; Banks et al., 2006; Baruch & Jenkins, 2007; Clark et al., 2013; Hellerstedt et al., 2022; Joshi et al., 2015; Mehra et al., 2023; O'Leary-Kelly & Newman, 2004; Phillips & Smith, 2003; Smith & Griffiths, 2022; Wilson et al., 2011). Federal, state, and local laws have been passed that support the protection of protected class employees in the workplace, and whistleblowing policies are designed to protect their anonymity (Crenshaw, 1989; Day & Schoenrade, 2000; Locke, 1997; Milliken et al., 2003; Near et al., 1993; Rubin, 1998) but some of these employees still do not feel protected. A culture that supports DQ could help these employees to communicate their true feelings with leaders who display genuine DQ.

Ethnic hatred is also a problem for US organizations, and unique cases arise for those organizations with multinational interests (Karsten, 2006; North et al., 2014; Perry, 2000; Petersen, 2002; Van Laer & Janssen, 2011). The Civil Rights Act of 1964 and its amendments define protected class groups and categories of people based upon race, color, national origin, sex, religion, age, disability, and family medical history and genetic information (U. S. EEOC Performance and Accountability Report, 2013). This definition reveals that there are very few individuals excluded from protected class groups within typical workplaces (Hughes, 2015). The few who are excluded are non-disabled, non-military veteran, non-LGBT, non-religious, White males under the age of 40 but their pay places them in a protected class category alongside every other employee who receives pay for their work. In response to White males' opposition to AA, White males were intentionally made a part of protected class groups and categories and diversity as noted by Peterson (1999):

The notion of "protected classes," beyond African Americans who suffered legal discrimination, also helped in the conception of diversity. Affirmative Action, and the benefits of Equal Employment Opportunity (EEO) laws, was extended to provide opportunity to white women, the disabled, Vietnam Veterans, persons over 40 and people with physical or mental handicaps; that is, all U.S. citizens are recognized as members of a protected class and entitled to the benefits of EEO. "However, the EEO laws were passed to correct a history of unfavorable treatment of women and minority group members." The new protected classes benefitted and protected white males by including them as victims of discrimination (on the basis of age, disability, etc.), and therefore providing a broader base for civil rights discussion. (p. 20)

Therefore, many organizations are more diverse than they may realize, and the organization leaders must address the problem of acceptance of diversity of thought and behavior within all employees despite their protected class affiliation.

A Call for Inclusiveness

There is a call for inclusiveness in the workplace (Foster, 1993). How is inclusiveness determined? When do protected employees feel included? Despite the calls for inclusiveness, protected class groups and categories of employees continue to face many forms of discrimination including stereotypes (Amodio, 2009; Banks, 2008; Pred, 2004; Wheeler et al., 2001); racism—both covert and overt (Doane & Bonilla-Silva, 2003; Fox & Stallworth, 2005; Katz & Moore, 2004; Kivel, 2002; Paradies, 2006); and sexism, primarily against women, deterring their advancement to executive leadership positions (Hughes, 2014; Karsten, 2006; Swim & Cohen, 1997). In some industries men also experience sexism (Swim et al., 2001), and some leaders show unconscious and/or conscious bias against protected class employees without any consequences for their actions (Van Laer & Janssens, 2011). The crux of the problem is the lack of consequences for leaders and holding leaders accountable for discriminatory behavior. Despite the formation of the Equal Employment Opportunity Commission (EEOC) on July 2, 1965, protected class employees are still discriminated against at work. The punishment from the EEOC has not been enough of a deterrent against continued discrimination (Hughes, in press).

Using Intelligence to Address
Chronic Workplace Problems

Covey (2006) recognized the importance of intelligence in resolving chronic workplace problems. He described four intelligences:

1. Mental Intelligence (IQ)—the ability of a person to analyze, reason, think abstractly, use language, visualize, and comprehend information.
2. Spiritual Intelligence (SQ)—an individual's drive for meaning and connection with the infinite.
3. Emotional Intelligence (EQ)—individual self-knowledge, self-awareness, social sensitivity, empathy, and the ability to communicate successfully with others and
4. Physical Intelligence (PQ)—a person's ability to maintain and develop his physical fitness.

Covey also described four roles of leadership as Pathfinding using IQ, Aligning using PQ, Empowering using EQ, and Modeling using SQ. If leaders are expected to display the roles described by Covey, how can a leader justify not supporting protected class employees if the leader claims to have high EQ? Where is the empowerment within discriminatory behaviors? Sometimes, if the person being discriminated against has high self-efficacy and has reached self-actualization, she may be empowered to use her efforts to fight back against those who discriminate against her. Covey also described the chronic problems of no shared vision/values associated with IQ, misalignment associated with PQ, disempowerment due to EQ, and low trust associated with SQ. These chronic problems are amplified more when there is no DQ. Leaders without DQ have no shared vision/values, are misaligned with, disempowers, and receive low trust from protected class employees.

It is very difficult for protected class employees to share the vision and/or values of those who marginalize them. They are also disempowered when they are excluded from opportunities to lead. There is often no trust as opposed to low trust from the maltreatment endured by protected class employees as they strive to maintain their job in a workplace environment that shows them that they are not wanted. Misalignment occurs when leaders do not place employees in appropriate positions, or their decisions are out of alignment with organization goals. Many organizations have stated diversity goals that leaders do not understand or choose not to follow (Banks et al., 2010).

IQ

Intelligent quotient (IQ) was derived in 1912 by Stern. IQ is determined by dividing and individual's mental age by the person's chronological age and multiplying the result by 100. The IQ was used to negatively categorize people who were of different races and social classes as less intelligent. It was also used to exclude some individuals from workplace participation. Thus, excluding them from earning income that was needed to survive within America's capitalistic society.

The extensive controversies that have arisen because of the discriminatory practices associated with IQ has lessened its use. *The Bell Curve* by Herrnstein and Murray (1994) was one way that the IQ was used to discredit others based on race and class but Kincheloe et al. (1997) and others debunked many of the lies asserted as truths within *The Bell Curve*. There are still questions as to whether IQ tests even measure intelligence. Without the controversies and protests made by protected class groups and categories of people against IQ bias, EQ, CQ, nor DQ would have been considered.

EQ

Peter Salovey and John Mayer (1990) created and described EQ as an ability to recognize the meaning of emotions and their relationships, and to reason and solve problems based on them. Their refined definition of EQ is "the ability to perceive accurately, appraise, and express emotion; … to access and/or generate feelings when they facilitate thought; … to understand emotion and emotional knowledge; and … to regulate emotions to promote emotional and intellectual growth" (Mayer & Salovey, 1997, p. 10). EQ consisted of three mental processes: appraising and expressing emotions in the self and others, regulating emotion in the self and others, and using emotions in adaptive ways (Salovey & Mayer, 1990). They further divided EQ into four mental abilities: perceiving emotions, integrating emotion into thought, understanding emotions, and managing emotions (Mayer & Salovey, 1997). With EQ individuals are thought to "be able to communicate and discuss feelings and develop expert knowledge in a particular emotional area such as aesthetics, moral or ethical feeling, social problem solving, leadership or spiritual feeling" (Mayer et al., 2000, p. 400). Despite the ability to measure and apply EQ, it has not been used extensively by leaders to resolve diversity issues within the workplace. The reasons for this is unknown; hence, the suggestion that DQ is needed.

Goleman (1995) defined EQ as an individual's ability to "motivate oneself and persist in the face of frustration; to control impulses and delay gratification; to regulate one's moods and keep distress from swamping the ability to think; to empathize and to hope" (p. 34). These characteristics are like those of protected class group members as they consistently endure mistreatment in the workplace. Protected class employees often have no choice but to persist in the face of frustration and control their impulses especially feelings of anger and disappointment. They must perform their job duties at optimum levels of excellence despite the loss of the hope of ever being promoted.

Goleman also identified five broad components of EQ: (a) self-awareness; (b) self-regulation; (c) motivation; (d) empathy; and (e) social skills. Only in the broad component of empathy is diversity mentioned. EQ grasps that humans are different but does nothing with that understanding of the difference. Empathy is sensing what people are feeling, being able to take their perspective, and cultivating rapport and harmony with a broad diversity of people (Goleman, 1995). Goleman (1998a) suggested that to achieve outstanding work performance individuals were required to have strengths dispersed across all five areas of EQ. This has not proven to be true for the success of protected class groups and categories of employees. Protected class employees can possess all five areas of EQ, and because of discrimination, never achieve outstanding work performance because individuals conducting performance ratings operate from a double standard and position of bias (D'Netto & Sohal, 1999; Fulkerson & Schuler, 1992; Gelfand et al., 2005; Jayne & Dipboye, 2004; Loden & Rosener, 1991; Morrison, 1992; Powell & Butterfield, 1994; Schreiber et al., 1993; Schuler et al., 1992; Shen et al., 2009; Triana et al., 2021). Many leaders possess strengths in the five areas but do not possess DQ to be fair and objective in their treatment of others who are different than them. Leaders do not need a reason to discriminate; they just choose to do so because there is often no deterrent for them not to be unfair and unethical (Hirsh, 2009; Mitchell et al., 2023; Treviño et al., 2006; Yang & Liu, 2021).

Goleman (1998a, 1998b) described EQ as a learnable construct that improves with age. This provides hope that individuals who do not yet possess DQ can learn how to integrate it into their EQ consciousness. EQ is necessary but it does not sufficiently address the issues that protected class employees encounter when interacting with leaders who lack DQ. Protected class employees possess enough EQ to know when they are being discriminated against. A discriminatory and negative workplace environment can stifle protected class employees' ability to truly display their EQ. David and Congleton (2014) suggested that effective leaders manage their negative thoughts and feelings through EQ and that they use their values to make decisions at work. What happens if the values of the leaders who are making decisions about and for protected class employees do not include DQ and are not supportive of protected class employees? If the many leaders who say that they have high EQ are not managing their negative thoughts and feelings toward protected class employees, should they still be allowed to lead? Should they not be asked to change their behavior?

EQ AND SOCIAL CAPITAL THEORY

Wieand (2002) stated that there "no psychological concept has had greater influence on leadership development than emotional intelligence" (p. 33). EQ impacts the psyche of the leader. Thus, it is surprising that leaders would not consider how their actions and behaviors effect the psyche of those they are entrusted to lead. They must be held accountable for how they treat protected class employees.

"Social capital theory was founded on the premise that a network provides value to its members by allowing them access to resources within the network" (Lin & Huang, 2005, p. 193). Similar to EQ, social capital is directly connected to an individual's ability to network or influence another individual, build trust, show concern for others, and living or adhering to a set of unspoken rules or norms in an organization (Dasgupta, 2005; Lin & Huang, 2005) resulting in a positive outcome on organizational performance.

"Building social capital is imperative for a leader today" (Wieand, 2002). If leaders are socializing with each other, it stands to reason that they know when their peers are not using their leadership to benefit protected class employees and should be able to influence their peers using their social capital. Hughes and Brown (2018) found that

100 percent of their participants saw protected class employees being mistreated in the workplace. Since individuals transact business because of the relationship that has been built (Dasgupta, 2005), they can communicate DQ using those same relationships; however, many relationships are lost or changed because of a lack of DQ and unwillingness to accept DQ. It may also be that individual leaders can use their social capital to increase DQ among their peers.

EQ AND LEADERSHIP STYLES

Goleman (2000, 2013) identified six leadership styles related to components of EQ. The leadership styles are as follows: (1) coercive as exemplified by the drive to achieve, initiative, and self-control; (2) authoritative by showing self-confidence, empathy, and acting as a change catalyst; (3) affiliative as represented by empathy, building relationships, and communication; (4) democratic using collaboration, team leadership, and communication; (5) pacesetting when showing conscientiousness, drive to achieve, and initiative; and (6) coaching by developing others, showing empathy, and self-awareness. EQ has been shown to have a strong positive effect on leadership strategies. Accepting Goleman's (1998a) belief that EQ is a learnable skill, EQ training sessions can be used to teach current and potential leaders how to integrate EQ with DQ concepts and strategies to accept and respect protected class employees, as they are. Often protected class employees are expected to assimilate as opposed to being accepted as they are. An example expressed that encapsulates this sentiment is from Rhett Hutchins:

> Cultural observation: a minority individual does something that doesn't meet majority expectations of a norm; the minority individual is a stereotypical example. A minority individual meets the majority cultural expectation; the minority individual is now an exception to their minority group instead of redefining the minority stereotype. (personal communication, FaceBook post, February 8, 2016)

CULTURAL INTELLIGENCE (CQ)

Earley and Mosakowski (2004) stated that "occasionally an outsider has a seemingly natural ability to interpret someone's unfamiliar and ambiguous gestures in just the way that person's compatriots and colleagues would, even to mirror them. We call that *cultural intelligence* or *CQ*" (p. 139). However, emulation is not always respectful behavior and can sometimes be perceived as cultural appropriation. Siems (2019) stated "Cultural appropriation is often defined as the 'taking of intellectual property, cultural expressions or artefacts, history, and ways of knowledge'" (p. 408). Some cultural behaviors should not be copied because some copying actions can be perceived as mockery or insulting. An example of this occurred when Louisville University's President chose to wear a Mexican poncho and sombrero and some Mexicans were offended by the stereotype. DQ can help leaders avoid some of these inappropriate actions. For some individuals and groups, cultural appropriation is wrong and harmful (Lalonde, 2021; Lenard & Balint, 2020) especially when it causes financial loss.

CQ is described by Mendenhall et al. (2013) as an individual's desire to understand differences in political, social, cultural, and ethical issues, and to experience diversity in human relations, work environments, and personal adventures. CQ links cultural competences to intelligence by (1) addressing how individuals adapt to the new environment of diversity that comes from globalization by shifting focus from culture-specific interpersonal types of intelligence (e.g., social intelligence, emotional intelligence) to a culture-free construct; and (2) expanding phenomena to be studied that are relevant to cultural adaptation as suggested by.

CQ is an emerging field (Gelfand et al., 2008) with four subdimensions: metacognitive, cognitive, motivational, and behavioral. The motivational factor of CQ is highly relevant to DQ because of its emphasis on contemporary globalization and how it highly encourages the mobility of labor across national and cultural boundaries (Templer et al., 2006). It is also relevant to DQ because of the challenges faced by leaders as they attempt to operate, successfully, within a different culture (Redmond, 2000). Motivational CQ is a key factor toward achieving the goal of operating in a different culture, but DQ is needed to help these individuals recognize that there are significant differences within cultures. People with higher levels of motivational CQ are said to be more motivated to engage in intercultural interactions. These people could also champion DQ efforts since they are also thought to be those who seek direct experiences in different cultures (Deci & Ryan, 1985).

CQ appears to place the onus for being accepted on the individual who is being discriminated against to make themselves understood and able to create fruitful collaborations in situations where cultural differences play a role. Why should the protected class employees be required to prove to those discriminating against them that they are worthy of their jobs? DQ would require discriminatory leaders to try to resolve their lack of understanding of those who are different than themselves. DQ of leaders can determine the success and/or failure of the organization in global business interactions.

DQ is needed and is distinctly different than CQ. CQ does not account for the differences found within specific human cultures. Not all Caucasians, Blacks, Europeans, Native Americans, or any other group of culturally similar people should be assumed to be the same. Culture has been defined as "the socially transmitted behavior patterns, beliefs, and products of work of a particular population, community, or group of people" (Cohen, 1994, p. 5). Group members may do similar things, but the individuals are not the same. Human beings have intercultural and multicultural differences; each individual human being is unique because his brain allows him to think differently, and his abilities allow him to behave differently. CQ can be taught and so can DQ.

Diversity Management in Practice

Indisputably, diversity management is a difficult and complex task. Significant barriers including human, psychological, organization, and institutional resistance challenge the execution of diversity to meet the business need (Avery, 2011; Konrad, 2006). Leaders must build "support for a diversity initiative [using] a clearly defined strategy for communicating the business case [with] clear roles and responsibilities for the senior leadership team, managers, and employees" (Jayne & Dipboye, 2004, p. 418). Why does there need to be a business case for diversity? Is it only about the money as opposed to doing the moral, legal, and ethical right thing for all employees?

Marques (2007) further explained that "if conscientiously applied and facilitated at all levels, diversity can elevate an organization's long-term performance to levels that are beyond all expectations" (p. 24). Hughes and Stephens (2014) suggested that the combination of all these dynamic elements provided evidence to support that diversity is not a legal issue but a constructive mindset which strongly influences individuals and organizations toward strategic thinking, interactive and collective discourse, and ethical behavior when dealing with protected class employees. If diversity is a legal issue, why are all the protected class laws not being enforced? Organization leaders should learn to use DQ to value the differences in personality styles and other inter-personnel characteristics of employees and use those differences to enhance the employee and the organization (Hughes, 2012).

POWER OF POSITION AND DIVERSITY MANAGEMENT

The success or failure of workplace diversity is often controlled by individuals with power and those who are a part of the power structure inside organizations. Leaders have power which is derived from their central position inside the organization (Brass & Burkhardt, 1993; Burkhardt & Brass, 1990). Jiang et al. (2022) described employees' perception of the extent to which an organization is fair and inclusive as the organization's diversity climate. Leaders influence employees' perception of the organization's diversity climate (Park & Park, 2022; Sakr et al., 2023). Leaders with power over diversity efforts must have DQ and use that DQ for the good of all stakeholders.

Many protected class employees, despite holding positions such as the Chief Diversity Officer for an organization, often lack the necessary power to affect change. A position must hold power as well as the person in the position. When the position is perceived to hold no power so is the person in the position perceived to be powerless. Protected class employees want powerful positions containing powerful people. A perfect example of this is the position of the President of the United States. The position is seen as the most powerful position in the world and the person in the position is perceived to be the most powerful person in the world. However, When President Barack Hussein Obama was elected, many individuals in the United States Congress and US society tried to diminish his power. By trying to diminish President Obama's power, they were essentially weakening the power of the presidency. Their blind ambitions against President Obama prevented them from seeing how their actions were also an attack on the power of the position. There has been a lot of evidence of this but none more poignant than Forbes magazine in 2010 deciding that the Chinese Premier was more powerful than their own President Barack Obama. This was the first time ever that Forbes had selected anyone other than the sitting US President.

Diversity and Human Resource Management (HRM)

A key to successful diversity efforts is "prioritizing diversity throughout organizational human-resource management practices" (Avery, 2011, p. 251). Avery (2011) also noted that:

> Through their human-resource management policies and procedures, organizations have a considerable impact on the diversity climates they facilitate and the employees they attract and retain. If they wish to encourage employee diversity activism, it is imperative that they take steps to ensure that the climates, supervisors, and coworkers employees routinely encounter convey that diversity is valued and supported. (p. 252)

To understand the effect of diversity on performance, organizations must also formulate a strategy to manage diversity that is connected to employees' career development plans (Pitts, 2006). Career development policies are usually managed within HRM departments and should encourage diversity and make it desirable for all employees, especially those in protected class groups and categories to remain in the organization (Pitts, 2006).

Visibility of Protected Class Employees

Often protected class employees are asked to assimilate into the organization; however, a specific example where this is not often possible and clearly visible is when dealing with the disabled. Accommodations must be made for the disabled. Many of their disabilities are visible while others are not. Some of the accommodations are simple to achieve while others require structural changes. Each protected class employee requires some form of accommodation as a part of their protected class status by organization leaders but not all of them receive the required accommodations. One accommodation policy for a specific protected class group or category may be enough. In many instances protected class employees are expected to assimilate and adapt to organization norms without fanfare. They can be seen but not heard within the organization. Some norms need to be reevaluated by DQ leaders.

Using Diversity Theories and Practices

Diversity theories (Nkomo et al., 2019; Post et al., 2021; Ray, 2019) and practices must be comprehensively learned and expressed in meaningful ways to drive change within organizations. To drive diversity, change leaders must have DQ. They must use DQ to recognize and leverage each employee's contribution for added success. The exponential capability that exists within an employee's location, use, maintenance, modification, and time value, and the personal diversity characteristics that everyone possesses bring extensive opportunities for organizations to succeed through the successful performance activities of their employees (Hughes, 2012). All employees must be perceived as valuable to the organization. If they are employed by the organization, they must contribute. The impact of the COVID-19 pandemic forced organizations to evaluate the contributions of all their employees. Organizational leaders are not required to "choose diverse employees over others, but ... they [should] acknowledge and understand all employees and use that knowledge to enhance and improve organizational performance" (Hughes & Stephens, 2012, p. 262). Employees' contributions can be stifled because of a lack of leader's DQ or enhanced by leader's DQ. Most employees are going to perform their job despite how they are treated because of obligations external to the organization. Their performance will often be less than what they are truly capable of producing because of the ill effects of discrimination. Quiet quitting is one way this is manifested in employee behavior.

The speed of demographic change has forced individuals and organizations to seek ways to change and adapt quickly. Each worker is different and finding a fit between organizational and individual goals is essential (Baird & Meshoulam, 1988; Becker et al., 2009; Delery, 1998; Vroom, 1973; Wright & McMahan, 1992). All workers including protected class employees who may not have been previously considered mainstream (Avery, 2011) must be allowed to fit within the organization. Organizations cannot continue to ostracize employees who are different and expect to sustain competitiveness in the constantly changing, global workplace.

Diversity among employees is not always recognizable by leaders, and, in some instances, leaders sometimes express their knowledge of protected class employees by discriminating against them through stereotyping. This is not the way to engender favor from protected class employees; by showing them that the only thing you know about them are the ways they have been discriminated against or stereotyped using disrespectful communications. Some leaders purposely make comments that do not add value to the conversation. Examples include comments such as telling a male employee that you had to make concessions for him because he took legally protected paternal leave. It is inexcusable and insulting.

The pragmatic approach to diversity management and procedural justice in the workplace requires the elimination of the cultural and environmental barriers that prevent the promotion of diversity across all organizational initiatives. If protected class employees appears content at work, it does not mean that they are satisfied with their treatment. Usually, it is when the worker decides to change jobs that the employer becomes aware that there is a problem.

Hughes (2012, 2018b) suggested that the five values, when recognized and understood, allow leaders the ability to clearly articulate measurable differences between employees without hindering or discriminating against another employee's ability to perform. There may be instances where employees feel slighted due to their protected class status; however, if the employee is allowed to recognize their own strengths within the five values and how those strengths align with organizational goals, the differences may not be seen as barriers to success.

Despite organization leaders' attempts to show their employees that they are all being treated fairly within the workplace, there continue to be instances of disparities (Folger & Greenberg, 1985; Jun et al., 2023; Quillian et al., 2017; Sonnemaker, 2021; Triana et al., 2021; Yang & Liu, 2021). As the workforce becomes more diverse with more protected class employees in the workplace (e.g., more employees over the age of 40, more women, and more disabled veterans), organizations must understand that providing their leaders with training in legal aspects of discrimination is not enough. Leaders must be equipped and capable with DQ to discern and document clear differences between employees. They must discern the difference from a positive perspective as opposed to the typical negative perspective where illegal discrimination occurs. The five values show employees that they are different, and that their unique contributions can be valued by the organization.

Diversity Training

It has been recognized by diversity scholars that the focus of diversity training has shifted from awareness of diversity to accountability for diversity (Hughes & Byrd, 2015; Triana et al., 2021; Yang & Liu, 2021). All employees are being encouraged to take responsibility for their own behaviors toward protected class employees. Diversity training can help to build a workplace environment where all employees feel valued and respected; however, the diversity training is just the beginning and, in many cases, can also be the end when those who received the training do not put their training to use to make the environment better. Diversity training that does not result in behavior modification is a wasted investment (Andoh et al., 2022; Deitch et al., 2003; Roberson et al., 2022; Roberts & Rizzo, 2021) for the organization especially if an employee who received training chooses to discriminate despite the training.

DQ can be taught to leaders so that they can develop methods of better interacting with protected employees. The foundational premise of DQ training must be assessing participants' knowledge of protected class employees and the laws that protect them; helping participants to fill in the gaps of what they are missing from a knowledge perspective; and ensuring that they apply current and new knowledge all the time during their interactions with protected class employees and others. Many of the problems occur when others who know how to do better intentionally choose not to do better or to help others do better. They do not intervene to help the person being mistreated nor do they hold leaders accountable for the inappropriate behavior.

Providing examples of problems and pitfalls to avoid is necessary within DQ training. Many individuals may believe that they are not discriminatory toward protected class employees because they have been allowed to perform bad behavior for such a long time (Anand et al., 2004); it has been normalized.

CONCLUSION

DQ needs to become a part of the mainstream conversation because of the disjointed diversity efforts that have not been successful. The attempt to mainstream acceptance of protected class employees began centuries ago; however, since 1965, the US Department of Labor's Office of Federal Contract Compliance Programs (OFCCP) has been responsible for enforcing Executive Order 11,246 (affirmative action or AA). There has been constant opposition to AA from, specifically, White males which led to the introduction of the term diversity which created confusion, ignorance, and chaos in the workplace. AA continues to have negative connotations because its opponents continue to tell those without DQ that AA does not support merit and that those who benefit from AA are incompetent (Banks, 2006a, b; Combs, 2003; Combs et al., 2005; Gutiérrez y Muhs et al., 2012; Heilman et al., 1992; Johnston & Teicher, 2010; Myrdal, 1944; Sinclair, 2000; Susskind et al., 2014; Thomas, 1990). Not all diversity efforts have failed and there is tolerance of others who are different within many workplaces. White women especially benefited from AA (Robinson, 2010). The commendable success of those efforts will be recognized within DQ.

The challenge will be having executive leaders accept DQ and recognize it as a benefit to the organization. In some instances, they may not want to know what is happening to protected class employees because of legal culpability. However, executive leaders must ask the following and similar questions of their organization leaders:

- In what ways can we assess the situation and obtain the facts regarding protected class employees in the workplace?
- In what ways can we generate possible solutions using non-judgmental thinking?
- In what ways can we share facts regarding protected class employee treatment without destructive repercussions?
- In what ways can we use factual information and not stereotypes about protected class employees that persist within our organization?
- In what ways can we obtain a commitment for improvement from leaders who are already paid to improve diversity?
- In what ways can we provide opportunities for sharing what has been learned from the DQ training?

Hughes and Liang (2020) developed a measure for examining a leader's DQ-like methods used to measure EQ, CQ, and IQ.

References

Amis, J. M., Mair, J., & Munir, K. A. (2020). The Organizational Reproduction of Inequality. *Academy of Management Annals, 14*(1), 195–230.

Amodio, D. M. (2009). Intergroup Anxiety Effects on the Control of Racial Stereotypes: A Psychoneuroendocrine Analysis. *Journal of Experimental Social Psychology, 45*(1), 60–67.

Anand, R., & Winters, M. F. (2008). A Retrospective View of Corporate Diversity Training from 1964 to the Present. *Academy of Management Learning & Education, 7*(3), 356–372.

Anand, V., Ashforth, B. E., & Joshi, M. (2004). Business as Usual: The Acceptance and Perpetuation of Corruption in Organizations. *The Academy of Management Executive, 18*(2), 39–53.

Avery, D. R. (2011). Support for Diversity in Organizations: A Theoretical Exploration of Its Origins and Offshoots. *Organizational Psychology Review, 1*(3), 239–256. https://doi.org/10.1177/2041386611402115

Baird, L., & Meshoulam, I. (1988). Managing Two Fits of Strategic Human Resource Management. *Academy of Management Review, 13*(1), 116–128.

Banks, C. H. (2006a). Career Planning: Toward an Inclusive Model. In M. Karsten (Ed.), *Gender, Race and Ethnicity in the Workplace* (Vol. III, pp. 99–116). Greenwood Publishing Group.

Banks, C. H. (2006b). Career Planning: Towards a More Inclusive Model for Women and Diverse Individuals. In F. Nafukho and H. Chen (Eds.), *Academy of Human Resource Development International Conference (AHRD) Proceedings. Symp. 31-1* (pp. 640–647). Academy of Human Resource Development.

Banks, C. H., Collier, M. M., & Preyan, L. M. (2010). Leveraging Diversity Through Faculty Perception of Their Power to Influence Diversity. *International Journal of Human Resource Development and Management, 10*(3), 208–223.

Banks, J. A. (2008). Diversity, Group Identity, and Citizenship Education in a Global Age. *Educational Researcher, 37*(3), 129–139.

Banks, K. H., Kohn-Wood, L. P., & Spencer, M. (2006). An Examination of the African American Experience of Everyday Discrimination and Symptoms of Psychological Distress. *Community Mental Health Journal, 42*(6), 555–570. https://doi.org/10.1007/s10597-006-9052-9

Baruch, Y., & Jenkins, S. (2007). Swearing at Work and Permissive Leadership Culture: When Anti-Social Becomes Social and Incivility is Acceptable. *Leadership & Organization Development Journal, 28*(6), 492–507.

Becker, B. E., Huselid, M. A., & Beatty, R. W. (2009). *The Differentiated Workforce: Transforming Talent into Strategic Impact*. Harvard Business Press.

Brass, D. J., & Burkhardt, M. E. (1993). Potential Power and Power Use: An Investigation of Structure and Behavior. *Academy of Management Journal, 36*(3), 441–470.

Brault, Matthew W. (2012). *Americans with Disabilities: 2010* (pp. P70–P131) (pp. 1–131). US Department of Commerce, Economics and Statistics Administration, US Census Bureau.

Burkhardt, M. E., & Brass, D. J. (1990). Changing Patterns or Patterns of Change: The Effects of a Change in Technology on Social Network Structure and Power. *Administrative Science Quarterly, 35*(1), 104–127.

Chow, R. M., Phillips, L. T., Lowery, B. S., & Unzueta, M. M. (2021). Fighting Backlash to Racial Equity Efforts. *MIT Sloan Management Review, 62*(4), 25–31.

Chua, A., & Rubenfeld, J. (2014). *The Triple Package: How Three Unlikely Traits Explain the Rise and Fall of Cultural Groups in America.* The Penguin Press.

Clark, C. M., Olender, L., Kenski, D., & Cardoni, C. (2013). Exploring and Addressing Faculty-To-Faculty Incivility: A National Perspective and Literature Review. *Journal of Nursing Education, 52*(4), 211–218.

Cohen, R. J. (1994). *Psychology and Adjustment: Values, Culture, and Change.* Allyn & Bacon.

Combs, G. M. (2003). The Duality of Race and Gender for Managerial African American Women: Implications of Informal Social Networks on Career Advancement. *Human Resource Development Review, 2*(4), 385–405.

Combs, G., Nadkarni, S., & Combs, M. W. (2005). Implementing Affirmative Action Plans in Multi-National Corporations. *Organizational Dynamics, 34*(4), 346–360.

Covey, S. R. (2006). Leading in the Knowledge Worker Age. *The Leader of the Future, 2,* 215–225.

Crenshaw, K. (1989). Demarginalizing the Intersection of Race and Sex: A Black Feminist Critique of Antidiscrimination Doctrine, Feminist Theory and Antiracist Politics. *University of Chicago Legal Forum, 1989,* 139–167.

D'Netto, B., & Sohal, A. S. (1999). Human Resource Practices and Workforce Diversity: An Empirical Assessment. *International Journal of Manpower, 20*(8), 530–547.

Dasgupta, P. (2005). Economics of Social Capital. *The Economic Record, 81*(s1), S2–S21.

David, S., & Congleton, C. (2014, Summer). Emotional Agility: How Effective Leaderrs Manage Their Negative Thoughts and Feelings. *Harvard Business Review Onpoint,* 88–92.

Day, N. E., & Schoenrade, P. (2000). The Relationship among Reported Disclosure of Sexual Orientation, Anti-Discrimination Policies, Top Management Support and Work Attitudes of Gay and Lesbian Employees. *Personnel Review, 29*(3), 346–363.

Deci, Edward L., & Ryan, Richard M. (1985). *Intrinsic Motivation and Self-Determination in Human Behavior*. Springer Science & Business Media.

Deitch, E. A., Barsky, A., Butz, R. M., Chan, S., Brief, A. P., & Bradley, J. C. (2003). Subtle Yet Significant: The Existence and Impact of Everyday Racial Discrimination in the Workplace. *Human Relations, 56*(11), 1299–1324. *Business Source Premier*, EBSCO*host* (Accessed 28 Dec 2014).

Delery, J. E. (1998). Issues of Fit in Strategic Human Resource Management: Implications for Research. *Human Resource Management Review, 8*(3), 289–309.

Dias, F. A. (2023). The (In) Flexibility of Racial Discrimination: Labor Market Context and the Racial Wage Gap in the United States, 2000 to 2021. *Socius, 9.* https://doi.org/10.1177/23780231221148932.

Doane, A. W., & Bonilla-Silva, E. (Eds.). (2003). *White Out: The Continuing Significance of Racism*. Psychology Press.

Dobbin, F., & Kalev, A. (2022). *Getting to Diversity: What Works and What Doesn't*. Harvard University Press.

Earley, P. C., & Mosakowski, E. (2004). Cultural Intelligence. *Harvard Business Review, 82*(10), 139–146.

Farley, J. E. (1987). Disproportionate Black and Hispanic Unemployment in US Metropolitan Areas: The Roles of Racial Inequality, Segregation and Discrimination in Male Joblessness. *American Journal of Economics and Sociology, 46*(2), 129–150.

Folger, R., & Greenberg, J. (1985). Procedural Justice: An Interpretive Analysis of Personnel Systems. *Research in Personnel and Human Resource Management, 3*(1), 141–183.

Foster, S. (1993). Difference and Equality: A Critical Assessment of the Concept of Diversity. *Wisconsin Law Review*, 105–161.

Fox, S., & Stallworth, L. E. (2005). Racial/Ethnic Bullying: Exploring Links between Bullying and Racism in the US Workplace. *Journal of Vocational Behavior, 66*(3), 438–456.

Fulkerson, J. R., & Schuler, R. S. (1992). Managing Worldwide Diversity at Pepsi-Cola International. In S. E. Jackson (Ed.), *Diversity in the Workplace: Human Resources Initiatives, Society for Industrial and Organisational Psychology* (The Professional Practice Series). Guildford Press.

Gelfand, M. J., Nishii, L. H., Raver, J. L., & Schneider, B. (2005). Discrimination in Organizations: An Organizational-Level Systems Perspective. *Discrimination at Work: Psychological and Organizational Bases, 104*, 117–144. Psychology Press.

Gelfand, M. J., L. Imai, & R. Fehr. (2008). Thinking Intelligently About Cultural Intelligence. In S. Ang & L. Van Dyne (Eds.), *Handbook on Cultural Intelligence: Theory, Measurement and Applications* (pp. 375–388). ME Sharpe.

Goleman, D. (1995). *Emotional Intelligence*. Bantam Books.

Goleman, D. (1998a). What Makes a Leader? *Harvard Business Review, 76*(1998b), 93–102.

Goleman, D. (1998b). *Working with Emotional Intelligence*. Bantam Books.

Goleman, D. (2000). Leadership That Gets Results. *Harvard Business Review, 78*(2), 78–93.

Goleman, D. (2013). Leadership that Gets Results. *Harvard Business Review, 78*(2), 26–38.

Gutiérrez y Muhs, G., Niemann, Y. F., Gonzalez, C. G., & Harris, A. P. (2012). *Presumed Incompetent: The Intersections of Race and Class for Women in Academia*. University Press of Colorado.

Gutman, A., Koppes, L. L., & Vodanovich, S. J. (2011). *EEO Law and Personnel Practices* (3rd ed.). Psychology Press.

Heilman, M. E., Block, C. J., & Lucas, J. A. (1992). Presumed Incompetent? Stigmatization and Affirmative Action Efforts. *Journal of Applied Psychology, 77*(4), 536–544.

Hellerstedt, K., Uman, T., & Wennberg, K. (2022). Fooled By Diversity? When Diversity Initiatives Exacerbate Rather Than Mitigate Inequality. *Academy of Management Perspectives*. https://doi.org/10.5465/amp.2021.0206

Herrnstein, R. J., & Murray, C. (1994). *The Bell Curve: Intelligence and Class Structure in American Life*. Free Press Enterprise.

Hirsh, C. E. (2009). The Strength of Weak Enforcement: The Impact of Discrimination Charges, Legal Environments, and Organizational Conditions on Workplace Segregation. *American Sociological Review, 74*(2), 245–271.

Holladay, C. L., Knight, J. L., Paige, D. L., & Quiñones, M. A. (2003). The Influence of Framing on Attitudes Toward Diversity Training. *Human Resource Development Quarterly, 14*(3), 245–263.

Hoynes, H. W., Miller, D. L., & Schaller, J. (2012). *Who Suffers During Recessions?* (No. w17951). National Bureau of Economic Research.

Hughes, C., & Byrd, M. (2015). *Managing HRD Programs: Current Issues and Evolving Trends*. Palgrave Macmillan.

Hughes, C., & Liang, X. (2020). *Hughes and Liang Diversity Intelligence® (DQ) Scale© 2020*. https://www.diversityintelligencellc.com

Hughes, C., & S. DeVaughn. (2012). Leveraging Workforce Diversity Through a Career Development Paradigm Shift. In C. L. Scott & M. Y. Byrd (Eds.), *Handbook of Research on Workforce Diversity in a Global Society: Technologies and Concepts* (pp. 262–272). IGI Global.

Hughes, C. (2012). *Valuing People and Technology in the Workplace: A Competitive Advantage Framework*. IGI Global.

Hughes, C. (2014). *American Black Women and Interpersonal Leadership Styles*. The Netherlands Sense Publishers.

Hughes, C. (2015). Valuing Diversity through a Career Development Paradigm Shift. *Academy of Business Research Journal, 2,* 40–67.

Hughes, C. (2018). *Workforce Inter-Personnel Diversity: The Power to Influence Human Productivity and Career Development.* Springer International Publishing.

Hughes, C., & Brown, L. M. (2018). Exploring Leaders' Discriminatory, Passive-Aggressive Behavior Toward Protected Class Employees Using Diversity Intelligence. *Advances in Developing Human Resources, 20*(3), 263–284.

Jayne, M. E. A., & Dipboye, R. L. (2004). Leveraging Diversity to Improve Business Performance: Research Findings and Recommendations for Organizations. *Human Resource Management, 43*(4), 409–424.

Jiang, Z., DeHart-Davis, L., & Borry, E. L. (2022). Managerial Practice and Diversity Climate: The Roles of Workplace Voice, Centralization, and Teamwork. *Public Administration Review, 82*(3), 459–472. https://doi.org/10.1111/puar.13494

Johnston, S., & Teicher, J. (2010). Is Diversity Management Past Its 'Use-By Date' for Professional and Managerial Women? *International Journal of Employment Studies, 18*(1, Special Edition), 34–62.

Joshi, A., Son, J., & Roh, H. (2015). When Can Women Close the Gap? A Meta-Analytic Test of Sex Differences in Performance and Rewards. *Academy of Management Journal, 58*(5), 1516–1545.

Jun, S., Phillips, L. T., & Foster-Gimbel, O. A. (2023). The Missing Middle: Asian Employees' Experience of Workplace Discrimination and Pro-Black Allyship. *Journal of Applied Psychology, 108*(2), 225–248. https://doi.org/10.1037/apl0001068.supp

Karsten, M. F. (Ed.). (2006). *Gender, Race, and Ethnicity in the Workplace: Management, Gender, and Ethnicity in the United States* (Vol. 1). Greenwood Publishing Group.

Kidder, D. L., Lankau, M. J., Chrobot-Mason, D., Mollica, K. A., & Friedman, R. A. (2004). Backlash Toward Diversity Initiatives: Examining the Impact of Diversity Program Justification, Personal and Group Outcomes. *International Journal of Conflict Management, 15*(1), 77–102.

Kincheloe, J. L., Steinberg, S. R., & Gresson III, A. D. (1997). *Measured Lies: The Bell Curve Examined.* St. Martin's Press, Scholarly and Reference Division.

Kivel, P. (2002). *Uprooting Racism: How White People can Work for Racial Justice.* New Society Publishers.

Konrad, A. M. (2006). Leveraging Workplace Diversity in Organizations. *Organization Management Journal, 3*(3), 194–189.

Konyu-Fogel, G. (2011). *Exploring the Effect of Global Mindset on Leadership Behavior: An Empirical Study of Business Leaders in Global Organizations.* Lap Lambert Academic Publishing GMBH & Co.

Lalonde, D. (2021). Does Cultural Appropriation Cause Harm? *Politics, Groups, and Identities, 9*(2), 329–346.

Lenard, P. T., & Balint, P. (2020). What Is (the Wrong of) Cultural Appropriation? *Ethnicities, 20*(2), 331–352.

Lin, S.-C., & Huang, Y.-M. (2005). The Role of Social Capital in the Relationship Between Human Capital and Career Mobility: Moderator Or Mediator? *Journal of Intellectual Capital, 6*(2), 191–205.

Livingston, R. (2020). How to Promote Racial Equity in the Workplace. *Harvard Business Review, 98*(5), 64–72.

Locke, S. S. (1997). Incredible Shrinking Protected Class: Redefining the Scope of Disability Under the Americans with Disabilities Act. *The University of Colorado Law Review, 68*, 107–127.

Loden, M., & Rosener, J. B. (1991). *Workforce America! Managing Employee Diversity as a Vital Resource*. Business One Irwin.

Marques, J. (2007). Diversity as a Win-Win Strategy. *Management Services, 51*(1), 22–24.

Mattingly, M. J., & Smith, K. E. (2010). Changes in Wives' Employment when Husbands Stop Working: A Recession-Prosperity Comparison. *Family Relations, 59*(4), 343–357.

Mayer, J. D., & Salovey, P. (1997). What Is Emotional Intelligence? In P. Salovey & D. Sluyter (Eds.), *Emotional Development and Emotional Intelligence: Educational Implications* (pp. 3–34). Basic Books.

Mayer, J. D., Salovey, P., & Caruso, D. R. (2000). Models of Emotional Intelligence. In R. J. Sternberg (Ed.), *Handbook of Human Intelligence* (2nd ed., pp. 396–422). Cambridge University Press.

Mehra, R., Alspaugh, A., Dunn, J. T., Franck, L. S., McLemore, M. R., Keene, D. E., Kershaw, T. S., & Ickovics, J. R. (2023). "'Oh Gosh, Why Go?' Cause They Are Going to Look at Me and Not Hire": Intersectional Experiences of Black Women Navigating Employment During Pregnancy and Parenting. *BMC Pregnancy and Childbirth, 23*(1), 1–13.

Milliken, F. J., Morrison, E. W., & Hewlin, P. F. (2003). An Exploratory Study of Employee Silence: Issues That Employees Don't Communicate Upward and Why. *Journal of Management Studies, 40*(6), 1453–1476.

Mitchell, M. S., Rivera, G., & Treviño, L. K. (2023). Unethical Leadership: A Review, Analysis, and Research Agenda. *Personnel Psychology, 76*, 1–37. Advance online publication. https://doi.org/10.1111/peps.12574

Morrison, A. M. (1992). *The New Leaders: Guidelines on Leadership Diversity in America*. Jossey- Bass Publishers.

Myrdal, G. (1944). *An American Dilemma*. Harper & Row.

Near, J. P., Dworkin, T. M., & Miceli, M. P. (1993). Explaining the Whistle-Blowing Process: Suggestions from Power Theory and Justice Theory. *Organization Science, 4*(3), 393–411.

Nkomo, S. M., Myrtle P. Bell, Laura M. R., Aparna J., & Sherry MB T. (2019). Diversity at a critical juncture: New theories for a complex phenomenon. *Academy of Management Review, 44*(3), 498–517.

North, C. S., Gordon, M., Kim, Y.-S., Wallace, N. E., Smith, R. P., Pfefferbaum, B., Hong, B. A., Ali, O., Wang, C., & Pollio, D. E. (2014). Expression of Ethnic Prejudice in Focus Groups from Agencies Affected by the 9/11 Attacks on the World Trade Center. *Journal of Ethnic and Cultural Diversity in Social Work, 23*(2), 93–109.

O'Leary-Kelly, A. M., & Newman, J. L. (2004). The Implications of Performance Feedback Research for Understanding Antisocial Work Behavior. *Human Resource Management Review, 13*(4), 605–629.

Paradies, Y. (2006). A Systematic Review of Empirical Research on Self-Reported Racism and Health. *International Journal of Epidemiology, 35*(4), 888–901.

Park, S., Park, S., & Shryack, J. (2022). Measures of Climate for Inclusion and Diversity: Review and Summary. *Human Resource Development Quarterly, 1–18.* https://doi.org/10.1002/hrdq.21493

Perry, B. (2000). Button-Down Terror: The Metamorphosis of the Hate Movement. *Sociological Focus, 33*(2), 113–131.

Petersen, R. D. (2002). *Understanding Ethnic Violence: Fear, Hatred, and Resentment in Twentieth-Century Eastern Europe.* Cambridge University Press.

Peterson, L. (1999). The Definition of Diversity: Two Views. A More Specific Definition. *Journal of Library Administration, 27*(1–2), 17–26. https://doi.org/10.1300/J111v27n01_03

Phillips, T., & Smith, P. (2003). Everyday Incivility: Towards a Benchmark. *The Sociological Review, 51*(1), 85–108.

Pitts, D. W. (2006). Modeling the Impact of Diversity Management. *Review of Public Personnel Administration, 26*(3), 245–268.

Post, C., Muzio, D., Sarala, R., Wei, L., & Faems, D. (2021). Theorizing Diversity in Management Studies: New Perspectives and Future Directions. *Journal of Management Studies, 58*(8), 2003–2023.

Powell, G. N., & Butterfield, D. A. (1994). Race, Gender and the Glass Ceiling: Empirical Study of Actual Promotions to Top Management. In *Annual Meeting of the Academy of Management*, Dallas, TX.

Pred, A. R. (2004). *The Past Is Not Dead: Facts, Fictions, and Enduring Racial Stereotypes.* University of Minnesota Press.

Quillian, L., Pager, D., Hexel, O., & Midtbøen, A. H. (2017). Meta-Analysis of Field Experiments Shows No Change in Racial Discrimination in Hiring Over Time. *Proceedings of the National Academy of Sciences, 114*(41), 10870–10875. https://doi.org/10.1073/pnas.1706255114

Ray, V. (2019). A Theory of Racialized Organizations. *American Sociological Review, 84*(1), 26–53.

Redmond, M. V. (2000). Cultural Distance as a Mediating Factor between Stress and Intercultural Communication Competence. *International Journal of Intercultural Relations, 24*(1), 151–159.

Roberson, Q., Moore, O. A., & Bell, B. S. (2022). An Active Learning Approach to Diversity Training. *Academy of Management Review.*

Roberts, S. O., & Rizzo, M. T. (2021). The Psychology of American Racism. *American Psychologist, 76*(3), 475–487.

Robinson, E. (2010). *Disintegration: The Splintering of Black America.* Doubleday.

Rubin, P. J. (1998). Equal Rights, Special Rights, and the Nature of Antidiscrimination Law. *Michigan Law Review, 97*(2), 564–598.

Sakr, N., Son Hing, L. S., & González-Morales, M. G. (2023). Development and Validation of the Marginalized-Group-Focused Diversity Climate Scale: Group Differences and Outcomes. *Journal of Business Psychology.* https://doi.org/10.1007/s10869-022-09859-3

Salovey, P., & Mayer, J. D. (1990). Emotional Intelligence. *Imagination, Cognition and Personality, 9*(3), 185–211.

Schreiber, C. T., Price, K. F., & Morrison, A. (1993). Workplace Diversity and the Glass Ceiling: Practices, Barriers, Possibilities. *Human Resource Planning, 16*(2), 51–69.

Schuler, R. S., Dowling, P. J., Smart, J. P., & Huber, V. L. (1992). *Human Resource Management in Australia* (2nd ed.). Harper Educational Publishers.

Shen, J., Chanda, A., D'netto, B., & Monga, M. (2009). Managing Diversity Through Human Resource Management: An International Perspective and Conceptual Framework. *The International Journal of Human Resource Management, 20*(2), 235–251.

Siems, M. (2019). The Law and Ethics of 'Cultural Appropriation.' *International Journal of Law in Context, 15*(4), 408–423.

Sinclair, A. (2000). Teaching Managers About Masculinities: Are You Kidding? *Management Learning, 31*(1), 83–101.

Smith, I. A., & Griffiths, A. (2022). Microaggressions, Everyday Discrimination, Workplace Incivilities, and Other Subtle Slights at Work: A Meta-Synthesis. *Human Resource Development Review, 21*(3), 275–299.

Sonnemaker, T. (2021). 2020 Brought a Wave of Discrimination and Harassment Allegations Against Major Companies Like Amazon, McDonald's, and Pinterest. These Are Some of the Year's High-Profile Legal Battles. *Business Insider.* https://www.businessinsider.com/every-company-that-was-sued-discrimination-and-harassment-lawsuits-2020-2021-1

Sum, A., & Khatiwada, I. (2010). The Nation's Underemployed in the 'Great Recession' of 2007–09. *Monthly Labor Review, 133*(11), 3–15.

Susskind, A. M., Brymer, R. A., Kim, W. G., Lee, H. Y., & Way, S. A. (2014). Attitudes and Perceptions Toward Affirmative Action Programs: An Application of Institutional Theory. *International Journal of Hospitality Management, 41*, 38–48.

Swim, J. K., & Cohen, L. L. (1997). Overt, Covert, and Subtle Sexism a Comparison Between the Attitudes Toward Women and Modern Sexism Scales. *Psychology of Women Quarterly, 21*(1), 103–118.

Swim, J. K., Hyers, L. L., Cohen, L. L., & Ferguson, M. J. (2001). Everyday Sexism: Evidence for Its Incidence, Nature, and Psychological Impact from Three Daily Diary Studies. *Journal of Social Issues, 57*(1), 31–53.

Taylor, P., Kochhar, R., Fry, R., Velasco, G., & Motel, S. (2011, July). *Wealth Gaps Rise to Record Highs Between Whites, Blacks, and Hispanics* (Vol. 26). Pew Research Center.

Templer, K. J., Tay, C., & Chandrasekar, N. A. (2006). Motivational Cultural Intelligence, Realistic Job Preview, Realistic Living Conditions Preview, and Cross-Cultural Adjustment. *Group & Organization Management, 31*(1), 154–173.

Thomas, D. A. (1990). *Strategies for Managing Racial Differences in Work-Centered Develop-Mental Relationships* (Working paper). Wharton School of Business, University of Pennsylvania.

Thomas, D. A., & Ely, R. J. (1996). Making Differences Matter: A New Paradigm for Managing Diversity. *Harvard Business Review, 74*(5), 79–90.

Treviño, L. K., Weaver, G. R., & Reynolds, S. J. (2006). Behavioral Ethics in Organizations: A Review. *Journal of Management, 32*(6), 951–990.

Triana, M. D., Carmen, P. G., Chapa, O., Richard, O., & Colella, A. (2021). Sixty Years of Discrimination and Diversity Research in Human Resource Management: A Review with Suggestions for Future Research Directions. *Human Resource Management, 60*(1), 145–204. https://doi.org/10.1002/hrm.22052

U.S. Equal Employment Opportunity Commission. (2013). *Fiscal Year 2013: Performance and Accountability Report.* http://www.eeoc.gov/eeoc/plan/upload/2013par.pdf

Van Laer, K., & Janssens, M. (2011). Ethnic Minority Professionals' Experiences with Subtle Discrimination in the Workplace. *Human Relations, 64*(9), 1203–1227.

Vroom, V. H. (1973). A New Look at Managerial Decision Making. *Organizational Dynamics, 1*(4), 66–80.

Wheeler, S. C., Jarvis, W. B. G., & Petty, R. E. (2001). Think Unto Others: The Self-Destructive Impact of Negative Racial Stereotypes. *Journal of Experimental Social Psychology, 37*(2), 173–180.

Wieand, P. (2002). Drucker's Challenge: Communication and the Emotional Glass Ceiling. *Ivey Business Journal, 66*(5), 32–37.

Wilson, B. L., Diedrich, A., Phelps, C. L., & Choi, M. (2011). Bullies at Work: The Impact of Horizontal Hostility in the Hospital Setting and Intent to Leave. *Journal of Nursing Administration, 41*(11), 453–458.

Wright, P. M., & McMahan, G. C. (1992). Theoretical Perspectives for Strategic Human Resource Management. *Journal of Management, 18*(2), 295–320.

Yang, J. R., & Liu, J. (2021, January 19). *Strengthening accountability for discrimination: Confronting Fundamental Power Imbalances in the employment relationship*. Economic Policy Institute. https://www.epi.org/unequalpower/publications/strengthening-accountability-for-discrimination-confronting-fundamental-power-imbalances-in-the-employment-relationship/

Diversity Intelligence and Leadership Development: How Allyship, Anti-Racism, and Inclusive Language Hinder Diversity Efforts

Leaders' behaviors, language, labels, and management can all hinder diversity efforts. Many leaders perceive their behaviors, language, labels that they use, and management actions differently than how they are received by protected class employees. Their inability to understand and accept that what they intended is not what occurs offers them room for growth through DQ.

Diversity Change and DQ

Change begins at the top of the organization. If organizations are truly seeking diversity change, leaders must have DQ. Leaders must disseminate DQ throughout the organization, and they cannot achieve this without being diversity intelligent themselves. Leaders must perceive that they have the power to influence diversity change and to lead diversity change efforts within their organization.

Implementing DQ throughout an organization would be a change effort, and executives at the highest hierarchical levels within the organization should introduce the organization's employees to this concept. Without the highest-level introduction, employees at the varying lower levels within the organization will feel comfortable with having differing

C. Hughes, *Diversity Intelligence*,
https://doi.org/10.1007/978-3-031-33250-0_4

views of DQ, despite the implicit mission and goals of the organization (Banks et al., 2010). For change efforts to be executed properly, communication between the executive leadership and employees must be clear. All organization members must exemplify respect and connectedness to authority figures in the organization (Wlodkowski & Ginsberg, 1995). It is difficult to feel included with leaders who do not value your existence within the organization (Hughes, 2012, in press). Executive leadership determines how the inclusion of protected class employees is established within the organization. Sometimes it takes executive leadership to compel their subordinate leaders to do their jobs. They cannot abdicate their power of influence and hope that their directives are executed properly especially as it relates to protected class employees.

Leaders may feel empowered to lead their departments or areas, but not feel empowered to implement inclusive practices that are in alignment with established local, state, and federal laws and policies because of weak enforcement of policies (Hirsh, 2009; Yang & Liu, 2021). Executive leaders must compel them to do the right thing even when no one is looking. Executive leaders must not just manage the knowledge about protected class employees, they must manage their leaders by ensuring that they have DQ and use their DQ (Hughes, 2018) for the betterment of the organization (Manville, 2001; Marquardt, 2002). It is of no consequence when guidelines have been established for working with protected class employees if leaders are not practicing the required measures. Banks et al. (2010) found that leaders must not only receive the communicated mission, but leaders must also understand how their position effects the overall goal of diversity for the organization.

Behavioral Channels

Beyond creating the necessary organizational structure to implement diversity change, executive leaders must employ behavioral channels of influence that will affect the behavior of their subordinates (Agote et al., 2016; Lipshitz et al., 2006; Stainback et al., 2010). Lipshitz et al. (2006) identified eight behavioral channels which are "agenda setting, allocating time and attention, selling and telling, walking the talk, exploiting moments of truth, providing support, coaching, and dispensing rewards and recognition" (p. 102). Executives must explicitly communicate the diversity mission to the employees and apply measures that reinforce and encourage compliant behavior. By creating an atmosphere of change and increasing communication channels utilizing the eight behavior channel techniques, leaders can inspire collaborative leveraging of DQ throughout the organization. If global organizations plan to be leaders with regard to diversity, corporate board members must practice inclusive DQ behavior and influence the performance of other leaders.

Diversity goals can be accomplished within any organization if the leadership effectively communicates the mission to those who are required to execute the mission and those affected by the mission. The diversity mission must be reflected in the behavior of all the employees within the organization. Putting the acquired DQ knowledge into practice can only be accomplished if the recipients comprehend the DQ information and know what it means to put DQ into action (Hughes, 2018). Empowering leaders to support the diversity ideals of the organization will require effort, and with proper planning, diversity can be a seamless transition of organizational change.

There is often a paradox for leaders who are tasked to lead diversity initiatives within the organization. Banks et al.'s (2010) findings revealed that leaders advocate that they have beliefs that are consistent with their organizations' diversity initiatives, however, they do not believe they have the power to positively impact those initiatives through their own actions. Banks et al. examined the role of leaders' power and key components of diversity training in leader's ability to implement diversity initiatives for their organization. They found that the leaders were far less interested in their organization's definition of diversity than the idea that they were acting consistently with their own personally held beliefs. The results also suggested that leaders seriously doubted their own personal capacity to bring about change or to successfully contribute to the diversity initiatives outlined by the organization.

Banks et al. (2010) suggested that improved diversity training programs that focused on the individual's capacity to enact positive change and impact the organization's capacity to achieve its diversity goals be implemented. The Hughes and Liang DQ scale © 2020 contains a workplace education and training subscale because the leaders felt that they needed more focused workplace education and training. DQ adds to the power of position (Pfeffer, 1994) of leaders. With DQ leaders would understand their power to influence diversity changes. Other research also suggested that organizations who leverage a cooperative environment versus position power tend to find more success in achieving their goals

(Medina et al., 2008). All leaders must be equipped with the knowledge needed to affect positive change within their organizations. DQ is one area of knowledge that is currently lacking in many organizations.

Personal Communication Cases

Case 1

Matt: Within the past year, my company has installed a new Chief Diversity Officer. The role has been in place for the past 5 years. I had the opportunity to hear the new Officer's diversity strategy this past year and wanted to hear your input on an item. The over-arching strategy hits on two main concepts: diversity in the workforce and diversity in the workplace. Workforce diversity is defined as ensuring a broad range of individuals from various backgrounds are part of our workforce and leadership team. Workplace diversity she defined as an environment where everyone's voice is respected, and ideas can come from anywhere. I thought it was an outstanding "big picture" plank. The question I have is what should the tactical elements look like? I can tell you that we already have in place things like financial risk/reward for executives in terms of diversity hiring, mentoring requirements, corporate sponsorship of resource groups, and required attendance at diversity events. It just feels like those things miss the mark of the overall strategy. Any ideas?

My Response: I agree with you and would tend not to like the overall statement because I believe that most organizations have diversity and are not leveraging it.... If stakeholders inside and outside the organization do not buy into the definition of diversity or the vision, mission, etc.... or do not perceive that they have the power to influence change, it will not happen.

Matt: Very interesting. So, part of a diversity education process might be simply helping participants discover the influence they have in accomplishing diversity objectives.

My Response: Exactly. I have noticed that many people do not act because they perceive that they do not have the power to do so. Personally, I recognize the fact that I do not have to tell people or remind them that I am Black—most of them can see. I allow that to speak for itself and I focus on excellence—nothing less. I will work with whomever, just about wherever necessary to achieve excellence. This is how you can leverage diversity. Do not allow the "isms" to limit your ability to act.

Matt: It feels odd to respond to my own post, however the final assignment has given me some time and reason to reflect a bit more on this concept. I think it ties back to the question I asked previously. In short, in what ways can an organization effectively bridge the gap between the theory of a diverse workplace and how that theory looks in practice with measurable objectives? Requiring individuals to execute around specific tasks is, in my mind, a power-limiting activity that may in fact be counterproductive. Self-discovery and self-charting activities may be more power-enhancing and thus more impacting to the overall vision of diversity. To that end, I intend to reach out to the Chief Diversity Officer and share the article Dr. Hughes posted and share with her some thoughts. I think we might be best served as an organization in constructing a framework in which each individual is permitted to chart their own course (within established guidelines) in executing the organization's diversity initiatives. In this way, individuals are more capable of seeing for themselves their own power in making a positive difference (Matt Gosney, Personal Communication, 2009).

Case 2

Carmen's response to my paper about power to influence diversity: Employees that have never experienced a diverse environment may not know what necessary factors influence or hinder that environment. Diversity is not a new concept but to some, it might be an overwhelming experience that garners more attention and focus than expected. Educating the workforce, in my opinion, begins with the understanding that diversity is a team effort. It cannot become second nature if only a few workers actually practice what is required. The organization's philosophy must be intertwined into the everyday practices of all employees, including upper management. This endeavor may seem challenging at first, but it can be easily implemented with collaborative action by workers. Involving all employees within the planning of diversity workshops, cultural competency seminars, and group ice breakers may bring a sense of empowerment and build worker-to-worker relationships. Empowerment has been the central theme to our readings this week, and for good reason. Employees hold the key to unleashing cultural acceptance within the organization but may not realize this power. It is the responsibility of upper management to communicate these messages to the workforce and to encourage the successful implementation of diversity initiatives. Employees are important facilitators of change but without acknowledgment that this power exists, it can remain embedded within and never utilized (Carmen Rogers, Personal Communication, 2009).

DQ and Leadership Strategy

Leadership is a broad concept and is a difficult endeavor in and of itself. Integrating DQ with leadership is not expected to be easy to accomplish. It should be a consistent, genuine, good faith effort intended to assist with maintaining as harmonious a workplace as possible for protected class employees and their peers. DQ requires a change of thought processes by executive leaders. In many organizations changes are occurring with regard to diversity efforts but leaders lack the diversity execution skills and strategies to be effective. Integrating DQ into the leadership strategy should assist in these efforts. One of the reasons for the absence of execution is a lack of knowledge about protected class employees' individual characteristics. Often the characteristics of protected class employees are assumed based on stereotypes and opinions as opposed to concrete empirical evidence/information, historical facts, or even talking directly to the affected protected class employees. It is difficult to obtain some of the facts since the history of protected class groups and categories are not taught in many educational curriculums at any level; k-12 or postsecondary institutions, and now—in 2023—there is a concerted effort going on throughout the United States not to teach it. Also, there is a lack of empirical research studies on these groups. For example, there is a limited available, global view of American Black females in leadership roles in the workplace because there are so few of them in any given workplace (Hughes, 2014; Jackson, 2012; Sims & Carter, 2019). The commonalities and differences that protected class employees bring to the workplace must be empirically explored to determine their unique characteristics. The understanding of this information is essential as the global workforce continues to evolve to include more protected class employees.

American Black Women, DQ, and Leadership

Leaders must realize that protected class employees are rallying around topics that support their interests. For example, women are interested in genderism and sexism in the workplace (Sandberg, 2013) while American Black women are sensitive to issues about colorism (Sims, 2010; Thompson & Keith, 2001), racism, sexism, genderism, classism, and ableism.

American Black women are directly affected by intersectionality (Bowleg, 2012; Crenshaw, 1989; Collins, 1990). Some of the elements of intersectionality may not be as prominent individually, but these elements always contribute collectively to intersectionality and negatively impact American Black women (Collins, 1990). Leaders cannot and usually do not include American Black women in with all other women when their needs are incongruent with typical women's groups (Bowleg, 2012). When the topic of women is used in the US, it usually does not include American Black women (Hughes, 2014; Johnson & Pietri, 2022). Specifically, the color Black has never been associated with privilege in US society and other societies outside the continent of Africa (Chua & Rubenfeld, 2014; Gates & Curran, 2022; Sue et al., 2007).

Groysberg and Connolly (2013) stated that there is one "single barrier that affects all women [in the workplace] which is exclusion from the networks and conversations that open doors to further development and promotion" (p. 71). Although it affects all women, the depth of that affect is felt the most by American Black women who are least represented in executive leadership roles (Dobbin & Kalev, 2022; Sims & Carter, 2019). Leaders must understand this barrier that disproportionally affects women but also understands the barriers that affect all other protected class employees and work to eradicate the barriers. Eradicating the barriers leads to organizational and procedural justice. Leaders must always be ready to lead and DQ can help them display interpersonal maturity or emotional agility (David & Congleton, 2014) when interacting with protected class employees.

External Obstacles

Some of the external obstacles that protected class employees encounter in the workplace can lead to the rise of internal, mental, and emotional experiences for affected individuals (Banks et al., 2006; Kidder et al., 2004; Pierce, 1970, 1995; Watson & Henderson, 2023). The mental and emotional energy required to recognize and address mistreatment at work can diminish the energy needed to perform required job tasks (Hughes, 2014; Schmader et al., 2008). If leaders know this, it may be a motivator for them to stop their destructive behavior but then again it may be the purpose of those who choose to intentionally mistreat protected class employees. They may want protected class employees to quit so that they can say that they were never suited for the job. Distracting protected class employees from their job task reduces their ability to meet organization goals when they clearly have the KSAs to successfully do their jobs. Collier (2003) noted that the "ideological forces, institutional policies and practices, and social norms that reinforce hierarchy and privileges [outnumber the] ideologies, policies, practices, and norms encouraging and rewarding intercultural alliances" (p. 14). Collier implied that there are not enough incentives in place within organizations to encourage the success of protected class employees and instead destroys the behavioral trust that protected class employees could provide to their leaders. Trust is almost impossible to rebuild once it has been lost because of intentional mistreatment.

Covey (2013) described 8 drivers of execution that leaders should employ for employees to execute strategy. Table 4.1 suggests implications for DQ as a part of each of the execution strategy drivers.

Using DQ can help leaders to be ethical and fair in their treatment of protected class employees. Some unethical leaders (Mitchell et al., 2023) have greed for money and power, and they are prone to exploit their power. "Today everything comes under the laws of competition and the survival of the fittest where the powerful feed upon the powerless. As a consequence, masses of people find themselves excluded and marginalized: without work, without possibilities, without any means of escape" (Pope Francis, July 26, 2014). Protected class employees want to be led by leaders who understand them and whom they can trust. They are seeking evidence of genuine interest in their development from organizational leaders. Otherwise, they may not feel that their efforts are worthwhile or will not be rewarded. The following list of implications can help leaders use DQ:

Table 4.1 Eight drivers of execution and DQ implications

The 8 drivers of execution	Implications for DQ
1. Clarity—Are people clear about key priorities?	To what extent are leaders clear and making it clear to their followers that DQ is valued and a key priority of organizational success?
2. Commitment—Are they committed to achieving them?	Are leaders committed to and encouraging their employees to be committed to diversity goals using DQ?
3. Translation—Do they know what to do about them?	Do leaders know what to do about DQ issues and have they taught their employees what to do about them?
4. Discipline—Do they follow through with discipline?	Do leaders have the self-discipline and focus to apply DQ knowledge? From another perspective, is there a discipline policy for leaders who do not follow DQ and for the employees who do not follow DQ?
5. Enabling—Does the organization enable them to execute?	Does the organization enable leaders and employees to execute DQ initiatives?
6. Collaboration—Do they work together well toward key goals?	Do leaders and employees work together to achieve key DQ goals?
7. Trust—Do they trust each other to move forward together?	Do leaders and protected class employees trust each other to move forward together?
8. Accountability—Do they hold each other accountable for key goals?	Are protected class employees allowed to hold leaders and themselves accountable for key goals? Protected class employees must hold themselves accountable to function toward goals even when leaders do not do their part

1. The implication for leaders and organization programs and policies is that leaders must take a stand one way or the other and get off the fence. They, along with everyone else in America, need to choose a side for or against these racist issues in all circumstances and move forward. Everyone continues to provide excuses and allow the issues to continue to be gray until they can go through life comfortably living as if the issues are no big deal or do not exist. Protected class individuals are often perceived as "blowing" things out of proportion when in fact it is a living, breathing issue for them every day.
2. Leaders must treat employees fairly in all situations. Leaders can almost be guaranteed that by the time protected class employees

arrive in their organization, they have been treated unfairly somewhere in American society and/or another organization. Be honest and upfront with your protected class employees, and they will respect you more than if you lied or provided information which you could not substantiate or on something which you could not follow through. Always follow through on a promise regardless of if it was because you did not have time; give the employee an answer. Do not give their minds a chance to deduce that you do not care enough to respond to them. An example of this is the University of Missouri case where the students felt that the university's system president did not want to listen to them.

3. Recognize protected class employees' contributions to the organization and society. Know something about their history besides the obvious. Show the protected class employees that you know something about their groups of people. Basically, let them know by your actions that you at least respect their difference, if not them personally. It's best that you respect both, but at least acknowledge your respect for their difference and its effect on them. They will know if you do not, and you will not have to tell them.

4. To educate employees, leaders must develop an understanding of their difference. Leaders need to allow their employees to express themselves in a way that is comfortable to them by not trying to mold them into behaviors that do not fit their individual norms. They must assign projects that allow for freedom of expression to the extent possible.

5. Leaders must not assume that protected class employees are ignorant or less intelligent. Allow employees an opportunity to prove that they cannot do the job and teach from that viewpoint. Once you have evidence of what employees cannot do, that is where the training and education efforts should begin. Low expectations often yield low results. Find out what they know first instead of assuming that they do not or are incapable of knowing. Employees will know by your actions how you feel about their potential. They will lose respect for you and will not want to learn anything you try to teach. Often, they will already know what you are trying to teach, but because they know that you have assumed they do not, they probably will not tell you.

The Power of Language and the Impact of Labels

Inclusive language, anti-racism, and allyship all became popular buzz words after the death of George Floyd. However, the key question is, who does these words benefit? Does it benefit the individuals who were denied allyship, experienced racism, and had to endure linguistic profiling in its many forms despite all of this being essentially taboo or against the law since the passage of the Civil Rights Act of 1964. What took individuals so long to begin acting as allies, stop being racist, and changing their discriminatory language? Do these topics truly fit into diversity initiatives since they typically make those who are trying to be allies, less racist, and no longer using exclusive language feel better about themselves. How does it make their recipients feel?

Detriment of Inclusive Language

It is also difficult to communicate appropriately when leaders are not receptive to or are biased against your presence and display deviant behaviors (Kaptein & Van Helvoort, 2019). They do not want protected class employees there which is why there is an emergence of the term belonging in the diversity vernacular. Why should an employee fight to feel that they belong? Did they not belong when they were hired? Robbins (2013) suggested that a culture of diversity must be communicated through both words and actions. What happens when that culture is full of negative words (Wolley, 2021; Zavattaro & Bearfield, 2022) and actions toward protected employees? This must not be allowed to happen, and leaders must be willing to obtain the DQ necessary to lead all employees not just the ones they prefer.

Anti-Racism

When minorities denounce the recent elevated attention of "anti-racism." They are told that this angle or justification seems unnecessary and potentially harmful. The perspective of not agreeing with all the anti-racism allyship is not denouncing the recent elevated attention of anti-racism. We are asking is who does it benefit? Why is it unnecessary and potentially harmful to point out that racism/colorism has been a protected class category since 1964 in the workplace? Yet it took a videotape of a Black man being murdered over a 9-minute timeframe for it to be acknowledged.

Despite, all the diversity conversations and training in the workplace, anti-racism did not receive attention for the minorities who were complaining about it happening to them at work. There can be a detriment to using positive diversity progress narratives (Kraus et al., 2022) that are not representative of all the barriers protected class employees encounter.

There are those who consider themselves to be allies who read the following three statements: Most of the language around the changes have been centered around anti-racism. Racism is but one area of protected class groups and categories in the workplace. Racism had been ignored and is still being ignored along with many of the other protected class categories. And they suggested that because of these statements, this book could be contributing to the deracialization of justice, equity, diversity, and inclusion (JEDI). Deracialization of JEDI is not the responsibility of this book. The fact that someone read those statements and made the leap to deracialization highlights the immense need for this book.

This book is focused on leaders who have had Civil Rights Laws to follow since 1964. This book points out that this work has not been done and is not being done by many leaders since many do not even know what the protected class laws and categories are (Hughes & Brown, 2018). The Hughes and Liang DQ scale© 2020, developed since the first edition of the book, continues to prove that leaders do not know or understand the protected class employees whom they are required to lead. Some of these leaders consider themselves to be allies and are in fact hindering diversity efforts because of their lack of knowledge and their inappropriate behaviors. Their lack of knowledge and inappropriate behavior makes them less diversity intelligent than they believe themselves to be. The DQ scale results, repeatedly, have revealed to leaders that they are less diversity intelligent than they think they are.

The fact that some people believe that the racial riots after George Floyd's death are the solution after Blacks in United States have been talking about and protesting for the thousands of other Black males murdered and lynched prior to George Floyd is part of the problem. The JEDI acronym means nothing if the allies need murderers for them to act. Therefore, my question remains, who is benefiting? Are the allies benefiting because they have finally decided to act? The dead men and their families are surely not benefiting. The heightened visibility is still not benefiting those who continue to suffer within workplaces where change is still not occurring.

Voice of Protected Class Employees

These employees need a voice of justice in the workplace, both procedural and organizational justice (Parker, 2001). Their own voices need to be heard and not just those of their allies (Knowlton et al., 2022; Rajesh, 2023). Why should an ally's voice mean more than the person enduring the injustices? Why should allies have to feel good about themselves to help those who are suffering? Why should allies be rewarded for enforcing the laws that have been on the books since 1964? Why should allies be rewarded for doing what is moral and ethical? Rajesh (2023) suggested that allies, "in their effort to uplift their marginalized colleagues using their personal privilege sometimes disrespect boundaries by silencing their colleagues' voices, assuming what their colleagues need, deciding for their colleagues, and making their colleagues dependent on them" (¶ 1). She also noted why allies overstep boundaries:

1. **Misunderstanding of the concept**: Some allies believe it is their responsibility to talk on behalf of their marginalized colleagues. What they misunderstand about allyship is that by becoming the voice of the underrepresented, there is actually very little benefit to the intended audience.
2. **Eagerness to help**: Allies-in-making are sometimes a little too keen to provide support and try to help in every possible way. This could translate into an overbearing and high-handed approach, not allowing the disadvantaged to actually improve their circumstances.
3. **To create tangible impact in the short term**: Allyship involves working for systemic change, which takes time. But some actions seem more effective in the short term and who can resist speedy gains?
4. **For personal benefit:** Some allies look to further their own interests and undertake activities that bring them more visibility. (¶ 1)

Passive Aggressive Behavior and Microaggressions

The DQ mindset of the leader should be known prior to placing a leader into a leadership position. It is very difficult to determine the mindset of the leader especially when they use passive aggressive behavior toward protected class employees (Hughes & Brown, 2018). Overt discriminatory behavior is obvious and can easily be addressed using policy and legal actions. It is the passive aggressive behavior that has allowed discrimination to permeate and remain a problem within organizations. Microaggression is one form of passive aggressive behavior that has been discussed in the race literature (Pierce, 1970, 1995). The indirectly expressed hostility is real and detrimental to relationship building especially when it is expressed by one's leader. Microaggression is a way to stereotype and discriminate against a person based on their race. The microaggressor uses statements that are stereotypically based to degrade a person and appears to not have said anything negative at all. An example is when a person says that I am sure there will not be an EEO problem with that hire because she is a Latino—meaning that despite the person's qualifications, she was hired because of her race only to meet an AA requirement.

Often these types of comments go unchecked even when reported to leadership because one cannot prove that the intent of the commenter was malicious. As these kinds of comments and behaviors are allowed to accumulate in the psyche of protected class employees, an insurmountable level of distrust is built. Microaggression is not a micro problem. It is a macro problem and should be dealt with in each instance with DQ. DQ must be mandatory, annual training like sexual harassment and other types of training are required each year.

SELF-MANAGEMENT OF INTELLIGENCES

Individuals can only speak for themselves with regard to their perception of their intelligence. Leaders must be held accountable and responsible for their own knowledge and action. When leaders are employed by an organization, they are asked to adhere to organization rules and policies. Leaders must be taught the rules and policies or be provided a copy of the rules and policies to read and learn on their own. Self-management of critical policies, especially legal policies and laws is important.

Leadership-Related Intelligence Assessments

There are scales available that are used to measure IQ, EQ, and CQ. EQ scales are used most frequently. Despite all the scales used, diversity concerns of protected class employees remain prevalent in organizations. DQ requires individuals to display both cognitive knowledge of protected class employees and positive behavioral actions toward all individuals who are different than oneself to be effective. There is now the Hughes and Liang Diversity Intelligence® (DQ) Scale© 2020 (Hughes & Liang, 2020). The Hughes and Liang DQ Scale© 2020 contain three subscales that measure leaders' DQ Knowledge, Workplace Education and Training, and Behavior.

DQ can be assessed at the individual and organizational levels. IQ, EQ, CQ, and DQ each contribute to leadership behavior since each of these intelligences can be learned and developed. These intelligences should be integrated into leaders' career development plans, leadership development training, and organizations' career management systems. Leaders who have problems relating to, valuing, and respecting workplace contributions of protected class employees can be a detriment to the organization's success and should not be in leadership positions.

Leaders must objectively examine themselves and their capability to lead others. Scores from EQ and CQ assessments typically show that the employee is self-aware, can self-manage, has social awareness, has relationship management skills, and is culturally aware—mainly from an international perspective. All these competencies come with expectations that if the leader has shown that they have them, they are expected to use them in their interactions on the job. This is not always the case. In some instances, leaders either have not learned the competencies, cannot apply the competencies, or intentionally choose not to use the competencies.

While some competency use may be optional, discrimination against protected class employees should not be an option. It appears, to protected class employees, that applying competencies that protect their rights in the workplace are optional; especially when the laws, policies, or rules are not followed and there are no consequences to the employees who are in violation. DQ must not be allowed to be optional.

Leaders should eliminate their personal biases regarding all the intelligences because the organization's goal, typically, is not for them to judge their employees' intelligences to the extent that the employee cannot perform at optimum levels. From a self-management perspective, leaders who consider themselves to have sufficient IQ, EQ, CQ, and DQ should ask themselves the following questions:

IQ

1. If we have all been hired by the organization, should I not expect that we have all met the hiring knowledge standard?
2. Do I assume that others are not as intelligent as me and why do I do that?
3. How do you manage your mental attitude toward the level of knowledge that you and others possess?
4. How do you balance your intellect to embrace not only your knowledge but the knowledge of your peers in regard to career development or career management?

EQ

1. How do you manage your emotions within yourself and toward others?
2. Are you motivated by negative or positive emotions?

CQ

1. How do you behave when interacting with someone from another international culture?
2. When you visit another country for work, do you expect the natives of that country to accept you as you are?

DQ

1. Do you know who members of protected class employees are and why they are protected?
2. Do you base your feelings toward protected class employees on opinions and stereotypes or on facts that you have researched and obtained?
3. Do you feel that it is the responsibility of the protected class employees to prove to you that they should be protected, or do you accept their status without expressing resentment toward them?
4. Why should protected class employees have to fight for inclusion, equity, equality, and belonging after being hired by an organization? Their rights are already protected, so why are their rights allowed to be violated at work?

Bradberry (2016) asserted that individuals with the listed EQ characteristics or competencies (see Table 4.2) are sure to have a high EQ. Having the competencies of high EQ still does not ensure that the individuals have DQ. DQ is not included in those competencies and has been allowed to be ignored. Here are ways to include DQ. Table 4.1 compares the high-EQ characteristics with what is needed for those individuals to have DQ and propositions to apply EQ and DQ together.

DQ provides the opportunity to move beyond EQ to create an inclusive environment.

Organization Management of Intelligences

Campbell's (1990) theory of job performance suggested that declarative knowledge, procedural knowledge, and skills and motivation are the three determinants of any component of job performance. These determinants are associated with cognitive theory and relate to intelligence. Organization leaders assess the job performance of employees to determine if they are using their cognitive skills to complete assigned job tasks. They also expect their leaders to have IQ, EQ, and CQ. Executive leaders must ensure that objective IQ, CQ, EQ, and DQ measurements are used and should not leave it to chance that all employees will be proficient at self-management of their intelligences. There must be enforcement of workplace laws, rules, and policies and consequences that occur when those laws, rules, and policies are not followed.

Inaccurate Performance Ratings

The performance of leaders must be accurately evaluated by executive leaders. Murphy and Cleveland (1991) stated that "Raters do not fail to give accurate ratings because they are incapable of accuracy but rather because they are unwilling to rate accurately" (p. 209). Harris (1994) found that evaluators' unwillingness to provide accurate performance appraisals was because of their personal motivations. This begs the question of whether executive leaders who do not provide accurate performance appraisals to workplace leaders (Joshi et al., 2015; Randel et al., 2018; Shore & Chung, 2023) do not care about how those leaders treat their subordinates. Do they not care whether their chosen leaders treat their employees fairly by adhering to workplace laws, rules, and policies that support protected class employees?

Table 4.2 High EQ versus DQ implications and propositions

High-EQ Characteristics (Bradberry, 2016, ¶ 5–23)	DQ Implications and Propositions
1. You have a robust emotional vocabulary Suggests that there are few people (36%) who can accurately identify their emotions as they occur. Not being able to recognize emotions is problematic because unlabeled emotions often go misunderstood, which leads to irrational choices and counterproductive actions. More specific and accurate word choices made by individuals with high EQs provide insight into exactly how they are feeling, what caused the feeling it, and what the individual should do about it	Individuals with high EQ also need DQ to describe how their feelings and emotions toward protected class group and category employees can be resolved. If they know that they have emotions that are counterproductive, they need to make decisions that will resolve the problem prior to making irrational choices **Proposition:** Some discriminatory leaders make frequent irrational choices with regard to protected class group employees
2. You're curious about people It doesn't matter if they're introverted or extroverted, EQ people are curious about everyone around them because they are empathetic. The more you care about other people and what they're going through, the more curiosity you're going to have about them	This would suggest that people with high EQ cares about the protected class group and category members; therefore, many leaders must not have high EQ because they do not show empathy toward protected class group and category members to the extent it is necessary for protected class group members to feel protected by their leaders in the workplace **Proposition:** Some leaders need to integrate DQ with EQ to be more empathetic toward their employees
3. You embrace change EQ people are flexible and are constantly adapting. They know that fear of change is paralyzing and a major threat to their success and happiness. They look for change and form a plan of action should these changes occur	Change has occurred with more protected class group and category members entering the workplace; yet many leaders have not embraced the change. **Proposition 1:** EQ is not enough alone and DQ is needed to reduce their fear, and they need to know that protected class group and category members are not a threat to their success and happiness. **Proposition 2:** Protected class group and category members are already perceived as a threat because of unfair perceptions that they are receiving an unwarranted advantage

High-EQ Characteristics (Bradberry, 2016, ¶ 5–23)	DQ Implications and Propositions
4. You know your strengths and weaknesses EQ people don't just understand emotions; they know what they're good at and what they're terrible at. They also know who pushes their buttons and the environments (both situations and people) that enable them to succeed. Having a high EQ means you know your strengths and how to lean into and use them to your full advantage while keeping your weaknesses from holding you back	If leaders with high EQ know their strengths and weaknesses with regards to situations and people, then **Proposition 1:** They know when they are being a detriment to protected class employees in the workplace. If they do not know this, then **Proposition 2:** Attaining DQ will strengthen their ability to improve the work environment for protected class employees
5. You're a good judge of character Much of EQ comes down to social awareness; the ability to read other people, know what they're about, and understand what they're going through. Over time, this skill makes you an exceptional judge of character. People are no mystery to you. You know what they're all about and understand their motivations, even those that lie hidden beneath the surface	DQ is needed by leaders who have high-EQ social awareness because if they are such a good judge of character, they must be totally ignorant of protected class group and category members. **Proposition:** There should be absolutely no diversity issues in the workplace if all leaders had social awareness and used it in the workplace
6. You are difficult to offend If you have a firm grasp of who you are, it's difficult for someone to say or do something that gets your goat. Emotionally intelligent people are self-confident and open-minded, which creates a pretty thick skin. You may even poke fun at yourself or let other people make jokes about you because you are able to mentally draw the line between humor and degradation	DQ is needed because if EQ people are open-minded, **Proposition:** They would not need to be convinced that protected class group and category members can benefit their organizations in leadership positions

(continued)

Table 4.2 (continued)

High-EQ Characteristics (Bradberry, 2016, ¶ 5–23)	DQ Implications and Propositions
7. You know how to say no (to yourself and others) Emotional intelligence means knowing how to exert self-control. You delay gratification and avoid impulsive action. Research conducted at the University of California, San Francisco, shows that the more difficulty that you have saying no, the more likely you are to experience stress, burnout, and even depression. Saying no is a major self-control challenge for many people, but "No" is a powerful word that you should be unafraid to wield. When it's time to say no, emotionally intelligent people avoid phrases such as "I don't think I can" or "I'm not certain." Saying no to a new commitment honors your existing commitments and gives you the opportunity to successfully fulfill them	Exerting leaders' self-control could be strengthened using DQ, and **Proposition:** Leaders could say no to peers who may want them to conform to an environmental norm that does not support protected class group and category members
8. You let go of mistakes EQ people distance themselves from their mistakes but do so without forgetting them. By keeping their mistakes at a safe distance, yet still handy enough to refer to, they are able to adapt and adjust for future success. It takes refined self-awareness to walk this tightrope between dwelling and remembering. Dwelling too long on your mistakes makes you anxious and gun shy, while forgetting about them completely makes you bound to repeat them. The key to balance lies in your ability to transform failures into nuggets of improvement. This creates the tendency to get right back up every time you fall down	**Proposition:** DQ could be used to help EQ leaders let go of past mistakes that may have been made against protected class group and category members and avoid potential future pitfalls

High-EQ Characteristics (Bradberry, 2016, ¶ 5–23)	DQ Implications and Propositions
9. You give and expect nothing in return When someone gives you something spontaneously, without expecting anything in return, this leaves a powerful impression. EQ people build strong relationships because they are constantly thinking about others	**Proposition 1:** EQ people cannot give to protected class group and category members if they do not have the DQ to know what protected class group members may need. **Proposition 2:** EQ people can benefit from DQ by having the knowledge necessary to build strong relationships with protected class group members **Proposition:** DQ can be used to help leaders avoid grudges because of perceived insurmountable differences
10. You don't hold grudges The negative emotions that come with holding onto a grudge are actually a stress response. Just thinking about the event sends your body into fight-or-flight mode, a survival mechanism that forces you to stand up and fight or run for the hills when faced with a threat. When the threat is imminent, this reaction is essential to your survival, but when the threat is ancient history, holding onto that stress wreaks havoc on your body and can have devastating health consequences over time. In fact, researchers at Emory University have shown that holding onto stress contributes to high blood pressure and heart disease. Holding onto a grudge means you're holding onto stress, and emotionally intelligent people know to avoid this at all costs. Letting go of a grudge not only makes you feel better now but can also improve your health	

(continued)

Table 4.2 (continued)

High-EQ Characteristics (Bradberry, 2016, ¶ 5–23)	DQ Implications and Propositions
11. You neutralize toxic people Dealing with difficult people is frustrating and exhausting for most. But high-EQ individuals control their interactions with toxic people by keeping their feelings in check. When they need to confront a toxic person, they approach the situation rationally. They identify their own emotions and don't allow anger or frustration to fuel the chaos. They also consider the difficult person's standpoint and are able to find solutions and common ground. Even when things completely derail, emotionally intelligent people are able to take the toxic person with a grain of salt to avoid letting him or her bring them down	Leaders who discriminate against the protected class group and category members are toxic, and executive leaders with the EQ competency of neutralizing toxic people and DQ need to understand that they cannot be passive aggressive toward this behavior. **Proposition:** Executive leaders with high EQ and DQ will remove toxic leaders who make the workplace unbearable for protected class group and category employees
12. You don't seek perfection Emotionally intelligent people won't set perfection as their target because they know that it doesn't exist. Human beings, by our very nature, are fallible. When perfection is your goal, you're always left with a nagging sense of failure that makes you want to give up or reduce your effort. You end up spending time lamenting what you failed to accomplish and should have done differently instead of moving forward, excited about what you've achieved and what you will accomplish in the future	If leaders with high EQ do not seek perfection, then they should understand that protected class group and category members are also not perfect and are not seeking perfection. However, protected class group and category members expect them to have DQ and to try to use their DQ to make the work environment better for protected class group and category employees **Proposition:** High-EQ leaders will learn DQ and use it to improve the environmental climate for protected class group and category employees

High-EQ Characteristics (Bradberry, 2016, ¶ 5–23)	DQ Implications and Propositions
13. You appreciate what you have Taking time to contemplate what you're grateful for isn't merely the right thing to do; it also improves your mood by reducing the stress hormone cortisol (in some cases by 23%). Research conducted at the University of California, Davis, found that people who work daily to cultivate an attitude of gratitude experience improved mood, energy, and physical well-being. It's likely that lower levels of cortisol play a major role in this	Leaders with high EQ and appreciate what they have should be less resentful of protected class group and category members. They need DQ to understand why protected class group and category members are not just grateful to have a job. They want to improve despite their situations and are grateful for opportunities to enhance their careers **Proposition:** Leaders with high EQ to appreciate what they have and DQ should be less resentful of protected class group and category members
14. You disconnect Taking regular time off the grid is a sign of a high EQ because it helps you to keep your stress under control and to live in the moment. When you make yourself available to your work 24/7, you expose yourself to a constant barrage of stressors. Forcing yourself offline and even–gulp!–turning off your phone gives your body and mind a break. Studies have shown that something as simple as an email break can lower stress levels. Technology enables constant communication and the expectation that you should be available 24/7. It is extremely difficult to enjoy a stress-free moment outside of work when an email with the power to bring your thinking (read: stressing) back to work can drop onto your phone at any moment	This competency should reveal to high-EQ leaders that protected class group and category members have stressors placed upon them by leaders who will not allow them to forget that they are different. Protected class group and category members need a break from constant mistreatment from leaders who lack DQ **Proposition:** High-EQ leaders who take time off the grid and have DQ will provide time off the grid for their protected class employees

(continued)

Table 4.2 (continued)

High-EQ Characteristics (Bradberry, 2016, ¶ 5–23)	DQ Implications and Propositions
15. You limit your caffeine intake Drinking excessive amounts of caffeine triggers the release of adrenaline, which is the primary source of a fight-or-flight response. The fight-or-flight mechanism sidesteps rational thinking in favor of a faster response to ensure survival. This is great when a bear is chasing you, but not so great when you're responding to a curt email. When caffeine puts your brain and body into this hyper-aroused state of stress, your emotions overrun your behavior. Caffeine's long half-life ensures you stay this way as it takes its sweet time working its way out of your body. High-EQ individuals know that caffeine is trouble, and they don't let it get the better of them	High-EQ leaders can use this competency to control their reactions to perceived advantages and use DQ to remain engaged in conversations with protected class group members
16. You get enough sleep It's difficult to overstate the importance of sleep to increasing your emotional intelligence and managing your stress levels. When you sleep, your brain literally recharges, shuffling through the day's memories and storing or discarding them (which causes dreams) so that you wake up alert and clearheaded. High-EQ individuals know that their self-control, attention, and memory are all reduced when they don't get enough—or the right kind—of sleep. So, they make sleep a top priority	This competency can help high-EQ leaders retain the DQ information needed, daily, to have positive interactions with protected class group members
17. You stop negative self-talk in its tracks The more you ruminate on negative thoughts, the more power you give them. Most of our negative thoughts are just that–thoughts, not facts. When it feels like something always or never happens, this is just your brain's natural tendency to perceive threats (inflating the frequency or severity of an event). Emotionally intelligent people separate their thoughts from the facts in order to escape the cycle of negativity and move toward a positive, new outlook	Leaders with this EQ competency to eliminate negative self-talk should be able to use DQ to accept facts about protected class group and category members **Proposition:** Leaders with High EQ who can eliminate negative self-talk and DQ should be able to help protected class employees improve their morale

High-EQ Characteristics (Bradberry, 2016, ¶ 5–23)	DQ Implications and Propositions
18. You won't let anyone limit your joy When your sense of pleasure and satisfaction are derived from the opinions of other people, you are no longer the master of your own happiness. When emotionally intelligent people feel good about something they've done, they won't let anyone's opinions or snide remarks take that away from them. While it's impossible to turn off your reactions to what others think, you don't have to compare yourself to others, and you can always take people's opinions with a grain of salt. That way, no matter what other people are thinking or doing, your self-worth comes from within	**Proposition:** High-EQ leaders with DQ will stop negatively comparing themselves to protected class group and category members and accept their differences

Most organizations conduct annual evaluations to determine the overall performance of employees. However, formative evaluations that seek to improve employee performance on a daily, weekly, or monthly basis may be more appropriate (Welch, 2005) because annual evaluations provide little opportunity for employees to improve their performance throughout the year. A system of continuous feedback can be established by formative evaluations (Banks, 2006a, b). The time required to provide continuous feedback would cost less than the settlements and payouts required should leaders treat employees in ways that violate protected class laws. Viswesvaran (2001) stated that "although a person's job performance depends on some combination of ability, motivation and situational constraints, it can be measured only in terms of some outcomes" (p. 114). The negative outcome associated with unfair treatment and lack of procedural justice of protected class group and category employees in the workplace is inexcusable when the information and time is available to avoid such occurrences. DQ can be taught and applied to avoid negative outcomes.

Organizations can be held accountable for the actions of their employees when they violate laws, policies, and rules, so they must communicate the laws, policies, and rules and ensure that their employees understand them. Cleveland and Murphy (1992) found that "organizations rarely reward good raters or punish bad ones" (p. 159) sending the message that organizations do not care about accurate performance evaluations, and subsequently, there is no consequence for not doing one's job. If there is a lack of respect for organizational policy, especially performance evaluation policy, then respect for laws, policies, and rules may also be suspect.

Organizations cannot just communicate policy to employees, they must make sure that their leaders understand how policy can have an impact upon themselves, their subordinates, and the organization. Organizations must also understand the capability of those they have placed in leadership positions. They should not ask leaders to try to execute policies and procedures that they do not understand. Organizations should ensure that their leaders are equipped with DQ and held accountable to justify their actions. Accountability can influence positive behavior but can also influence negative behavior in leaders (Mero & Motowidlo, 1995). Leaders who are not sure that they possess the proper tools and resources to be effective may not do anything to help protected class employees

(Harris, 1994). From an organization management perspective, leaders who consider themselves to have sufficient IQ, EQ, CQ, and DQ should ask themselves the following questions:

IQ

1. Do organizations value the intellect of employees to the extent that they allow inappropriate behavior toward protected class group and category employees?

EQ

1. Are organizations cognizant of the EQ of employees and hold them accountable for it as a part of its evaluation system?
2. Does the organization understand that motivation effects an individual's energy and activity level and directs the individual toward goals, promotes initiation and persistence in certain activities, and affect the learning strategies and cognitive processes employed by individuals?

CQ

1. Do organizations reflect an attitude of embracement and acceptance of different international cultures and recognize inter-personnel diversity within cultures?

DQ

1. Does the organization publicly embrace diversity of appearance and diversity of thought and action?
2. Does the organization publicly ensure that all employees feel appreciated for their contribution to the success of the organization despite their differences?

Conclusion

Personal variables including the amount of information, self-efficacy, and mood influences how individuals perform on their jobs. Employees respond to motivational factors including rewards, negative consequences, and impression management. Organizations establish the situational circumstances including accountability, organizational HRM strategy, task/outcome dependence, trust, and forms that leaders need to perform their jobs. They must encourage all leaders to be honest with themselves about how they apply the IQ, EQ, CQ, and DQ intelligences in the workplace, respecting the presence of all employees despite known and unknown differences.

Rajesh (2023) offered some suggestions that allies should consider for understanding allyship boundaries:

1. Speak out in public on various issues that the disadvantaged sections face, AFTER holding conversations with them and educating yourself about their needs. Don't assume what your marginalized colleagues need.
2. Champion for your colleagues' rights without killing their voices. Your responsibility is to amplify their voices, not to speak on their behalf.
3. When a woman faces harassment or discrimination, call out the sexist behavior, but do not try to crack the issue for your colleague by chastising the offender. Instead, guide her to speak up about the incident, while you advocate for company-wide change to tackle the biased work culture.
4. When a woman is overlooked for promotion, request details about the factors that resulted in the decision—this will make the manager take a step back and reflect. Do not actively advocate for her promotion, but mentor her on the areas she needs to focus on for favorable results in future appraisals. Demand fair, transparent, and equitable measures of appraisal for all employees.
5. Do not make decisions for your colleagues. Discuss openly the pros and cons of all options but leave the final judgment to them.
6. When women or other disadvantaged colleagues are ignored, interrupted, or spoken over in meetings—an everyday reality—redirect the conversation back to them. You could say, "Kiara's suggestion sounds interesting. Can we try to get a deeper understanding of her idea?"
7. Mentor women and LGBTQ colleagues and provide resources that will help your colleagues progress in their work, but do not do the work for them.

8. Do not micro-manage while guiding colleagues in their work projects. Ensure that they have limitless creative freedom to explore and learn. (¶ 1)

REFERENCES

Agote, L., Aramburu, N., & Lines, R. (2016). Authentic Leadership Perception, Trust in the Leader, and Followers' Emotions in Organizational Change Processes. *The Journal of Applied Behavioral Science, 52*(1), 35–63.

Banks, C. H. (2006a). Career Planning: Toward an Inclusive Model. In M. Karsten (Ed.), *Gender, Race and Ethnicity in the Workplace* (Vol. III, pp. 99–116). Greenwood Publishing Group.

Banks, C. H. (2006b). Career Planning: Towards a More Inclusive Model for Women and Diverse Individuals. In F. Nafukho and H. Chen (Eds.), *Academy of Human Resource Development International Conference (AHRD) Proceedings. Symp. 31–1* (pp. 640–647). Academy of Human Resource Development.

Banks, C. H., Collier, M. M., & Preyan, L. M. (2010). Leveraging Diversity Through Faculty Perception of Their Power to Influence Diversity. *International Journal of Human Resource Development and Management, 10*(3), 208–223.

Banks, K. H., Kohn-Wood, L. P., & Spencer, M. (2006). An Examination of the African American Experience of Everyday Discrimination and Symptoms of Psychological Distress. *Community Mental Health Journal, 42*(6), 555–570. https://doi.org/10.1007/s10597-006-9052-9

Bowleg, L. (2012). The Problem with the Phrase Women and Minorities: Intersectionality—An Important Theoretical Framework for Public Health. *American Journal of Public Health, 102*(7), 1267–1273.

Bradberry, T. (2015). *18 Behaviors of Emotionally Intelligent People: Emotional Intelligence is a Huge Driver of Success* (pp. ¶ 5–23). Retrieved February 12, 2016, from http://time.com/3838524/emotional-intelligence-signs/

Campbell, J. P. (1990). Modeling the Performance Prediction Problem in Industrial and Organizational Psychology. In M. D. Dunnette & L. M. Hough (Eds.), *Handbook of Industrial and Organizational Psychology* (2nd ed., Vol. 1, pp. 687–732). Consulting Psychologists Press.

Chua, A., & Rubenfeld, J. (2014). *The Triple Package: How Three Unlikely Traits Explain the Rise and Fall of Cultural Groups in America*. The Penguin Press.

Cleveland, J. N., & Murphy, K. R. (1992). Analyzing Performance Appraisal as Goal-Directed Behavior. *Research in Personnel and Human Resources Management, 10*(2), 121–185.

Hughes, C. (in press). *Valuing People and Technology in the Workplace: Ethical Implications and Imperatives for Success*. IGI Global.

Collier, M. J. (2003). *Intercultural Alliances: Critical Transformation*. Sage.

Collins, P. H. (1990). *Black Feminist Thought: Knowledge, Consciousness, and the Politics of Empowerment*. Routledge.

Covey, S. R. (2013). *The 8th Habit: From Effectiveness to Greatness*. Simon and Schuster.

Crenshaw, K. (1989). Demarginalizing the Intersection of Race and Sex: A Black Feminist Critique of Antidiscrimination Doctrine, Feminist Theory and Antiracist Politics. *University of Chicago Legal Forum, 1989*, 139–167.

David, S., & Congleton, C. (2014, Summer). Emotional Agility: How Effective Leaderrs Manage Their Negative Thoughts and Feelings. *Harvard Business Review Onpoint*, 88–92.

Dobbin, F., & Kalev, A. (2022). *Getting to Diversity: What Works and What Doesn't*. Harvard University Press.

Gates, H. L., Jr, & Curran, A. S. (Eds.). (2022). *Who's Black and Why? A Hidden Chapter from the Eighteenth-Century Invention of Race*. Harvard University Press.

Groysberg, B., & Connolly, K. (2013). Great Leaders Who Make the Mix Work: Twenty-Four CEOS on Creating Diverse and Inclusive Organizations. *Harvard Business Review, 91*(9), 68–76.

Harris, M. M. (1994). Rater Motivation in the Performance Appraisal Context: A Theoretical Framework. *Journal of Management, 20*(4), 737–756.

Hirsh, C. E. (2009). The Strength of Weak Enforcement: The Impact of Discrimination Charges, Legal Environments, and Organizational Conditions on Workplace Segregation. *American Sociological Review, 74*(2), 245–271.

Hughes, C., & Liang, X. (2020). *Hughes and Liang Diversity Intelligence® (DQ) Scale© 2020*. https://www.diversityintelligencellc.com

Hughes, C., & Brown, L. M. (2018). Exploring Leaders' Discriminatory, Passive-Aggressive Behavior Toward Protected Class Employees Using Diversity Intelligence. *Advances in Developing Human Resources, 20*(3), 263–284.

Hughes, C. (2012). *Valuing People and Technology in the Workplace: A Competitive Advantage Framework*. IGI Global.

Hughes, C. (2014). *American Black Women and Interpersonal Leadership Styles*. The Netherlands Sense Publishers.

Hughes, C. (2018). Conclusion: Diversity Intelligence as a Core of Diversity Training and Leadership Development. *Advances in Developing Human Resources, 20*(3), 370–378.

Jackson, L. R. (2012). *The Self-Efficacy Beliefs of Black Women Leaders in Fortune 500 Companies* (Unpublished doctoral dissertation). University of Arkansas, Fayetteville, AR.

Johnson, I. R., & Pietri, E. S. (2022). An Ally You Say? Endorsing White Women as Allies to Encourage Perceptions of Allyship and Organizational Identity-Safety Among Black Women. *Group Processes & Intergroup Relations, 25*(2), 453–473.

Joshi, A., Son, J., & Roh, H. (2015). When Can Women Close the Gap? A Meta-Analytic Test of Sex Differences in Performance and Rewards. *Academy of Management Journal, 58*(5), 1516–1545.

Kaptein, M., & Van Helvoort, M. (2019). A Model of Neutralization Techniques. *Deviant Behavior, 40*(10), 1260–1285. https://doi.org/10.1080/01639625.2018.1491696

Kidder, D. L., Lankau, M. J., Chrobot-Mason, D., Mollica, K. A., & Friedman, R. A. (2004). Backlash Toward Diversity Initiatives: Examining the Impact of Diversity Program Justification, Personal and Group Outcomes. *International Journal of Conflict Management, 15*(1), 77–102.

Knowlton, K., Carton, A. M., & Grant, A. M. (2022). Help (Un) Wanted: Why the Most Powerful Allies Are the Most Likely to Stumble—And When They Fulfill Their Potential. *Research in Organizational Behavior*, 100180.

Kraus, M. W., Torrez, B., & Hollie, LaStarr. (2022). How Narratives of Racial Progress Create Barriers to Diversity, Equity, and Inclusion in Organizations. *Current Opinion in Psychology, 43*, 108–113. https://doi.org/10.1016/j.copsyc.2021.06.022

Lipshitz, R., Friedman, V., & Popper, M. (2006). *Demystifying Organizational Learning.* Sage.

Manville, B. (2001). Learning in the New Economy. *Leader to Leader, 20,* 36–45.

Marquardt, M. J. (2002). *Building the Learning Organization: Mastering the 5 Elements for Corporate Learning.* Davies-Black Publishing.

Medina, F. J., Munduate, L., & Guerra, J. M. (2008). Power and Conflict in Cooperative and Competitive Contexts. *European Journal of Work and Organizational Psychology, 17*(3), 349–362.

Mero, N. P., & Motowidlo, S. J. (1995). Effects of Rater Accountability on the Accuracy and the Favorability of Performance Ratings. *Journal of Applied Psychology, 80*(4), 517–524.

Mitchell, M. S., Rivera, G., & Treviño, L. K. (2023). Unethical Leadership: A Review, Analysis, and Research Agenda. *Personnel Psychology, 76,* 1–37. Advance online publication. https://doi.org/10.1111/peps.12574

Murphy, K. R., & Cleveland, J. N. (1991). *Performance Appraisal: Organizational Perspective.* Allyn & Bacon.

Parker, P. S. (2005). *Race, Gender, and Leadership: Re-Envisioning Organizational Leadership from the Perspectives of African American Women Executives.* Lawrence Erlbaum Associates, Publishers.

Pfeffer, J. (1994). *Competitive Advantage Through People: Unleashing the Power of the Work Force.* Harvard Business School Press.

Pierce, C. M. (1970, November). Black Psychiatry One Year After Miami. *Journal of the National Medical Association, 62*(6), 471–473. PMID: 5493608; PMCID: PMC2611929.

Pierce, C. (1995). Stress Analogs of Racism and Sexism: Terrorism, Torture, and Disaster. *Mental Health, Racism, and Sexism, 33,* 277–293.

Pope Francis. (2014). *The Joy of the Gospel* (p. 21). BookBaby.

Rajesh, S. (2023, March 19). *Being a Diversity Ally—How Much Is Too Much? Allies at Workplaces Must Champion Their Marginalised Colleagues' Voices Without Being Patronising Towards Them.* https://www.thehindubusinessline.com/opinion/being-a-diversity-ally-how-much-is-too-much/article66639186.ece

Randel, A. E., Galvin, B. M., Shore, L. M., Ehrhart, K. H., Chung, B. G., Dean, M. A., & Kedharnath, U. (2018). Inclusive Leadership: Realizing Positive Outcomes Through Belongingness and Being Valued for Uniqueness. *Human Resource Management Review, 28*(2), 190–203.

Robbins, S. (2013, Fall). Culture as Communication. *Harvard Business Review Onpoint,* 18–20.

Sandberg, S. (2013). *Lean In: Women, Work, and the Will to Lead.* Alfred Knopf.

Schmader, T., Johns, M., & Forbes, C. (2008). An Integrated Process Model of Stereotype Threat Effects on Performance. *Psychological Review, 115*(2), 336–356.

Shore, L. M., & Chung, B. G. (2023). Enhancing Leader Inclusion While Preventing Social Exclusion in the Work Group. *Human Resource Management Review, 33*(1), 100902.

Sims, C. M., & Carter, A. D. (2019). Revisiting Parker & Ogilvie's African American Women Executive Leadership Model. *The Journal of Business Diversity, 19*(2), 99–112.

Sims, C. (2010). The Impact of African American Skin Tone Bias in the Workplace: Implications for Critical Human Resource Development. *Online Journal for Workforce Education and Development, 3*(4), 1–17.

Stainback, K., Tomaskovic-Devey, D., & Skaggs, S. (2010). Organizational Approaches to Inequality: Inertia, Relative Power, and Environments. *Annual Review of Sociology, 36,* 225–247. https://www.annualreviews.org/doi/pdf/10.1146/annurev-soc-070308-120014

Sue, D. W., Capodilupo, C. M., Torino, G. C., Bucceri, J. M., Holder, A., Nadal, K. L., & Esquilin, M. (2007). Racial Microaggressions in Everyday Life: Implications for Clinical Practice. *American Psychologist, 62*(4), 271–286.

Thompson, M. S., & Keith, V. M. (2001). The Blacker the Berry: Gender, Skin Tone, Self-Esteem, and Self-Efficacy. *Gender and Society, 15*(3), 336–357.

Visweswaran, C. (2001). Assessment of Individual Job Performance: A Review of the Past Century and a Look Ahead. In N. Anderson, D. S. Ones, H.

K. Sinangil, & C. Viswesvaran (Eds.), *Handbook of Industrial, Work and Organizational Psychology* (Vol. 1, pp. 110–126). Sage.

Watson, L. B., & Henderson, J. (2023). The Relation Between Gendered Racial Microaggressions and Traumatic Stress Among Highly Educated Black Women. *The Counseling Psychologist, 51*(2), 210–241.

Welch, J. (2005). *Winning*. HarperCollins.

Wlodkowski, R. J., & Ginsberg, M. B. (1995). *Diversity & Motivation: Culturally Responsive Teaching. Jossey-Bass Higher and Adult Education Series. Jossey-Bass Education Series, Jossey-Bass Social and Behavioral Science Series.* Jossey-Bass.

Wolley, M. (2021). Making Diversity and Equity Bad Words Is Problematic. *Indianapolis Business Journal, 42*(21).

Yang, J. R., & Liu, J. (2021, January 19). *Strengthening accountability for discrimination: Confronting Fundamental Power Imbalances in the employment relationship.* Economic Policy Institute. https://www.epi.org/unequalpower/publications/strengthening-accountability-for-discrimination-confronting-fundamental-power-imbalances-in-the-employment-relationship/

Zavattaro, S. M., & Bearfield, D. (2022). Weaponization of Wokeness: The Theater of Management and Implications for Public Administration. *Public Administration Review, 82*(3), 585–593. https://doi.org/10.1111/puar.13484

CHAPTER 5

Diversity Intelligence, Career Development, and Digital/Virtual Work

DQ is needed in many aspects of career development and even more so in the prevalent nature of digital, virtual, and remote work. As we transition from Industry 4.0 of digitization and technology enhancement and enter into Industry 5.0 which represents human–computer interaction, it is imperative that leaders have DQ. The Great Resignation and quiet quitting during the COVID-19 pandemic have revealed the lack of career development strategies and planning that organizations and employees need (Hughes & Niu, 2021a, b). This chapter looks at ways DQ can and has influenced career development and digital/virtual workplace changes. Digital/virtual work does not lessen the need for diversity efforts. There are specific protected class groups and categories (i.e., disability, sex, and colorism) that have been negatively affected by AI and other digital technologies (McDonnell et al., 2019; Tambe et al., 2019). Leaders must have talent development strategies that can contribute directly to the career development of all employees (Kaliannan et al., 2022).

It is not Always What a Leader Does, It is What the Leader Does not Do

Workplace conflicts occur because leaders are either insensitive or uncaring with regard to the needs of those who are different. Some protected class employees are never made aware of talent development

C. Hughes, *Diversity Intelligence*, https://doi.org/10.1007/978-3-031-33250-0_5

opportunities that are supposed to be shared with them. Often they are denied the funding needed to attend external development activities and/ or not even made aware that funding exists for their development.

The withholding of resources is the most notorious tactic used by leaders to prevent the development of protected class employees. It is very convenient for unscrupulous leaders to say that there is no money in the budget because they never have to show the budget data to subordinates. This has been extensively used to deny equal pay to minorities and women in the workplace. Talent development strategies for leaders must include DQ criteria, and leaders must show DQ when interacting with subordinate employees in these efforts. DQ must be applied by leaders, measured by executive leadership, and assessed for effectiveness.

Talent Development Strategies

Organizations are losing talent and have inexperienced managerial talent available for senior and executive leadership positions because of their leaders' inability to view talent in terms of protected class employees (Houser, 2019; Shaw et al., 2022; Warren, 2009). Because of this inability to view talent in terms of protected class employees, organizations' work environments are perceived to be supportive of embedded biases that serve as barriers against protected class employees' development and advancement.

Talent development strategies are supposed to be used to develop all within organizations; yet many individuals, because of the negativity associated with their protected class status, are excluded from talent development activities. They are often subjected to biased activities such as unfair testing, physical obstacles, and other barriers that require more effort to overcome than those in leadership positions were required to endure. The procedural justice efforts are not used by leaders in these instances.

DIGITAL AND VIRTUAL WORK

Some organizations are looking to artificial intelligence (AI) to help make hiring decisions to eliminate bias against protected class employees (Bigman et al., 2021; Houser, 2019; Raghavan et al., 2020). While there are many instances where AI has the potential to make bad decisions, those decisions are because of the humans who are designing and inputting the algorithm (Hughes et al., 2019; Kane, 2019; Kane et al., 2019). Sometimes, programmers cannot separate their bias from their AI work.

In other instances, protected class employees are choosing to work remotely to avoid bias and discrimination in the workplace. While this may remove them from networks that could lead to advancement (Bachrach et al., 2022), many see remote work as a positive opportunity to protect their mental health. It also protects their psychological well-being and provides them with a better work-life balance. White women have found remote work more beneficial than Black women who were already invisible in the workplace. Working remotely renders Black women even more unlikely to advance. Protected class employees need career development that will include all their talents.

Diversity and Career Development

Organizational leaders, HR professionals and practitioners, and career development professionals and practitioners are often asked to help manage the careers of diverse employees. It is difficult for these leaders to integrate diverse individuals within their strategies without a clear and agreed upon definition of diversity. They need to know that protected class employees deserve the same attention as others and that competing forces within the same organization reduces effectiveness. In many organizations, despite the organization's pledge to increase diversity, protected class employees are diminished and/or ignored.

Protected class employees must be identified and developed to be successors within talent succession planning strategies. If they are continuously excluded, turnover problems among protected class employees will not be alleviated as was seen during the Great Resignation during the COVID-19 pandemic. The cost of replacing employees who choose to leave adverse work environments is high and very few ever tell why they leave so that true root cost of the lost is unknown and potential remedies uncertain. Some protected class employees will leave mentally and emotionally while remaining physically as is seen with quiet quitting which has also been highlighted during the COVID-19 pandemic. The following questions provide a potential research agenda to further understand why protected class group members leave organizations and how DQ could reduce these problems:

1. What type of support is needed from leaders with DQ to make all protected class employees' career development and retention programs effective?
2. What evidence exists to suggest that leaders with DQ and organizations are meeting the socialization for career development needs of all protected class employees, in-person and virtually?
3. How are the unmet needs of protected class employees compounding the employee retention and non-promotion phenomenon?
4. How can organizations reduce any negative impact associated with possessing a protected class employee characteristic to advocate for employee retention and promotion?
5. To what degree do protected class employees conform to the traditional career development models? If they do not conform to these models what types of new models should be proposed to better meet the career development needs of protected class employees?
6. Are protected class employees who are being promoted and succeeding in their career goals realizing the full benefit of their success on their terms? In other words, has the attainment of a promotion or career goal led to further career progression and higher paying jobs?
7. What role can leaders with DQ play in assisting protected class employees with career development? Is there a way to better integrate protected class employees into better careers within the workplace?

Career Development Theories

Most career development theories can be attributed to Super's (1953) Life-Career Rainbow which includes six life roles. Super (1953) associated age with five stages of career development: growth (4–13), exploration (14–24), establishment (25–44), maintenance (45–65), and decline (65 and over). He suggested that individuals develop at different stages and would not progress through the model at the same pace. The model provided by Super was revised in 1990 with the Segmental Model of Career Development containing 14 propositions which may be based upon individual biographical and geographical influences (Super, 1990).

As more protected class employees entered the workplace, the applicability of Super's models to all employees has been questioned because his models were based on white males who initially made up the workplace when the models were developed. Questions of interest include:

1. What aspect of the model is relevant and/or applicable to protected class employees?
2. In what way(s) can Super's model be modified and effectively used by protected class employees?
3. How can leaders and professional career development advisors best help employees use Super's model?

Holland's Theory, Career Development, and the Work Environment

Holland considered personality as a major aspect in career development and choice. His theory is based on six personality types: realistic, investigative, artistic, social, enterprising, and conventional. Holland believed that people in similar vocations had similar personality traits, and an individual's success might be attributed to the compatibility of his personality with the work environment (Isaacson & Brown, 1997). Leaders must be cognizant of how adverse treatment of protected class employees can affect their personality and career choice and use DQ to ensure that they (leaders) do not impede protect class employees' career progress.

Holland's theory may need to be considered for use by protected class employees for career development because it focuses on individual personality traits. Unscrupulous leaders who oppose protected class employees' personality differences in a biased work environment hinders their career success. Unfair limitations are often placed upon protected class group members' career development because of inherent and systemic biases due to leaders' lack of DQ. Career development extends beyond the individual worker to include the work environment. Holland (1959) suggested that an individual wants and actively seeks work environments that align with their goals, values, and skills.

CAREER DEVELOPMENT IN PRACTICE

Career Development is essential for individuals who would like to have successful, long-term careers. Individuals are being asked to be responsible for their own career development. Historically, employees only had to follow the script within their workplace and were allowed to maintain their job until retirement. In today's high-powered workplaces, the speed of change has forced individuals and organizations to change and adapt, not always in the best interest of the employee. Understanding of the career development process and the potential benefits for both employees and organizations are key to success.

An exploration of the different types of resources that are available to assist in the successful development and execution of a career development program within an organization is needed to determine what the best career plan may be for each employee. The key is to choose the career development program that is most appropriate for the organization and the individuals who will be impacted, and the expectations, goals, and/or aspirations of all employees including those in protected class employees must be assessed and included. This would include protected class employees being involved in the design process. There is no absolute right choice, but one can strive to be as close to right as possible so that there will be a return on investment from a people and cost perspective. In a fast paced, global economic environment, all employees need to be up to speed in all areas of their development. System-wide, flexible, and appropriate career development resources must be chosen.

Leaders must find the right people to their open positions. Questions for leaders to consider are:

- How do we develop current employees to fill the jobs within our organization without having to look outside?

- How do we determine what the employee values and what skills they have that they are not having to use within their current position?
- How do we avoid having the wrong people in our organization?
- How do we avoid having the right people doing the wrong job?

Employees and leaders seek to optimize their career options in the workplace. The control which an employee or leader has in truly optimizing his or her options in the workplace remains debatable. A past Society of Human Resource Management (SHRM) survey revealed that over 90% of Human Resource (HR) professionals were not comfortable with current performance appraisal systems. Yet, millions of employees have placed their faith in receiving adequate and accurate feedback through these systems in the workplace. Their options for enrichment, vertical movement, lateral movement, realignment, relocation, and exploration of possible options have all been dictated by performance appraisal systems within the workplace. If 90% of the individuals enforcing this system are not confident in the system, have employees been misled into using the results of these systems for career development in workplaces around the country?

One option for HR professionals and other leaders is to help all employees to create a career map which can, at least, help them to get started on the way to at least document where they are in their careers. This will provide the employees with a starting point for a career development strategy. It is hard to know where you are going if you have no idea where you are. There are millions of employees or hopeful employees who have no idea where they are in their career, what they want to do, or how they plan to get there. This is especially true for protected class group members who receive no mentorship or guidance from biased leaders. One of the most popular tools today is the employee development plan (EDP) that leaders should use to assist employees with their career development.

Leaders must know that an individual employees' behavior and expectations on the job are directly impacted by the environment in which they work and can assist with making the environment conducive for the success of all employees. Dawis et al. (1964) in the theory of work adjustment (TWA) noted that the behavior an individual exhibit at work is reflective of the inputs received from the work environment. Social Cognitive Career Theory (SCCT) suggests that the work environment directly impacts the experience, behavior, and self-efficacy of American Black females in leadership positions (Hughes, 2014).

DQ has the potential to positively impact the career development of all employees. Some employees have been denied career development opportunities because of a lack of understanding of their ability to learn and attain new KSAs. Many false assumptions are held by leaders that have been allowed to hinder the career development potential of protected class group members.

Career development can occur inside or outside the organization. Once employees know where they are within their career plans, they began pursuing and achieving the goals of the plan, only if the plan aligns with a career path that is applicable within that organization or to an external organization if the employee intends to leave. Visiting the training and education departments is often the first step that employees take. Another step should be taken prior to meeting with a training or education representative and that completing an assessment of the employees' resource needs based upon their protected class status. Some protected class employees need learning accommodations, etc. Not providing learning opportunities because of limitations beyond the employees' control is inexcusable. Without the proper resources, the training content may be correct but is not effectively delivered. Methods that meet employees' needs will result in a better implementation of their career development plan. Actively involving the employees in projects that allow them to have influence should be the overall objective of any training and education that is meant to help them implement their career plan. Training and education that employees receive must be relevant to what they are doing and to what the organization that they are working for or hope to obtain employment with expects. There should be constant communication and feedback throughout the process to ensure relevancy.

Practitioners within the field of career development have a hard job. They must stay abreast of trends within the career development field and constantly assess their own professional development. As the global workplace expands, they must be well versed in the different needs of protected class employees and be diversity intelligent. As economic conditions change; organizations continue to restructure and reinvent themselves; the need for dedicated practitioners in the career development field will only increase. The impact of the COVID-19 pandemic has proven the need for career development.

All employees deserve leaders' best efforts in helping them determine and achieve their career goals. Robbins (2005) describes a career as a pattern of work-related experiences that encompass the course of a person's life. He noted that careers are boundaryless. The boundaryless method depends on individuals taking responsibility for their own future.

Unfair Workplace Environment and Career Advancement

Leaders are responsible for the workplace environment that an employee encounters upon hire and thereafter. Some workplace environmental conditions are inherently unfair to protected class employees (Lee, 2022; Wolfgruber et al., 2022) and are often more obvious to the disabled when they cannot find a place to park or enter buildings comfortably. There are empirically supported, compelling accounts of differential treatment, exclusion, isolation, and career advancement opportunities not commensurate with the KSAs of highly qualified protected class employees in organizations (Cose, 1993; Dobbin & Kalev, 2022; Feagin & Sikes, 1994). The disparity in opportunities in instrumental relationships reduced the positive experiences for protected class employees (Bell & Nkomo, 2001; Combs, 2003; Dickens & Dickens, 1982; Talley-Ross, 1995). Some work environments continue to reflect race as a negative factor (Alderfer, 2000; Ferdman, 1999; Grossman, 2000; John J. Heldrich Center, 2002; Thomas, 2001). Fernandez (1991) noted that protected class employees are excluded from informal activities of their work groups and view them as a major obstruction to their career advancement. One example described by Combs (2003) occurs when White peers only speak to American Black leaders when they are spoken to; otherwise, they obviously avoid any unnecessary contact with American Blacks in the workplace.

Conditions in the Workplace Environment and Career Advancement

Hofacker (2014) found nine workplace environmental conditions that are detrimental to the success of protected class employees: bias, homophily, homosocial reproduction, occupational segregation, social segregation, spatial segregation, stereotype threat, structural segregation, and subtle forms of racism. The condition of the workplace environment has shown that protected class employees are less likely to advance than their white counterparts (Dobbin & Kalev, 2022; Maume, 1999; Tang, 2000; Vallas, 2003); because they are subject to:

1. Homosocial reproduction (April et al., 2023; Kanter, 1977; Hudson et al., 2017; Galea et al., 2023; Zietsman & Kurt, 2021). Homosocial reproduction is evident when "Managers tend to carefully guard power and privilege for those who fit in, for those they see as 'their kind' … reproducing themselves "in their own image"" (Kanter, 1977, p. 48).
2. Structural segregation (Kalev, 2009; Ray, 2019; Shin & Kim, 2022; Sokoloff, 1992; Tomaskovic-Devey, 1993). Structural segregation occurs when minorities are overrepresented at the lower levels of the organization and underrepresented at the higher levels (Thomas, 2005; Giscombe & Mattis, 2002).
3. Social segregation (Giscombe & Mattis, 2002; Maume, 1999; Pullen et al., 2023; Sun et al., 2023). Social segregation is shown when "minorities lack access to important workplace relationships that are important in developing one's career" (Thomas, 2005, p. 79).
4. Occupational segregation (Albelda, 1985; Buhai & van der Leij, 2023; Glass, 1990; Kaida & Boyd, 2022; Maume, 1999; Thomas, 2005; Tomaskovic-Devey, 2006; Sokoloff, 1992). Occupational segregation occurs when a minority is channeled into what is considered to be a minority job such as Director of Diversity (Albeda, 1985; Maume, 1999; Sokoloff, 1992; Tatum, 1999; Thomas, 2005; Vallas, 2003).
5. Homophily (Ertug et al., 2022; Jung & Welch, 2022; McPherson et al., 2001). "Homophily is the principle that a contact between similar people occurs at a higher rate than among dissimilar people" McPherson et al., 2001, p. 416).
6. Stereotype threat (Perna et al., 2009; Schmader et al., 2008: Woodcock et al., 2012; VanLandingham et al., 2022). Stereotype threat is when "stereotypes and negative expectations often create obstacles and difficulties for minority employees in U.S. organizations" (Chemers et al., 2011, p. 486).
7. Spatial segregation (Vallas, 2003). Spatial segregation happens when occupational segregation is facilitated by locating minorities in minority jobs together in the workplace (Albelda, 1985; Vallas, 2003).
8. Racism (Bell, 1980; Elias, 2023; Thomas, 2005). Subtle forms of racism occurs when White prejudice is conveyed toward protected class group and category members by White opposition to demands

and resentment at their protected class group and category members' presumed special treatment (Feldman & Huddy, 2005; Thomas, 2005). Racial harassment (Bell, 1980) was prevalent in organizations and continues to be a problem (Avery et al., 2023).

9. Bias (Avery et al., 2022; Tversky & Kahneman, 1983; Heffernan, 2022; Hughes & Dodge, 1997; Joshi et al., 2015). The workplace environment condition of bias is manifested by "stereotyping and bias among managers who make hiring and promotion decisions" (Dobbin et al., 2007, p. 23).

The protected class employees' relationships with leaders who are important to their career advancement are affected by environments where resentment, discrimination, and prejudice are present (Cohen, 2002; Hirsh, 2009; National Academies of Sciences, Engineering, and Medicine, 2023; Plitmann, 2022). These conditions contribute to the lack of encouragement and isolation that protected class employees experience. Protected class employees often cannot quit their jobs because of economic needs, so they typically establish coping (Dickens & Chavez, 2018; Dickens et al., 2019; Hall et al., 2012) mechanisms to endure unfair treatment. DQ and Fair Process training is needed to help leaders restore a workplace environment that has been corrupted by unfair treatment (Brockner, 2014; Fleming et al., 2005; Kim & Mauborgne, 2003). Fairness process training has been shown to be effective for organizations and needs to be extended to include DQ to improve the treatment of protected class employees in the workplace and address unfair workplace environment conditions.

The work environment or organization culture has been shown to explain some of the self-efficacy belief patterns of employees (Lent et al., 2002), their interpersonal styles, and can impact the physical, mental, and emotional well-being of employees. Individuals, especially women, who are assertive and display no-nonsense interpersonal leadership styles tend to make others uncomfortable. American Black women are labeled as angry when their interpersonal leadership style is fierce and effective (Doyle, 2011), and they have great power and influence. Dickens and Dickens (1982) noted that the environment impacts American Black managers' performance and that these managers are dissatisfied with their environment, the injustice, and inequity in treatment that becomes visible to them. They also noted that over time spent in an inequitable environment, American Black managers experience a low sense of self ability, capability, and/or confidence which was not present upon entry into the environment. As issues of inclusion, professional identity, and interpersonal leadership ability are questioned by the American Black managers and those who lead them, their ability to grow is diminished. Therefore, the premise that women need to lean in (Sandberg, 2013) is not valid for all women, especially American Black women. American Black women who are pursuing positions of authority are being unacknowledged, excluded, and pushed out despite their efforts to lean in and seek authority (Hughes, 2014). Leaders without DQ will not help protected class employees progress within organizations when they clearly have the capability to succeed.

Personal Obstacles and Career Advancement

Protected class employees understand that not all the responsibility for their success is the responsibility of the leader. They must overcome personal/internal obstacles that could prevent them from achieving their goals (Sandberg, 2013). Microaggression, discrimination, and racism limits protected class employees' potential to ascend to higher levels within the workplace (Avery et al., 2023; Cartwright et al., 2009; King et al., 2022; Smith & Griffiths, 2022). However, the protected class employees must be capable of addressing their own reaction to individuals who have limited or non-existent DQ. They should control their response to overt and covert discriminatory treatment and follow the organizations' laws, policies, and rules when they respond. Hence, the importance of organizations ensuring that all employees know their rights according to the laws, policies, and rules. When an organization does not make this information known to employees or enforce their own policies effectively (Hirsh, 2009; Hirsh & Kornrich, 2008; Nishii et al., 2018; Yang & Liu, 2021) there is more of a tendency for the employee to seek retribution beyond the confines of the organizational structure (Stainback et al., 2010) and file EEOC complaints and/or seek legal representation to file lawsuits outside the EEOC.

Sandberg (2013) noted that for women the internal obstacles can be more difficult to overcome than the institutional obstacles of sexism, discrimination, and/or sexual harassment. They are more difficult to overcome because some women lack the DQ to personally recognize the obstacle and do not understand the extent to which they are affected by their own internal obstacles. American Black Women, more so than some other protected class employees, tend to make excuses for others' misbehavior toward them and blame themselves for others' actions (Smith, 2002; Johnson et al., 2021). Women may perceive themselves to be oversensitive because of the stereotype that women are oversensitive (Joshi et al., 2015).

No one likes to be devalued or have their credentials diminished. This is especially true of protected class employees who often must observe others with less skills and credentials advance ahead of them. It is difficult for protected class employees to interpersonally communicate or say just the right thing or make the apt symbolic gesture at just the right moment as Goleman (2000) suggested when they are dealing with the shock attributable to the mistreatment they have received from their leaders (Johnson et al., 2021). The level of trauma after the murder of George Floyd in 2020, and the way businesses began to adjust to racism is one example of this. Protected class employees who were enduring racism in the workplace for many years were shocked at the overnight changes in some treatment and some policies by leaders who could have made those same changes years before.

Protected Class Employee Voice and Career Advancement

There is a need to hear the individual and collective voices of protected class employees within the workplace. The interpersonal skills of protected class employees have been and are still being manipulated, exploited, and negatively distributed by leaders who profess to know better, within the workplace. Protected class employees are being presented by their leaders to other leaders as incompetent and this must stop. DQ of all leaders is required to end the negativity perpetrated against those who are different within the workplace. Communication among and between those who are different is essential for continued organization success. Collective voices are often minimized and summarized to align with the organizations' goals even if they diverge. The true feelings and perceptions of employees become diluted and distorted in the summaries. Why should the feelings of protected class employees be validated? Most protected class laws are based on a reasonable person standard. How does one define a reasonable person who has never experienced discrimination?

TEAM PLAYER AND CAREER ADVANCEMENT

Some leaders measure and judge protected class employees based upon the perception of others regarding the protected class employee being a team player. Those others and the leaders themselves are often not judged based upon their lack of teamwork toward the protected class employees. How can one be a team player when they have never been allowed to be a team member? The focus on belonging reveals that some protected class employees were never considered to be a team member. In many organizations, there is clearly a double standard regarding interpersonal skills displayed within the workplace. Interpersonal skills are subjective, unmeasurable criteria and should never be used as a part of a performance evaluation system, yet many career aspirations have been derailed because of these criteria. How do you measure the people interaction of leaders who lack DQ? Hughes and Liang's (2020) DQ Scale © 2020 measures leader's perception of their behavior toward protected class employees whom they lead. How do you measure the social communication of leaders who lack DQ? How do you measure the emotional intelligence of leaders who lack DQ? As Hughes (2014) asked, why is it wrong to be different?

Leaders are allowed to determine what disagreeable is and often determine that American Black women and other protected class employees are disagreeable when they seek to be better understood by their leaders. Leaders use stereotypes to hinder the success of protected class employees because very few individuals inside the organization are willing to challenge their power to do so. Leaders are not challenged because of the threat of retaliation. If all individuals inside the organization had DQ, they would know that they are protected from retaliations and may be more likely to help foster a culture that supports difference.

FROM CAREER DEVELOPMENT TO LEADERSHIP DEVELOPMENT FOR PROTECTED CLASS EMPLOYEES

A recurring theme in the literature regarding leadership development of executives stems from the notion of succession planning coupled with EQ. Succession planning and EQ together have not solved the problem of the underrepresentation of protected class employees in executive leadership development programs and the progression to leadership positions. DQ is the missing link that is needed for leaders to understand how to truly incorporate and integrate protected class employees in positions that they are often overqualified to fill.

Organizations have found value in developing talent from the inside out, and high potential employees are provided opportunities to showcase their KSAs (Ross, 2005); yet very few of those leader development employees represent protected class groups. Protected class employees are often left out because of fear. It is fear of the unknown which is why DQ should be integrated into leadership development training. Most protected class employees have the best interest of the organization in mind and only want the opportunity to provide their best work performance for their organization. They are often stymied by leaders who are ignorant of their abilities and personal motivations for success.

Informal networks, relationships, trust, and credibility are all components of a workplace culture or work environment that supports and nurtures the development of leaders (Johnson & Pietri, 2022), but these components are not openly provided or offered to protected class employees (Alvarado & Lynham, 2005; Amis et al., 2020; Combs, 2003; Mor Barak, 2015, 2017; Slepian & Jacoby-Senghor, 2021). Protected class employees are not provided equal access to mentoring, they lack access to informal networks, and they endure discrimination and stereotypes that are designed by those who oppose their presence in the organization to hinder their career development, advancement, and retention.

The systemic blockage of protected class employees is not a hidden agenda. It is known but there has been little success in alleviating the problem because not enough protected class employees are in positions to affect change, and the current leaders in the positions of influence are not using their power, influence, and authority to make necessary changes. For example, the term "concrete ceiling" was used by the Federal Glass Ceiling Commission (1995) over 25 years ago and represents the internal barriers perceived and experienced by American Black women in corporate America (Hughes, 2014; Jackson, 2012: Sims & Carter, 2019). The relationship of the concrete ceiling to the work environment was described by the Federal Glass Ceiling Commission (1995) as a place of isolation that resulted in the invisibility of American Black women (Buchanan & Settles, 2019; McCluney et al., 2019; Obasi, 2022; Sesko & Biernat, 2010; Smith et al., 2019) by decision makers for leadership opportunities. When protected class employees can be rendered invisible (Bhattacharyya & Berdahl, 2023; Buchanan & Settles, 2019) by leaders who profess to care about their presence in their organizations (, it represents a huge, almost insurmountable problem as it relates to ascension to leadership ranks within organizations. Many individuals are familiar with the term "glass ceiling," and there is a distinct difference between "concrete ceiling" and "glass ceiling." The difference between the concept of the "concrete ceiling" and the "glass ceiling" is that the glass allows the imagination of possibilities and observation because that which is above the glass is visible. The "concrete ceiling" does not offer visibility or insight into activities happening beyond the wall and reinforces the lack of opportunities for advancement because of negative environmental influences. The concrete ceiling must be eliminated for all protected class employees to attain their career goals.

The citizenry within America and the employee composition within organizations are rapidly becoming diverse. These individuals are repeating many of the old and making new demands for fair treatment in society and the workplace. Organizations are also fighting to maintain a competitive advantage in this global climate and are finding this endeavor to be difficult (Cox & Blake, 1991; Kick et al., 2006; Stata, 1989). The paradox is that protected class employees are fighting to participate within organizations that are stifling their contributions while the organization is fighting to survive. The solution is within the organization's reach through the use of DQ to begin to leverage diversity through career development interventions. Organization leaders must stop the infighting against some of their employees if they are going to regain and maintain competitive advantage (Cummings & Worley, 2005; Herring, 2009; Hughes, 2014; Hughes & Stephens, 2012; Kick et al., 2006; Mackey et al., 2021; Stata, 1989) with a competent and diverse workforce.

Career Management Systems

Protected class employees must be provided with a supportive climate where they feel comfortable interacting with leaders and co-workers as mentors for career development (Thomas et al., 2005; Thomas, 2008). If leaders followed Boudreaux's (2001) suggestion that career development focuses "on the alignment of individual subjective career aspects and the more objective career aspects of the organizations in order to achieve the best fit between individual and organizational needs as well as personal characteristics and career roles" (p. 806), they would seek ways to understand the personal characteristics of protected class employees to enhance their career development success. Hughes's (2010, 2012, in press b) five values align with the personal characteristics of the employees and can be used by organization leaders for career development of protected class employees. Many organizations and employees had no career strategy or career plan for successful transitioning or adaptation to the rapid changes during the Great Recession (Friedman & Mandelbaum, 2011) nor during the COVID-19 pandemic (Hughes in pressb) and without a clear strategy employees move from job to job seeking a career (Banks, 2006a, b; Hayes, 2000; Karsten & Igou, 2005).

Organizations must also expand beyond the typical career development models and understand how protected class employees can influence their own career development strategy (Banks, 2006a, b; Hughes, 2014). Protected class employees must not excluded from nor should they exclude themselves from their own career development. They must be in positions to network with individuals who can influence their career success.

Career management includes mindsets of personal ownership, accountability, and responsibility that individuals hold toward their career development. Career management systems offer employees and organization leaders the opportunity to create a model for employee development that benefits both the employee and the organization. Some career management systems include performance-based and skill-based pay systems that contain detailed career development strategies and opportunities for employees to enhance their careers within the organization.

Hughes (2015a) suggested that the four intelligences could be developed into a typology for a career development evaluation system measurement tool (pp. 4–5). She suggested that leaders could examine each of the four intelligences diversity perspective. DQ can be used to guide the diversity perspective of the leader and content within this book can be extended and empirically examined to develop a career development evaluation tool. Hughes provided the following questions for further examination.

1. In what way(s) can the career development evaluation systems be developed to benefit protected class employees and the organizations?
2. To what extent is diversity significant enough to the organization to warrant a clear definition and its inclusion in annual training programs?

3. If diversity becomes a part of annual training programs, what effect does it have on the culture of the organization? Will the workplace environment be changed for the betterment of protected class employees?
4. To what extent can organization leaders leverage their understanding of workforce inter-personnel diversity, legally mandated diversity, and DQ?

CONCLUSION

Organizations can begin to leverage diversity by improving advancement opportunities in leadership positions for protected class employees, specifically, minorities and American Black women (Sims & Carter, 2019). According to Cummings and Worley (2005), "only 5% and less than 1% of management and senior executive [positions]" (p. 413) were held by Blacks. Less than 16 percent of top officers were female and only 3.2 percent of board seats held in Fortune 500 companies were held by women of color (Byrnes & Crockett, 2009; Catalyst, 2008). Those numbers have not improved much since 2005 (Dobbin & Kalev, 2022). The ratio of American Black women participation in executive leadership is 1% in comparison to a total of 21% women in executive leadership (Connley, 2021). Efforts to diversify organizations at the executive level have shown minimal success. DQ can offer opportunities for improvement to change the systemic environmental influences that are negatively impacting career development aspirations of protected class employees.

Concerted efforts using DQ to address the problems within workplace environments that have limited networking opportunities, little access to mentors, stereotypes and discrimination, and other undermining efforts to prevent protected class employees from becoming effective leaders. The superiority complex is so engrained in some leaders that they never want to be led by a protected class employee. They want the protected class employees' KSAs, but they do not want the protected group employee. So, they steal ideas, marginalize their KSAs, and under pay the protected employees.

REFERENCES

Alderfer, C. P. (2000). National Culture and the New Corporate Language for Race Relations. In R. T. Carter (Ed.), *Addressing Cultural Issues in Organizations Beyond the Corporate Context* (pp. 19–33). Sage.

Alvarado, M., & Lynham, S. (2005). Experiences of Hispanic Executives in the USA Workplace: An Exploratory Overview of Current Knowledge and Understanding. In L. Morris, & F. Nafukho (Eds.), *Proceedings of the Academy of Human Resource Development Annual Research Conference* (pp. 890–897). Academy of Human Resource Development.

Amis, J. M., Mair, J., & Munir, K. A. (2020). The Organizational Reproduction of Inequality. *Academy of Management Annals, 14*(1), 195–230.

April, K., Dharani, B., & April, A. (2023). Contextualised Discrimination. In *Lived Experiences of Exclusion in the Workplace: Psychological & Behavioural Effects* (pp. 109–153). Emerald Publishing Limited.

Avery, D. R., Dumas, T. L., George, E., Joshi, A., Loyd, D. L., van Knippenberg, D., Wang, M., & Xu, H. (2022). Racial Biases in the Publication Process: Exploring Expressions and Solutions. *Journal of Management, 48*(1), 7–16.

Avery, D. R., Hall, A. V., Preston, McKenzie, Ruggs, E. N., & Washington, E. (2023). Is Justice Colorblind? A Review of Workplace Racioethnic Differences Through the Lens of Organizational Justice. *Annual Review of Organizational Psychology and Organizational Behavior, 10*, 389–412.

Bachrach, D. G., Patel, P. C., & Pratto, F. (2022). As Clear as Black and White: Racially Disparate Concerns Over Career Progression for Remote Workers Across Racial Faultlines. *Business & Society*, 1–28. https://doi.org/10.1177/00076503221121823

Banks, C. H. (2006a). Career Planning: Toward an Inclusive Model. In M. Karsten (Ed.), *Gender, Race and Ethnicity in the Workplace* (Vol. III, pp. 99–116). Greenwood Publishing Group.

Banks, C. H. (2006b). Career Planning: Towards a More Inclusive Model for Women and Diverse Individuals. In F. Nafukho and H. Chen (Eds.), *Academy of Human Resource Development International Conference (AHRD) Proceedings. Symp. 31–1* (pp. 640–647). Academy of Human Resource Development.

Bhattacharyya, B., & Berdahl, J. L. (2023). Do You See Me? An Inductive Examination of Differences Between Women of Color's Experiences of and Responses to Invisibility at Work. *Journal of Applied Psychology*. https://doi.org/10.1037/apl0001072

Bell, D. (1980). Brown v. Board of Education and the Interest-Convergence Dilemma. *Harvard Law Review, 93*, 518–533.

Bell, E. L. J., & Nkomo, S. M. (2001). *Our Separate Ways: Black and White Women and the Struggle for Professional Identity*. Harvard University Press.

Bigman, Y. E., Yam, K. C., Marciano, D., Reynolds, S. J., & Gray, K. (2021). Threat of Racial and Economic Inequality Increases Preference for Algorithm Decision-Making. *Computers in Human Behavior, 122*, 106859.

Boudreaux, M. A. (2001). Career Development: What Is Its Role in Human Resource Development? In O. A. Aliaga (Ed.), *Academy of HRD 2001 Conference Proceedings* (pp. 805–812). Academy of Human Resource Development.

Brockner, J. (2014, Summer). Why It's So Hard to Be Fair. *Harvard Business Review Onpoint*, pp. 44–51.

Buchanan, N. T., & Settles, I. H. (2019). Managing (in) Visibility and Hypervisibility in the Workplace. *Journal of Vocational Behavior, 113*, 1–5.

Buhai, I. S., & van der Leij, M. J. (2023). A Social Network Analysis of Occupational Segregation. *Journal of Economic Dynamics and Control, 147*, 1–23. https://doi.org/10.1016/j.jedc.2022.104593

Byrnes, N., & Crockett, R. O. (2009, May 28). Ursula Burns: An Historic Succession at Xerox. *BusinessWeek*.

Cartwright, B. Y., Washington, R. D., & McConnell, L. R. (2009). Examining Racial Microaggressions in Rehabilitation Counselor Education. *Rehabilitation Education, 23*(2), 171–182.

Catalyst, I. (2008). *2008 Catalyst Census of Women Corporate Officers and Top Earners of the Fortune 500*. Catalyst Inc.

Chemers, M. M., Zurbriggen, E. L., Syed, M., Goza, B. K., & Bearman, S. (2011). The Role of Efficacy and Identity in Science Career Commitment among Underrepresented Minority Students. *Journal of Social Issues, 67*(3), 469–491.

Cohen, C. F. (2002). Glass Ceilings and Glass Slippers: Still Stereotyping After All These Years? In P. J. Frost, W. R. Nord, & L. A. Krefting (Eds.), *HRM Reality: Putting Competence in Context* (pp. 205–213). Prentice Hall.

Combs, G. M. (2003). The Duality of Race and Gender for Managerial African American Women: Implications of Informal Social Networks on Career Advancement. *Human Resource Development Review, 2*(4), 385–405.

Connley, C. (2021, January 12). *How Corporate America's Diversity Initiatives Continue to Fail Black Women*. CNBC. https://www.cnbc.com/2020/07/01/how-corporate-americas-diversity-initiatives-continue-to-fail-black-women.html

Cose, E. (1993). *The Rage of a Privileged Class*. HarperCollins.

Cox, T. H., & Blake, S. (1991). Managing Cultural Diversity: Implications for Organizational Competitiveness. *Academy of Management Executive, 5*(3), 45–56.

Cummings, T. G., & Worley, C. G. (2005). Human Resources Management Interventions: Developing and Assisting Members. In *Organization Development and Change* (8th ed., pp. 396–433). South-Western, Thomson Corporation.

Dawis, R., England, G. W., & Lofquist, L. H. (1964). *A Theory of Work Adjustment. Minnesota Studies in Vocational Rehabilitation, XV* (pp. 1–27). University of Minnesota, Industrial Relations Center.

Dickens, D. D., & Chavez, E. L. (2018). Navigating the Workplace: The Costs and Benefits of Shifting Identities at Work Among Early Career U.S. Black Women. *Sex Roles, 78*(11–12), 760–774. https://doi.org/10.1007/s11199-017-0844-x

Dickens, D. D., Womack, V. Y., & Dimes, T. (2019). Managing Hypervisibility: An Exploration of Theory and Research on Identity Shifting Strategies in the Workplace Among Black Women. *Journal of Vocational Behavior, 113*, 153–163.

Dobbin, F., & Kalev, A. (2022). *Getting to Diversity: What Wrks and What Doesn't*. Harvard University Press.

Dobbin, F., Kalev, A., & Kelly, E. (2007). Diversity Management in Corporate America. *American Sociological Association, 6*(4), 21–27.

Doyle, A. (2011). *Powering Up: How America's Women Achievers Become Leaders*. Xlibris Corporation.

Elias, A. (2023). Racism as Neglect and Denial. *Ethnic and Racial Studies*, 1–23.

Ertug, G., Brennecke, J., Kovacs, B., & Zou, T. (2022). What does homophily do? A review of the consequences of homophily. *Academy of Management Annals, 16*(1), 38–69. https://doi.org/10.5465/annals.2020.0230

Feagin, J. R., & Sikes, M. P. (1994). *Living with Racism: The Black Middle-Class Experience*. Beacon.

Federal Glass Ceiling Commission. (1995). *Good for Business: Making Full Use of the Nation's Human Capital*. Retrieved April 7, 2012, from http://www.dol.gov/oasam/programs/history/reich/reports/ceiling.pdf

Feldman, S., & Huddy, L. (2005). Racial Resentment and White Opposition to Race-Conscious Programs: Principles or Prejudice? *American Journal of Political Science, 49*(1), 168–183.

Ferdman, B. M. (1999). The Color and Culture of Gender in Organizations: Attending to Race and Ethnicity. In G. N. Powell (Ed.), *The Handbook of Gender and Work* (pp. 17–34). Sage.

Fernandez, J. P. (1991). *Managing a Diverse Workforce: Regaining the Competitive Edge*. Lexington Books.

Fleming, J. H., Coffman, C., & Harter, J. K. (2005, July–August). Manage Your Human Sigma. *Harvard Business Review, 83*(7), 106–114.

Friedman, T. L., & Mandelbaum, M. (2011). *That Used to Be Us: How America Fell Behind in the World It Invented and How We can Come Back*. Farrar, Strauss, and Giroux.

Galea, N., Powell, A., & Salignac, F. (2023). The role of homosociality in maintaining men's powerfulness in construction companies. *Construction Management and Economics, 41*(2), 172–182.

Giscombe, K., & Mattis, M. C. (2002). "Leveling the Playing Field for Women of Color in Corporate Management: Is the Business Case Enough? *Journal of Business Ethics, 37*(1), 103–119.

Glass, J. (1990). The impact of occupational segregation on working conditions. *Social Forces, 68*(3), 779–796. https://doi.org/10.1093/sf/68.3.779

Goleman, D. (2000). Leadership That Gets Results. *Harvard Business Review, 78*(2), 78–93.

Grossman, R. J. (2000, March). Race in the Workplace. *HR Magazine*, pp. 41–45.

Hall, D. T., Briscoe, J. P., Dickmann, M., & Mayrhofer, W. (2012). Implications of the Management of People and Organizations. In J. P. Briscoe, D. T. Hall, & W. Mayrhofer (Eds.), *Careers Around the World: Individual and Contextual Perspectives* (pp. 166–186). Routledge.

Hayes, K. H. (2000). *Managing Career Transitions: Your Career as a Work in Progress* (2nd ed.). Prentice Hall.

Heffernan, T. (2022). Sexism, Racism, Prejudice, and Bias: A Literature Review and Synthesis of Research Surrounding Student Evaluations of Courses and Teaching. *Assessment & Evaluation in Higher Education, 47*(1), 144–154.

Heldrich, J. J. (2002). Center for Workforce Development. *Work Trends Survey Report. A Workplace Divided: How Americans View Discrimination and Race on the Job*. Rutgers University.

Herring, C. (2009). Does Diversity Pay? Race, Gender, and the Business Case for Diversity. *American Sociological Review, 74*(2), 208–224.

Hirsh, C. E. (2009). The Strength of Weak Enforcement: The Impact of Discrimination Charges, Legal Environments, and Organizational Conditions on Workplace Segregation. *American Sociological Review, 74*(2), 245–271.

Hirsh, C. E., & Kornrich, S. (2008). The Context of Discrimination: Workplace Conditions, Institutional Environments, and Sex and Race Discrimination Charges. *American Journal of Sociology, 113*(5), 1394–1432.

Hofacker, S. A. (2014). Diversity and Inclusion in the Engineering Workplace: A Call for Majority Intentionality to Increase Career Self-Efficacy. In *American Society for Engineering Education: 2014 ASEE Southeast Section Conference*.

Holland, J. L. (1959). A Theory of Vocational Choice. *Journal of Counseling Psychology, 6*(1), 35–45.

Houser, K. A. (2019). Can AI Solve the Diversity Problem in the Tech Industry: Mitigating Noise and Bias in Employment Decision-Making. *Stanford Technology Law Review, 22*, 290–354.

Hudson, M., Netto, G., Noon, M., Sosenko, F., De Lima, P., & Kamenou-Aigbekaen, N. (2017). Ethnicity and Low Wage Traps: Favouritism, Homosocial Reproduction and Economic Marginalization. *Work, Employment and Society, 31*(6), 992–1009.

Hughes, C. (2010). People as Technology Conceptual Model: Towards a New Value Creation Paradigm for Strategic Human Resource Development. *Human Resource Development Review, 9*(1), 48–71. https://doi.org/10.1177/1534484309353561

Hughes, C. (2014). *American Black Women and Interpersonal Leadership Styles*. The Netherlands Sense Publishers.

Hughes, C. (Ed.). (2015). *The Impact of Diversity on Organization and Career Development*. IGI Global.

Hughes, C., & DeVaughn, S.. (2012). Leveraging Workforce Diversity Through a Career Development Paradigm Shift. In C. L. Scott & M. Y. Byrd (Eds.), *Handbook of Research on Workforce Diversity in a Global Society: Technologies and Concepts* (pp. 262–272). IGI Global.

Hughes, D., & Dodge, M. A. (1997). African American Women in the Workplace: Relationships between Job Conditions, Racial Bias at Work, and Perceived Job Quality. *American Journal of Community Psychology, 25*(5), 581–599.

Hughes, C., & Liang, X. (2020). *Hughes and Liang Diversity Intelligence®(DQ) Scale© 2020*. https://www.diversityintelligencellc.com

Hughes, C., & Niu, Y. (2021a). Preface: Shifting Career Realities and Navigating Career Journeys. *Advances in Developing Human Resources, 23*(3), 195–202.

Hughes, C., & Niu, Y. (2021b). Responding to Career Development Uncertainties and Successfully Navigating Career Journeys. *Advances in Developing Human Resources, 23*(3), 267–272.

Hughes, C., Robert, L., Frady, K., & Arroyos, A. (2019). *Managing Technology and Middle and Low Skilled Employees: Advances for Economic Regeneration*. Emerald Publishing.

Isaacson, L. E., & Brown, D. (1997). *Career Information, Career Counseling, and Career Development* (6th ed.). Allyn & Bacon.

Jackson, L. R. (2012). *The Self-Efficacy Beliefs of Black Women Leaders in Fortune 500 Companies*. Unpublished doctoral dissertation, University of Arkansas, Fayetteville, AR.

Johnson, I. R., & Pietri, E. S. (2022). An Ally You Say? Endorsing White Women as Allies to Encourage Perceptions of Allyship and Organizational Identity-Safety Among Black Women. *Group Processes & Intergroup Relations, 25*(2), 453–473.

Johnson, V. E., Nadal, K. L., Sissoko, D. R. G., & King, R. (2021). "It's Not in Your Head": Gaslighting, 'Splaining, Victim Blaming, and Other Harmful Reactions to Microaggressions. *Perspectives on Psychological Science, 16*(5), 1024–1036.

Joshi, A., Son, J., & Roh, H. (2015). When Can Women Close the Gap? A Meta-Analytic Test of Sex Differences in Performance And Rewards. *Academy of Management Journal, 58*(5), 1516–1545.

Jung, H., & Welch, E. W. (2022). The Impact of Demographic Composition of Social Networks on Perceived Inclusion in the Workplace. *Public Administration Review, 82*(3), 522–536. https://doi.org/10.1111/puar.13470

Kaida, L., & Boyd, M. (2022). Revisiting Gender Occupational Segregation Trends in Canada: 1991–2016. *Canadian Review of Sociology/Revue Canadienne de Sociologie, 59*(S1), 4–25.

Kalev, A. (2009). Cracking the Glass Cages? Restructuring and Ascriptive Inequality at Work. *American Journal of Sociology, 114*(6), 1591–1643.

Kaliannan, M., Darmalinggam, D., Dorasamy, M., & Abraham, M. (2022). Inclusive Talent Development as a Key Talent Management Approach: A Systematic Literature Review. *Human Resource Management Review, 33*(1), 100926. https://doi.org/10.1016/j.hrmr.2022.100926

Kane, G. (2019). The Technology Fallacy: People Are the Real Key to Digital Transformation. *Research-Technology Management, 62*(6), 44–49.

Kane, G. C., Phillips, A. N., Copulsky, J. R., & Andrus, G. R. (2019). *The Technology Fallacy: How People Are the Real Key to Digital Transformation.* MIT Press.

Kanter, R. M. (1977). *Men and Women of the Corporation.* Basic Books.

Karsten, M. F., & Igou, F. (2005). Career Planning: A Model for a Diverse Workforce. In *Refereed Proceedings of the North American Management Society Track at the 2005 Midwest Business Administration Association Conference.* MBAA.

Kick, E. L., Fraser, J. C., & Davis, B. L. (2006, February). Performance Management, Managerial Citizenship and Worker Commitment: A Study of the United States Postal Service with Some Global Implications. *Economic and Industrial Democracy, 27*(1), 137–172.

Kim, W. C., & Mauborgne, R. (2003, January). Fair Process: Managing the Knowledge Economy. *Harvard Business Review Classics, 81*(1), 127–136.

King, D. D., Fattoracci, E. S. M., Hollingsworth, D. W., Stahr, E., & Nelson, M. (2022). When Thriving Requires Effortful Surviving: Delineating Manifestations and Resource Expenditure Outcomes of Microaggressions for Black Employees. *Journal of Applied Psychology, 108*(2), 183–207.

Lee, J. (2022). A Critical Review and Theorization of Workplace Backlash: Looking Back and Moving Forward Through the Lens of Social Dominance Theory. *Human Resource Management Review*, 100900.

Lent, Robert W., Steven D. Brown, and Gail Hackett. 'Social Cognitive Career Theory." In *Career Choice and Development* (4th ed) edited by D. Brown and Associates. (San Francisco, CA: Jossey-Bass, 2002): 255–311.

Mackey, J. D., Ellen III, B. P., McAllister, C. P., & Alexander, K. C. (2021). The Dark Side of Leadership: A Systematic Literature Review and Meta-Analysis of Destructive Leadership Research. *Journal of Business Research, 132*, 705–718.

Maume, D. J. (1999). Glass Ceilings and Glass Escalators Occupational Segregation and Race and Sex Differences in Managerial Promotions. *Work and Occupations, 26*(4), 483–509. https://doi.org/10.1177/073088849902600 4005

McCluney, C. L., & Rabelo, V. C. (2019). Conditions of Visibility: An Intersectional Examination of Black Women's Belongingness and Distinctiveness at Work. *Journal of Vocational Behavior, 113*, 143–152.

McDonnell, M., & Baxter, D. (2019). Chatbots and Gender Stereotyping. *Interacting with Computers, 31*(2), 116–121.

McPherson, M., Smith-Lovin, L., & Cook, J. M. (2001). Birds of a Feather: Homophily in Social Networks. *Annual Review of Sociology, 27*, 415–444.

Mor Barak, M. E. (2015). Inclusion is the Key to Diversity Management, But What is Inclusion? *Human Service Organizations: Management, Leadership & Governance., 39*(2), 83–88.

Mor Barak, M. E. (2017). *Managing Diversity: Toward a Globally Inclusive Workplace* (4th ed.). SAGE.

National Academies of Sciences, Engineering, and Medicine. (2023). *Advancing Antiracism, Diversity, Equity, and Inclusion in STEMM Organizations: Beyond Broadening Participation*. The National Academies Press. https://doi.org/ 10.17226/26803

Nishii, L. H., Khattab, J., Shemla, M., & Paluch, R. M. (2018). A Multi-Level Process Model for Understanding Diversity Practice Effectiveness. *Academy of Management Annals, 12*(1), 37–82.

Obasi, C. (2022). Black Social Workers: Identity, Racism, Invisibility/ Hypervisibility at Work. *Journal of Social Work, 22*(2), 479–497.

Perna, L., Lundy-Wagner, V., Drezner, N. D., Gasman, M., Yoon, S., Bose, E., & Gary, S. (2009). The Contribution of HBCUs to the Preparation of African American Women for STEM Careers: A Case Study. *Research in Higher Education, 50*(1), 1–23.

Plitmann, Y. (2022). Authentic Compliance with a Symbolic Legal Standard? How Critical Race Theory Can Change Institutionalist Studies on Diversity in the Workplace. *Law & Social Inquiry, 47*(1), 331–346. https://doi.org/ 10.1017/lsi.2021.38

Pullen, E., Fischer, M. W., Morse, G., Garabrant, J., Salyers, M. P., & Rollins, A. L. (2023). Racial Disparities in the Workplace: The Impact of Isolation on Perceived Organizational Support and Job Satisfaction. *Psychiatric Rehabilitation Journal, 46*(1), 45–52. https://doi.org/10.1037/prj0000543

Raghavan, M., Barocas, S., Kleinberg, J., & Levy, K. (2020). Mitigating Bias in Algorithmic Hiring: Evaluating Claims and Practices. In *Proceedings of the 2020 Conference on Fairness, Accountability, and Transparency* (pp. 469–481).

Ray, V. (2019). A Theory of Racialized Organizations. *American Sociological Review, 84*(1), 26–53.

Robbins, S. P. (2005). *Organizational Behavior* (11th ed.). Pearson Prentice Hall.

Ross, E. (2005, April). Find Talent and Use It. *Business Review Weekly, 27*(4), 66–68.

Sandberg, S. (2013). *Lean In: Women, Work, and the Will to Lead.* Alfred Knopf.

Schmader, T., Johns, M., & Forbes, C. (2008). An Integrated Process Model of Stereotype Threat Effects on Performance. *Psychological Review, 115*(2), 336–356.

Sesko, A. K., & Biernat, M. (2010). Prototypes of Race and Gender: The Invisibility of Black Women. *Journal of Experimental Social Psychology, 46*(2), 356–360.

Shaw, J., Wickenden, M., Thompson, S., & Mader, P. (2022). Achieving Disability Inclusive Employment–Are The Current Approaches Deep Enough? *Journal of International Development, 34*(5), 942–963.

Shin, H., & Kim, S. (2022). Overcoming Women's Isolation at Work: The Effect of Organizational Structure and Practices on Female Managers' Workplace Relationships. *International Sociology, 37*(3), 330–354. https://doi.org/10.1177/02685809211051282

Sims, C. M., & Carter, A. D. (2019). Revisiting Parker & Ogilvie's African American Women Executive Leadership Model. *The Journal of Business Diversity, 19*(2), 99–112.

Slepian, M. L., & Jacoby-Senghor, D. S. (2021). Identity Threats in Everyday Life: Distinguishing Belonging from Inclusion. *Social Psychological and Personality Science, 12*(3), 392–406.

Smith, A. N., Watkins, M. B., Ladge, J. J., & Carlton, P. (2019). Making the Invisible Visible: Paradoxical Effects of Intersectional Invisibility on the Career Experiences of Executive Black Women. *Academy of Management Journal, 62*(6), 1705–1734.

Smith, I. A., & Griffiths, A. (2022). Microaggressions, Everyday Discrimination, Workplace Incivilities, and Other Subtle Slights at Work: A Meta-Synthesis. *Human Resource Development Review, 21*(3), 275–299.

Smith, R. A. (2002). Race, Gender, and Authority in the Workplace: Theory and Research. *Annual Review of Sociology, 28*(1), 509–542.

Sokoloff, N. J. (1992). *Black Women and White Women in the Professions: Occupational Segregation by Race and Gender, 1960–1980*. Routledge.

Stainback, K., Tomaskovic-Devey, D., & Skaggs, S. (2010). Organizational Approaches to Inequality: Inertia, Relative Power, and Environments. *Annual Review of Sociology, 36*, 225–247. https://www.annualreviews.org/doi/pdf/10.1146/annurev-soc-070308-120014

Stata, R. (1989). Organizational Learning: The Key to Management Innovation. *Sloan Management Review, 30*(3), 63–74.

Sun, T., Schilpzand, P., & Liu, Y. (2023). Workplace Gossip: An Integrative Review of Its Antecedents, Functions, and Consequences. *Journal of Organizational Behavior, 44*(2), 311–334. https://doi.org/10.1002/job.2653

Super, D. E. (1953). A Theory of Vocational Development. *American Psychologist, 30*(5), 88–92.

Super, D. E. (1980). A Life-Span, Life-Space Approach to Career Development. *Journal of Vocational Behavior, 16*(3), 229–298.

Talley-Ross, N. C., & Edges, J. (1995). *Black Professional Women in White Male Worlds*. Peter Lang.

Tambe, P., Cappelli, P., & Yakubovich, V. (2019). Artificial Intelligence in Human Resources Management: Challenges and a Path Forward. *California Management Review, 61*(4), 15–42.

Tang, J. (2000). *Doing Engineering: The Career Attainment and Mobility of Caucasian, Black, and Asian-American Engineers*. Rowman & Littlefield.

Tatum, B. D. (1999). *Why Are All the Black Kids Sitting Together in the Cafeteria?* Basic Books.

Thomas, D. A. (2001). The Truth About Mentoring Minorities: Race Matters. *Harvard Business Review, 79*(4), 98–112.

Thomas, K. M. (2005). *Diversity Dynamics in the Workplace*. Wadsworth.

Thomas, K. M., Hu, C., Gewin, A. G., Bingham, K., & Yanchus, N. (2005). The Roles of Protégé Race, Gender, and Proactive Socialization Attempts on Peer Monitoring. *Advances in Developing Human Resources, 7*(4), 540–555.

Thomas, K. M. (2008). *Diversity Resistance in Organizations*. Lawrence Erlbaum.

Tomaskovic-Devey, D. (1993). *Gender & Racial Inequality at Work: The Sources and Consequences of Job Segregation*. Cornell University ILR Press.

Tomaskovic-Devey, D., Zimmer, C., Stainback, K., Robinson, C., Taylor, T., & McTague, T. (2006). Documenting Desegregation: Segregation in American Workplaces by Race, Ethnicity, and Sex, 1966–2003. *American Sociological Review, 71*(4), 565–588.

Tversky, A., & Kahneman, D. (1983). Judgment Under Uncertainty: Heuristics and Biases. In D. Kahneman, P. Slovic, & A. Tversky (Eds.), *Judgement Under Uncertainty* (pp. 3–22). Cambridge University Press.

Vallas, S. P. (2003). Rediscovering the Color Line with Work Organizations: The 'Knitting of Racial Groups' Revisited. *Work and Occupations, 30*(4), 379–400.

VanLandingham, H., Ellison, R. L., Laique, A., Cladek, A., Khan, H., Gonzalez, C., & Dunn, M. R. (2022). A Scoping Review of Stereotype Threat for BIPOC: Cognitive Effects and Intervention Strategies for the Field of Neuropsychology. *The Clinical Neuropsychologist, 36*(2), 503–522.

Warren, A. K. (2009). *Cascading Gender Biases, Compounding Effects: An Assessment of Talent Management Systems*. Catalyst.

Wolfgruber, D., Einwiller, S., & Wloka, M. (2022). *Tackling the Backlash: Dealing with Internal and External Criticism of D&I Initiatives* (No. 16). Communication Insights.

Woodcock, A., Hernandez, P. R., Estrada, M., & Schultz, P. (2012). The Consequences of Chronic Stereotype Threat: Domain Disidentification and Abandonment. *Journal of Personality and Social Psychology, 103*(4), 635.

Yang, J. R., & Liu, J. (2021, January 19). *Strengthening accountability for discrimination: Confronting Fundamental Power Imbalances in the employment relationship*. Economic Policy Institute. https://www.epi.org/unequalpower/publications/strengthening-accountability-for-discrimination-confronting-fundamental-power-imbalances-in-the-employment-relationship/

Zietsman, D., & April, K. (2021). Homosocial Reproduction: The Lived Workplace Experiences of Diverse Millennial Women—Part II. *Effective Executive, 24*(4)(12), 37–61. https://www.proquest.com/scholarly-journals/homosocial-reproduction-lived-workplace/docview/2622691488/se-2

CHAPTER 6

Diversity Intelligence and the Need for Diversity Expertise

Leaders who do not have a frame of reference for the lived experiences of protected class employees can be open to learning and being educated about some of the experiences. They can learn enough to be fair in their treatment of protected class employees. Leaders can listen to employees but there is a limit to the empathy that they can offer (Waytz, 2016). The limitations of empathy are that it can be exhausting, zero sum, and erode ethics. The limitations are compounded for leaders as they try to focus on everyone's problems and not the problems that they are legally required to address. How does one gain diversity intelligence expertise? Why is there no specific degree required for those who lead diversity efforts in organizations? What criteria is needed for leaders of diversity efforts (Mallick, 2020), and how can they share that expertise with others in the workplace? How does one lead inclusive workflows/processes without expertise?

FUTILE EFFORTS AND EXHAUSTION

Some protected class employees are exhausted by the continuous efforts to obtain fairness at work (Dwivedi et al., 2022) and were traumatized by the speed of change within some organizations after the murder of George Floyd (Carter, 2020). Organizations throughout the country were releasing anti-racism position statements. Protected class employees were wondering why it took the publicly, brutal death of a Black man to influence changes against racism (Ruggs et al., 2023). Yet, some leaders want to feel good about themselves before they even attempt to help others. Some protected class employees are tired of being placed within the zero-sum calculations with others who have not been treated unfairly, and they are tired of watching their leaders' ethics being eroded while mistreating them and other protected class employees. Leaders should abdicate their leadership roles if they cannot work with all protected class employees.

Legislation, including the Equal Pay Act of 1963, is still being pursued to minimize the adverse impact that women and minorities are experiencing in workplace environments including entry, barriers to entry, and barriers to re-entry. The Equal Pay Act of 1963 was an amendment to the Fair Labor Standards Act (FLSA) of 1938 and "prohibited sex discrimination in the payment of wages" (Cascio & Aguinis, 2005, p. 22). The Equal Pay Act of 1963 states:

> (d) (1) No employer having employees subject to any provisions of this section shall discriminate, within any establishment in which such employees are employed, between employees on the basis of sex by paying wages to employees in such establishment at a rate less than the rate at which he pays wages to employees of the opposite sex in such establishment for equal work on jobs the performance of which requires equal skill, effort, and responsibility, and which are performed under similar working conditions. (U.S. Department of Labor, 2011)

The signing of the Lilly Ledbetter Fair Pay Act to require and accelerate equal pay for women in January 2009 by President Barak Obama still faces opposition despite continued disparate treatment with regard to pay. The following list contains the 13 types of discrimination enforced by the Equal Employment Opportunities Commission (EEOC):

1. Age—Age Discrimination in Employment Act of 1967 (ADEA)
2. Disability—Americans with Disabilities Act of 1990 (ADA)
3. Equal Pay/Compensation
4. Genetic Information—Genetic Information Nondiscrimination Act of 2008
5. Harassment—Title VII of the Civil Rights Act of 1964
6. National Origin

7. Pregnancy—Pregnancy Discrimination Act (PDA) of 1978
8. Race/Color
9. Religion
10. Retaliation
11. Sex
12. Sexual Harassment
13. Sexual Orientation and Gender Identity (EEOC Laws and Guidance, 2023).

Organizations that have federal contracts are required to follow federal laws and guidelines and their employees are protected by the EEOC. Some veterans are protected under the Vietnam Era Veterans' Readjustment Assistance Act of 1974 and Uniformed Services Employment and Reemployment Rights Act.

The fact that many workplace leaders know of the existence of the above mentioned and other workplace laws and mandates to protect certain employees in the workplace, suggests that they are being recklessly stubborn against the application of the laws and mandates because there is not enough consequences (Hirsh, 2009; Yang & Liu, 2021) to compel them to act otherwise.

The role of the leader can be described as a visible role in the organization in which individuals have demonstrated the ability to execute the organizations vision and strategies. A leader focuses on the knowledge, skills, and values that help her lead other people and functions as well as deliver the expected organizational performance results (Charan et al., 2001; Drucker, 2004; Goleman, 1996; Ulrich & Smallwood, 2007). Thus, leaders should acquire DQ knowledge to help lead all their employees.

Stereotyping

One of the biggest problems that leaders must overcome is stereotyping of protected class employees (Avery et al., 2023; Brinson, 2006; Catalyst, 1999; Lipman-Blumen, 1992; Salcedo et al., 2022; Triana et al., 2021). Sanders (2004) suggested that the gender gap existed in work organizations because of stereotypical, evolutionary, biological, and social differences. She along with other authors (Sandberg, 2013; Warren, 2009) suggests one way to close the gender gap in the workplace is to increase awareness and understanding of gender stereotypes (Tabassum & Nayak, 2021). The awareness and understanding of all protected class employees' stereotypes need to be addressed using DQ (Hughes & Brown, 2018). Sandberg (2013) and many other researchers and writers sometimes miss opportunities to help other protected class employees because they fixate on one group such as women and often, they do not mean American Black women. American Black women are frequently stereotyped in the workplace because of their race and gender (Burrows et al., 2022; Hughes, 2014; Jackson, 2012; Parker & oglivie, 1996; Sims & Carter, 2019; Tomaskovic-Devey & Stainback, 2007) and when the focus is just on gender, they are left out of the discussions (Parker & oglivie, 1996). DQ is needed so that all protected class employees are always included and not selectively excluded. Stereotyping is an inaccurate science (Prime, 2005) that is used to destroy individuals' chances to achieve career success.

Researchers have tried to explain why stereotyping and unconscious bias are incorrect using the concept of unconscious incompetence when it comes to perceptions of individuals (Gutiérrez & Muhs et al., 2012). They assert that some stereotypical views are made without conscious knowledge that the perception or judgment was occurring. This may have been true with the first stereotype but repeated use of stereotypes across generations suggests that it is intentional and those using the stereotypes believe they are correct, and they are uncaring about its effect on those being stereotyped. Stereotypes are taught during the socialization within organizational, cultural, social, and familial environments (Anand et al., 2004; Ashforth & Anand, 2003). Stereotypes are also used to classify individuals in specific groups to certain behaviors, heedlessly of the true competency or behavior that the individual may have exhibited that contradicts the stereotype (Prime, 2005; Hughes, 2014). Stereotyping has proven negative consequences (Burgess & Borgida, 1999; Cheung et al., 2016; Eagly & Karau, 2002; Heilman, 2001; Heilman et al., 2004; Ridgeway, 1982; Rudman, 1998); for example, gender stereotyping was one of the factors that caused lowered self-efficacy beliefs in women (Barbulescu & Bidwell, 2013; Pajares, 1996; Schunk & Pajares, 2002; Tabassum & Nayak, 2021) and when women's self-efficacy beliefs were low, they were less likely to have the self-confidence to lead others and/ or seek higher ranks within organizations. Stereotypes have led to some women wanting to be liked in the workplace to the extent that it has been detrimental to their opportunities for advancement because in research from 1957 to 2008 Judge et al. (2012) revealed that disagreeable people, both men and women, consistently earned more than agreeable people. Thus, being disliked has not been the penalty some people think it should be. However, it is unknown how many of those individuals represented protected class groups who are explicitly disliked in the workplace and endure untold frustration because of their difference (Benard & Correll, 2010; Correll, 2013; Correll et al., 2007; Johnson-Bailey & Cervero, 2008; Reynolds-Dobbs et al., 2008).

Organizational Mindsets

In organization environments where networks, role models, and mentors are part of the leader development opportunities that can lead to career advancement, protected class employees must be provided access to the leadership development opportunities. Stereotypes and negative self-efficacy beliefs held by white males and others in leadership positions toward protected class employees' leadership behavior must end. The organizational mindset must shift from one of indifference to the needs of protected class employees to one on acceptance of practical reality.

Theory of Successful Intelligence

Sternberg (Sternberg & Vroom, 2002) described three components of leadership in what he termed the Wisdom, Intelligence, and Creativity Synthesized (WICS) model. He noted that the three components must work together for the leader to be a highly effective leader. They must impart their wisdom, intelligence, and creativity together for the institutional mindset to be affected. Sternberg focused on intelligence that was based on his theory of successful intelligence (Sternberg, 1997, 1999, 2002) and defined successful intelligence as "the ability to succeed in life, given one's own conception of success, within one's sociocultural environment" (Sternberg & Vroom, 2002, p. 302). He focused the theory on academic and practical intelligence with academic intelligence being related to "the abilities needed to recall and recognize but also to analyze, evaluate, and judge information" (p. 302). When it comes to protected class employees, leaders are failing at academic intelligence because they are stereotyping without obtaining any information about the protected class employees. Sternberg defined practical intelligence as "the ability to solve everyday problems by utilizing knowledge gained from experience in order purposefully to adapt to, shape, and select environments" (Sternberg & Vroom, 2002, p. 303). If leaders were to apply Sternberg's practical intelligence with regard to protected class group members, they would use DQ to correct environments that are non-conducive to the well-being and career success of protected class employees. He further described practical intelligence as the ability to change oneself to suit the environment, change the environment to suit oneself, or finding a new environment in which to work and to use those skills to manage oneself, manage others, and manage tasks. Many protected class employees are at a disadvantage because they are not in positions to apply the abilities of practical intelligence as described by Sternberg. They have no power to change the environment and often their color, disability, gender, and other characteristics are unchangeable. Smithey and Lewis (1998) argued that training and perceived differences in interpersonal skills, or lack thereof, are barriers that cause problems for protected class employees. Their focus on self-reliance and well-developed interpersonal skills allows leaders, who assume or perceive that protected class employees do not possess these skills, to place protected class employees in disadvantageous situations. Hill and Ragland (1995) noted that leadership aspirations and opportunities of protected class employees are often obstructed by historical and contemporary myths that have been allowed to permeate the organization and become a part of the organization members' mindset.

Leadership styles vary between and among identity groups (Ely & Thomas, 2001; Sims & Carter, 2019) and the organization's mindset must be one of acceptance toward these differences. The leadership styles of some protected class employees are clearly not valued by their organizations as evidenced by the paucity of American Black women leaders in executive leadership positions (de Leon & Rosette, 2022; Hughes, 2014; Jackson, 2012). Advancement opportunities into leadership positions within organizations are as important as or more so than the entry movement that first opened the doors of organizations for protected class employees. Protected class employees want entry and advancement as they seek successful careers that will allow them to support or help support their families (Sims & Carter, 2019; Whitmarsh et al., 2007).

The adverse organizational mindset toward protected class employees often also leads to negative organization structure problems. Its employee structure may be one in which protected class employees never achieve sustainable success. They are often promoted and made visible when there is a diversity crisis or image problem for the organization and once the crisis passes, they are relegated back into invisible status (de Leon & Rosette, 2022).

Melissa Harris-Perry's situation (Gabriel, 2016; Koblin, 2016) on MSNBC can be perceived as one example. After the Election of President Obama, her network wanted to make visible Black political pundits; yet, in 2016 when there was no viable Black candidate in the political news cycle, her show was taken off the air without warning for many days. Dr. Harris-Perry decided to quit because of the perceived structural problem. The organization does not perceive that there is a problem but because of Dr. Harris-Perry's public email about the problem, the show was canceled. The lack of DQ is evident because of the public nature to the disagreement. Why were the MSNBC leaders and Melissa Harris-Perry not able to communicate privately about the show's schedule? Why did the MSNBC leaders only respond after Melissa Harris-Perry went public? Why did Melissa Harris-Perry not know that she was a pawn (or Black voice only when needed) before ill treatment escalated to an untenable crisis for her? Did MSNBC need to conduct an environmental scan or self-examination to determine what their organizational efficacy is as it relates to American Black women and other protected class employees? An environmental examination or climate survey may help organizations discover and uncover barriers that may persist within the culture which could serve as an underlying impairment to advancement or development of American Black women (Hughes, 2014). Women continue to encounter extensive barriers and work hard to achieve goals, but if the evaluations of their achievements (Nkomo, 1992) are not perceived as fair, how can they ever advance? If the organizational efficacy does not support an environment conducive to self-development and/or cultural change, if and where warranted, it may be that protected class employees will continue to face obstacles to acquiring executive leadership positions (Hughes, 2014; Jackson, 2012; Parker & olgivie, 1996; Sims & Carter, 2019) and remain underutilized and underappreciated in organizations.

Protected class employees should not have to pursue paths that are vastly different than others to become successful in organizations (Amis et al., 2020). Protected class employees are often encouraged to seek highly visible positions, develop expertise in an area where accomplishments are easily measured, and avoid roles that typecast them and/or force them to become the token protected class employee (Prasad, 2022; Strach & Wicander, 1993). They should also evaluate whether they are being tracked into a specific type of job upon entry to the organization. The onus should not be placed on the protected class employee to be totally responsible for their own success when all types of barriers have been positioned against them. Protected class employees are often characterized as playing the victim; they do not have to play the victim when they are the victim of implicit bias, unfair judgment, stereotyping, and discrimination because of how they look and who they are (Avery et al., 2023; Jost et al., 2009; Tetlock & Mitchell, 2009; Triana et al., 2021). Protected class employees must absorb and ignore mistreatment because there are no laws that protect against implicit bias, rhetoric, and stereotypes, and along with sexual harassment victims, other protected class employees also endure hostile work environments.

Within Group Diversity

Protected class employees sometimes experience unfair pressure inherent to the organization's culture to represent their group even when they have no interest in representing their group or participating in protected class group-based activities. Their personal interests may not even align with the protected class group of which they are a member. This is one reason why DQ is needed. Everyone employee in each group is not the same. The within group diversity must be understood by organization leaders. Executive leadership can benefit from understanding and valuing the unique perspective that protected class group members can bring to their organizations.

Organization leaders including career counselors, human resource development, and human resource management professionals should consider reexamining their use of the varying perceptions and perspectives regarding existing leadership competencies based on research primarily done with white male participants (Banks, 2006a, b; Fitzgerald & Betz, 1994; Heifetz, 1994; Hekman et al., 2017; Savickas & Lent, 1994) and consider research that examined protected class employees. Without these considerations, it will be difficult for DQ to be integrated into the leadership and career development areas within organizations. Protected class employees continue to leave organization environments that do not value their contributions or quietly quit. The competencies that protected class employees display may not align because their leadership competencies were never examined (Parker & olgivie, 1996) and their effectiveness is unknown or is not empirically sanctioned (Gotsis & Grimani, 2016; Sims & Carter, 2019). The anecdotal evidence of their success should not be discounted especially when it continuously meets stated organizational goals. Executive leaders must consider and answer the question: Why is a different method of achieving organizational goals perceived as wrong when the method originates from protected class employees? Executive leaders must provide career opportunities for protected class employees (Alfred, 2001; Hughes, 2014).

Leaders' DQ Workforce Education and Training

Leaders must develop their DQ so that they can stop being afraid to interact with protected class employees. They are often afraid of saying the wrong thing and being criticized or fired. It behooves leaders to take ownership of their DQ development and do so with a positive attitude. It should not be a burden to respect the differences of others who are protected by law. Training is not the answer to every problem, but if a leader lacks DQ, they need to figure out how to obtain it. Leaders need to determine their DQ deficiencies through targeted needs assessment and seek the necessary education, training, development, and resources to correct all deficiencies. The Hughes and Liang DQ Scale© 2020 solves this education and training needs assessment problem.

Training and development are necessary to address KSA gaps (Silberman, 1998); however, it is not enough to consider the person's ability but also their capability to perform their jobs. Leaders must consider whether their frame of reference for developing protected class employees is sufficient (Hughes, 2014, 2016, 2018)? Human resource professionals must categorize training programs to help develop DQ content that is most relevant for developing leaders who can effectively manage protected class employees alongside all employees. Training programs should be developed based upon unbiased, empirical evidence, and customized to organizational needs (Hughes, 2014).

HR professionals encounter learning transfer issues that have not demonstrated return on investment for the organization (Rouiller & Goldstein, 1993) especially with regard to diversity training (Dobbin & Kalev, 2022; Triana et al., 2021). One reason for the lack of diversity learning transferred to the workplace may be due to the lack of power to influence change of the individuals who have participated in the training or because unwilling leaders have not committed to the training. Many leaders and employees appear to not be interested in diversity training despite the billions spent on the efforts because it is not reflected on the job. Leaders must buy into the diversity intervention prior to training implementation, thereby increasing the likelihood that the objectives of the program will be reinforced by the leaders. Leaders are known to control the flow of information downward throughout the organization and can a delay productivity effort (Callan, 1993; DiPadova & Faerman, 1993; Johlke & Duhan, 2001) when the communication is not quickly disseminated. There appears to be very little desire to quickly disseminate diversity efforts information throughout organizations especially from executive leadership unless some type of diversity crisis has occurred that has affected or could affect the bottom-line profits of the organization. George Floyd's murder, the Great Resignation, Quiet Quitting, and impacts of the COVID-19 pandemic are all examples that have affected or could affect the organization, so there have been some efforts from 2019 to 2023 toward anti-racism in organizations. There has also been a backlash against these changes.

Self-Efficacy and Diversity Training

Combs and Luthans (2007) defined diversity self-efficacy (DSE) as "the perception and belief (confidence) that one can marshal the necessary motivation, cognitive resources, and courses of action to change behaviors and successfully attain desired diversity goals and initiatives in the workplace" (p. 92). They suggested that by improving diversity training with self-efficacy components (enactive mastery, modeling, verbal and social persuasion, and psychological arousal) a positive relationship with trainee intentions to engage in positive diversity initiatives would occur. They have also developed the diversity efficacy questionnaire (DEQ) which "not only allowed a reliable and initially valid way to measure the confidence and belief of individuals to successfully value and promote diversity initiatives, but also, at least to some extent, gages the effectiveness of diversity training" (p. 115). They discovered that a positive relationship existed between diversity self-efficacy beliefs and diversity-related desirable intentions which have the potential to meet diversity challenges of organizations (Combs & Luthans, 2007). While the intentions and the DSE may be present for leaders, implementation, and execution of diversity efforts will not occur without DQ. Research with regard to the relationship between DSE and DQ could potentially solve leadership and career development problems by helping to integrate DQ into the development efforts. Organizations must have leaders who are engaged, have self-efficacy, and are supportive of diversity efforts to benefit all employees.

Protected Class Employees and Work Engagement

Kahn (1990) defined engagement as "the harnessing of organizational members' selves to their work role" (p. 693) and focused on the personal engagement of organizational members to emphasize aspects of work performance improvement on physical, cognitive, and emotional levels while performing their job. Employee engagement relates to job satisfaction, employees' work-related passion, and organizational commitment (Federman, 2009; Igbaria & Guimaraes, 1993; Leiter & Bakker, 2010; Zigarmi et al., 2009). Jones and Harter (2005) found that employee engagement determined the employees' tendency to remain with their organization. Protected class employees' level of engagement is dependent upon leaders in the organization and their willingness to engage with them (Bao et al., 2021). Badal and Harter (2013) found a business-unit level, financial benefit to organizations that have strong employee engagement and gender diversity and suggested that having diversity as an organizational priority within an engaged culture could produce cumulative financial benefit. Dedicated leaders with DQ who inspire supportive peers could increase the level of protected class employees' work engagement and improve overall organizational performance.

CONCLUSION

Leaders have ample opportunities to include protected class employees in organizational leadership and career development initiatives. However, many of these leaders do not have DQ nor do they have the diversity expertise to leverage the differences among their protected class employees. There are diversity professionals and practitioners who have the expertise to help become DQ and apply their DQ within their leadership role (Hughes, in press).

DQ can enhance the mindset development of leaders if they are open to changing how they think about and treat others who are different than themselves. DQ is not passive knowledge, it must be proactively used by leaders as they integrate it with their other leadership characteristics and competencies to remain highly effective when managing a diverse workforce. Leaders must be objective and avoid tendencies to revert to comfortable acceptance of stereotypes and biases against protected class employees that may be inherent within the workplace environment.

REFERENCES

Alfred, M. (2001). Expanding Theories of Career Developoment: Adding the Voices of African American Women in the White Academy. *Adult Education Quarterly, 51*(2), 108–127.

Amis, J. M., Mair, J., & Munir, K. A. (2020). The Organizational Reproduction of Inequality. *Academy of Management Annals, 14*(1), 195–230.

Anand, V., Ashforth, B. E., & Joshi, M. (2004). Business as Usual: The Acceptance and Perpetuation of Corruption in Organizations. *The Academy of Management Executive, 18*(2), 39–53.

Ashforth, B. E., & Anand, V. (2003). The Normalization of Corruption in Organizations. *Research in Organizational Behavior, 25*, 1–52.

Avery, D. R., Hall, A. V., Preston, M., Ruggs, E. N., & Washington, E. (2023). Is Justice Colorblind? A Review of Workplace Racioethnic Differences Through the Lens of Organizational Justice. *Annual Review of Organizational Psychology and Organizational Behavior, 10*, 389–412. https://www.annualreviews.org/doi/abs/10.1146/annurev-orgpsych-120920-052627

Badal, S., & Harter, J. K. (2013). Gender Diversity, Business-Unit Engagement, and Performance. *Journal of Leadership & Organizational Studies, 21*(4), 2–12. https://doi.org/10.1177/1548051813504460

Banks, C. H. (2006a). Career Planning: Toward an Inclusive Model. In M. Karsten (Ed.), *Gender, Race and Ethnicity in the Workplace* (Vol. III, pp. 99–116). Greenwood Publishing Group.

Banks, C. H. (2006b). Career Planning: Towards a More Inclusive Model for Women and Diverse Individuals. In F. Nafukho and H. Chen (Eds.), *Academy of Human Resource Development International Conference (AHRD) Proceedings. Symp. 31-1* (pp. 640–647). Academy of Human Resource Development.

Bao, P., Xiao, Z., Bao, G., & Noorderhaven, N. (2021). Inclusive Leadership and Employee Work Engagement: A Moderated Mediation Model. *Baltic Journal of Management, 17*(1), 124–139. https://doi.org/10.1108/bjm-06-2021-0219

Barbulescu, R., & Bidwell, M. (2013). Do Women Choose Different Jobs from Men? Mechanisms of Application Segregation in the Market for Managerial Workers. *Organization Science, 24*(3), 737–756.

Benard, S., & Correll, S. J. (2010). Normative Discrimination and the Motherhood Penalty. *Gender & Society, 24*(5), 616–646.

Brinson, H. (2006). *The Effect of Race and Gender in Organizational Leadership Success: A Study of African American Women and Their Challenges to Become Leaders in Corporate America* [Unpublished Doctoral Dissertation]. Capella University, Dissertation Abstracts International.

Burgess, D., & Borgida, E. (1999). Who Women Are, Who Women Should Be: Descriptive and Prescriptive Stereotyping in Gender Discrimination. *Psychology, Public Policy and Law, 5*(3), 665–692.

Burrows, D., Pietri, E. S., Johnson, I. R., & Ashburn-Nardo, L. (2022). Promoting Inclusive Environments: In-Group Organizational Endorsement as a Tool to Increase Feelings of Identity-Safety Among Black Women. *Sex Roles, 86*(1–2), 67–88. https://doi.org/10.1007/s11199-021-01253-2

Callan, V. J. (1993). Subordinate-Manager Communication in Different Sex Dyads: Consequences for Job Satisfaction. *Journal of Occupational and Organizational Psychology, 66*(1), 13–27.

Carter, E. R. (2020). Restructure Your Organization to Actually Advance Racial Justice. *Harvard Business Review*, 1–5.

Cascio, W. F., & Aguinis, H. (2005). *Applied Psychology in Human Resource Management* (6th ed.). Pearson Education.

Catalyst. (1999). *Women of Color in Corporate Management: Opportunities and Barriers*. Catalyst.

Charan, R., Drotter, S., & Noel, J. (2001). *The Leadership Pipeline: How to Build the Leadership Powered Company*. Jossey-Bass.

Cheung, H. K., King, E., Lindsey, A., Membere, A., Markell, H. M., & Kilcullen, M. (2016). Understanding and Reducing Workplace Discrimination. *Research in Personnel and Human Resources Management, 34*, 101–152.

Combs, G. M., & Luthans, F. (2007). Diversity Training: Analysis of the Impact of Self-Efficacy. *Human Resource Development Quarterly, 18*(1), 91–120.

Correll, S. J. (2013). Minimizing the Motherhood Penalty: What Works, What Doesn't and Why. In *Research Symposium: Gender & Work: Challenging Conventional Wisdom* (pp. 80–86). Harvard Business School.

Correll, S. J., Benard, S., & Paik, I. (2007). Getting a Job: Is There a Motherhood Penalty? *American Journal of Sociology, 112*(5), 1297–1339.

de Leon, R. P., & Rosette, A. S. (2022). "Invisible" Discrimination: Divergent Outcomes for the Nonprototypicality of Black Women. *Academy of Management Journal, 65*(3), 784–812.

DiPadova, L. N., & Faerman, S. R. (1993). Using the Competing Values Framework to Facilitate Managerial Understanding Across Levels of Organizational Hierarchy. *Human Resource Management, 32*(1), 143–174.

Dobbin, F., & Kalev, A. (2022). *Getting to Diversity: What Works and What Doesn't*. Harvard University Press.

Drucker, P. F. (2004). What Makes an Effective Executive? *Harvard Business Review, 86*(2), 58–63.

Dwivedi, P., Gee, I. H., Withers, M. C., & Boivie, S. (2022). No Reason to Leave: The Effects of CEO Diversity-Valuing Behavior on Psychological Safety and Turnover for Female Executives. *Journal of Applied Psychology*. Advance online publication. https://doi.org/10.1037/apl0001071

Eagly, A. H., & Karau, S. J. (2002). Role Congruity Theory of Prejudice Toward Female Leaders. *Psychological Review, 109*(3), 573–598.

EEOC. (2023). *Laws & Guidance*. U.S. Equal Employment Opportunity Commission (eeoc.gov). https://www.eeoc.gov/laws-guidance.

Ely, R. J., & Thomas, D. A. (2001). Cultural Diversity at Work: The Effects of Diversity Perspectives on Work Group Processes and Outcomes. *Administrative Science Quarterly, 46*(2), 229–273.

Federman, B. (2009). *Employee Engagement: A Roadmap for Creating Profits, Optimizing Performance, and Increasing Loyalty*. Jossey-Bass.

Fitzgerald, L. F., & Betz, N. E. (1994). Career Development in Cultural Contexts: The Role of Gender, Race, Class and Sexual Orientation. In M. L. Savickas & R. W. Lent (Eds.), *Convergence in Career Development Theories* (pp. 103–117). CPP Books.

Gabriel, A. *MSNBC Has Been Whitewashed: Melissa Harris-Perry Exits, Buffoonish White Pundits Rule Once More*. Retrieved March 1, 2016, from http://www.salon.com/2016/03/01/msnbc_has_been_whitewashed_melissa_harris_perry_exits_buffoonish_white_pundits_rule_once_more/

Goleman, D. (1996). *Emotional Intelligence: Why It Can Matter More Than IQ*. Bantam Books.

Gotsis, G., & Grimani, K. (2016). Diversity as an Aspect of Effective Leadership: Integrating and Moving Forward. *Leadership & Organization Development Journal, 37*(2), 241–264. https://doi.org/10.1108/lodj-06-2014-0107

Gutiérrez y Muhs, G., Niemann, Y. F., Gonzalez, C. G., & Harris, A. P. (2012). *Presumed Incompetent: The Intersections of Race and Class for Women in Academia*. University Press of Colorado.

Heifetz, R. A. (1994). *Leadership Without Easy Answers*. Belkap Press of Harvard University Press.

Heilman, M. E. (2001). Description and Prescription: How Gender Stereotypes Prevent Women's Ascent Up the Organizational Ladder. *Journal of Social Issues, 57*(4), 657–674.

Heilman, M. E., Wallen, A. S., Fuchs, D., & Tamkins, M. M. (2004). Penalties for Success: Reactions to Women Who Succeed at Male Gender Typed Tasks. *Journal of Applied Psychology, 89*(3), 416–427.

Hekman, D. R., Johnson, S. K., Foo, M.-D., & Yang, W. (2017). Does Diversity-Valuing Behavior Result in Diminished Performance Ratings for Non-White and Female Leaders? *Academy of Management Journal, 60*(2), 771–797.

Hill, M. S., & Ragland, J. C. (1995). *Women as Educational Leaders: Opening Windows, Pushing Ceilings*. Corwin Press.

Hirsh, C. E. (2009). The Strength of Weak Enforcement: The Impact of Discrimination Charges, Legal Environments, and Organizational Conditions on Workplace Segregation. *American Sociological Review, 74*(2), 245–271.

Hughes, C. (2014). *American Black Women and Interpersonal Leadership Styles.* The Netherlands Sense Publishers.

Hughes, C. (2016). *Diversity Intelligence: Integrating Diversity Intelligence Alongside Intellectual, Emotional, and Cultural Intelligence for Leadership and Career Development.* Palgrave Macmillan.

Hughes, C. (2018). Conclusion: Diversity Intelligence as a Core of Diversity Training and Leadership Development. *Advances in Developing Human Resources, 20*(3), 370–378.

Hughes, C. (2023, in press). The Intersection of Diversity, Equity, and Inclusion (DEI), Diversity Intelligence, and Ethics with the Role of HRD Scholars, Professionals, and Practitioners. In D. Russ-Eft & A. Alizadeh (Eds.), *Ethics in Human Resource Development.* Palgrave Macmillan.

Hughes, C., & Brown, L. M. (2018). Exploring Leaders' Discriminatory, Passive-Aggressive Behavior Toward Protected Class Employees Using Diversity Intelligence. *Advances in Developing Human Resources, 20*(3), 263–284.

Igbaria, M., & Guimaraes, T. (1993). Antecedents and Consequences of Job Satisfaction Among Information Center Employees. *Journal of Management Information Systems, 9*(4), 145–175. https://doi.org/10.1145/144 001.372749

Jackson, L. R. (2012). *The Self-Efficacy Beliefs of Black Women Leaders in Fortune 500 Companies.* Unpublished doctoral dissertation, University of Arkansas, Fayetteville, AR.

Johlke, M. C., & Duhan, D. F. (2001). Testing Competing Models of Sales Force Communication. *The Journal of Personal Selling and Sales Management, 21*(4), 265–277.

Johnson-Bailey, J., & Cervero, R. (2008). Different Worlds and Divergent Paths: Academic Careers Defined by Race and Gender. *Harvard Educational Review, 78*, 311–332.

Jones, J. R., & Harter, J. K. (2005). Race Effects on the Employee Engagement-Turnover Intention Relationship. *Journal of Leadership & Organizational Studies, 11*(2), 78–88.

Jost, J. T., Rudman, L. A., Blair, I. V., Carney, D. R., Dasgupta, N., Glaser, J., & Hardin, C. D. (2009). The Existence of Implicit Bias Is Beyond Reasonable Doubt: A Refutation of Ideological and Methodological Objections and Executive Summary of Ten Studies that No Manager Should Ignore. *Research in Organizational Behavior, 29*, 39–69.

Judge, T. A., Livingston, B. A., & Hurst, C. (2012). Do Nice Guys—And Gals—Really Finish Last? The Joint Effects of Sex and Agreeableness on Income. *Journal of Personality and Social Psychology, 102*(2), 390–407.

Kahn, W. A. (1990). Psychological Conditions of Personal Engagement and Disengagement at Work. *Academy of Management Journal, 33*(4), 692–724. https://doi.org/10.2307/256287

Koblin, J. (2016). *Melissa Harris-Perry Walks Off Her MSNBC Show After Pre-emptions.* Retrieved February 26, 2016, from http://www.nytimes.com/2016/02/27/business/media/melissa-harris-perry-walks-off-her-msnbc-show-after-pre-emptions.html?_r=0

Leiter, M. P., & Bakker, A. B. (2010). Work Engagement: Introduction. In A. B. Bakker & M. P. Leiter (Eds.), *Work Engagement: A Handbook of Essential Theory and Research* (pp. 1–9). Psychology Press.

Lipman-Blumen, J. (1992). Connective Leadership: Female Leadership Styles in the 21st Century Workplace. *Sociological Perspectives, 35*(1), 183–203.

Mallick, M. (2020). Do You Know Why Your Company Needs a Chief Diversity Officer. *Harvard Business Review*, 1–5.

Nkomo, S. M. (1992). The Emperor Has No Clothes: Rewriting "Race in Organizations." *Academy of Management Review, 17*(3), 487–513.

Pajares, F. (1996). Self-Efficacy Beliefs in Academic Settings. *Review of Educational Research, 66*(4), 543–578.

Parker, P. S., & dt olgivie. (1996). Gender, Culture, and Leadership: Toward a Culturally Distinct Model of African-American Women Executives' Leadership Strategies. *The Leadership Quarterly, 7*(2), 189–214.

Prasad, A. (2022). The Model Minority and the Limits of Workplace Inclusion. *Academy of Management Review.* https://doi.org/10.5465/amr.2021.0352

Prime, J. L. (2005). *Women "Take Care", Men "Take Charge".* Catalyst Inc.

Reynolds-Dobbs, W., Thomas, K. M., & Harrison, M. S. (2008, January). From Mammy to Superwoman: Images That Hinder Black Women's Career Development. *Journal of Career Development, 35*(2), 129–150.

Ridgeway, C. L. (1982). Status in Groups: The Importance of Motivation. *American Sociological Review, 47*(1), 76–88.

Rouiller, J. Z., & Goldstein, I. L. (1993). The Relationship Between Organizational Transfer Climate and Positive Transfer of Training. *Human Resource Development Quarterly, 4*(4), 377–390.

Rudman, L. A. (1998). Self-Promotion as a Risk Factor for Women: The Costs and Benefits of Counter Stereotypical Impression Management. *Journal of Personality and Social Psychology, 74*(3), 629–645.

Ruggs, E. N., Hebl, M., & Shockley, K. M. (2023). Fighting the 400-Year Pandemic: Racism Against Black People in Organizations. *Journal of Business and Psychology, 38*(1), 1–5.

Salcedo, A., Williams, P., Elias, S., Valencia, M., & Perez, J. (2022). Future Direction in HRD: The Potential of Testimonio as an Approach to Perturb the Dominant Practices in the Workplace. *European Journal of Training and*

Development, 46(7/8), 727–739. https://doi.org/10.1108/ejtd-07-2021-0109.

Sandberg, S. (2013). *Lean In: Women, Work, and the Will to Lead.* Alfred Knopf.

Sanders, J. (2004). *Understand Behavioral Style Differences.* Get GenderSmart! Empowerment Enterprises.

Savickas, M., & Lent, R. W. (1994). *Convergence in Career Development Theories.* Consulting Psychologists Press.

Schunk, D. H., & Pajares, F. (2002). The Development of Academic Self-Efficacy. In A. Wigfield & J. S. Eccles (Eds.), *Development of Achievement Motivation* (pp. 15–31). Academic Press. https://doi.org/10.1016/B978-012750053-9/50003-6

Silberman, M. L. (1998). *Active Training* (2nd ed.). Jossey-Bass/Pfeiffer.

Sims, C. M., & Carter, A. D. (2019). Revisiting Parker & ogilvie's African American Women Executive Leadership Model. *The Journal of Business Diversity, 19*(2), 99–112.

Smithey, P. N., & Lewis, G. B. (1998). Gender, Race and Training in the Federal Civil Service. *Public Administration Quarterly, 22*(2), 204–228.

Sternberg, R. J. (1997). *Successful Intelligence.* Plume.

Sternberg, R. J. (1999). The Theory of Successful Intelligence. *Review of General Psychology, 3*(4), 292–316. https://doi.org/10.1037/1089-2680.3.4.292

Sternberg, R. J. (2002). Successful Intelligence: A New Approach to Leadership. In R. E. Riggio, S. E. Murphy, & F.J. Pirozzolo (Eds.), *Multiple Intelligences and Leadership,* (pp. 9–28). Erlbaum.

Sternberg, R. J., & Vroom, V. H. (2002). The Person Versus the Situation in Leadership. *The Leadership Quarterly, 13*(3), 301–323.

Strach, L., & Wicander, L. (1993). Fitting In: Issues of Tokenism and Conformity for Minority Women. *S.A.M. Advanced Management Journal, 59*(3), 22–25.

Tabassum, N., & Nayak, B. S. (2021). Gender Stereotypes and Their Impact on Women's Career Progressions from a Managerial Perspective. *IIM Kozhikode Society & Management Review, 10*(2), 192–208.

Tetlock, P. E., & Mitchell, G. (2009). Implicit Bias and Accountability Systems: What Must Organizations Do to Prevent Discrimination? *Research in Organizational Behavior, 29,* 3–38.

Tomaskovic-Devey, D., & Stainback, K. (2007). Discrimination and Desegregation: Equal Opportunity Progress in US Private Sector Workplaces Since the Civil Rights Act. *The Annals of the American Academy of Political and Social Science, 609*(1), 49–84.

Triana, M. D., Carmen, P. G., Chapa, O., Richard, O., & Colella, A. (2021). Sixty Years of Discrimination and Diversity Research in Human Resource Management: A Review with Suggestions for Future Research Directions.

Human Resource Management, 60(1), 145–204. https://doi.org/10.1002/hrm.22052

U.S. Department of Labor. (2011). *Equal Pay Act of 1963, as Amended.* Retrieved October 19, 2011, from United States Department of Labor. http://www.dol.gov/oasam/regs/statutes/equal_pay_act.htm

Ulrich, D., & Smallwood, N. (2007). *Leadership Brand: Developing Customer-Focused Leaders to Drive Performance and Build Lasting Value.* Harvard Business School Press.

Warren, A. K. (2009). *Cascading Gender Biases, Compounding Effects: An Assessment of Talent Management Systems.* Catalyst.

Waytz, A. (2016). The Limits of Empathy. (Cover Story). *Harvard Business Review, 94*(1), 68–73.

Whitmarsh, L., Brown, D., Cooper, J., Hawkins-Rodgers, Y., & Wentworth, D. K. (2007, March). Choices and Challenges: A Qualitative Exploration of Professional Women's Career Patterns. *The Career Development Quarterly, 55*(3), 225–236.

Yang, J. R., & Liu, J. (2021, January 19). *Strengthening accountability for discrimination: Confronting Fundamental Power Imbalances in the employment relationship.* Economic Policy Institute. https://www.epi.org/unequalpower/publications/strengthening-accountability-for-discrimination-confronting-fundamental-power-imbalances-in-the-employment-relationship/

Zigarmi, D., Nimon, K., Houson, D., Witt, D., & Diehl, J. (2009). Beyond Engagement: Toward a Framework and Operational Definition for Employee Work Passion. *Human Resource Development Review, 8*(3), 300–326. https://doi.org/10.1177/1534484309338171

CHAPTER 7

Current Issues and Evolving Trends

There are many benefits of examining leadership DEI competencies through a DQ lens. This book demonstrates a strong knowledge of the conceptual forebears of diversity and provides evidence of the reasons why promoting DQ among workplace leaders is important. Critical HRD/ social justice has emerged as a topic in the field of HRD. How does this topic enhance diversity efforts? Where does diversity fit within this narrative? Are HRD professionals, practitioners, and scholars willing to critically examine their record as it relates to the failure of diversity efforts in organizations and educational institutions in the areas of training and development, organization development, and career development? How do HRD professionals, practitioners, and scholars explain their willingness to ignore the expertise of true diversity, equity, and inclusion (DEI) experts. They publish and communicate about definitions of diversity and inclusion without any application and understanding of why it has been a failure. If all these Human Resource Development (HRD) and Human Resource Management (HRM) certified professionals (PHR, SPHR, etc.) have not been successful with diversity since 1964, why are they continuing to write about and teach the same content over and over?

Hearing someone say I am tired of being politically correct is code speak for I am tired of following anti-discrimination laws. W. E. B. Dubois in 1906 stated that "Either the United States will destroy ignorance or

C. Hughes, *Diversity Intelligence*,
https://doi.org/10.1007/978-3-031-33250-0_7

153

ignorance will destroy the United States" (Dubois & Blaisdell, 2013). It seems that the United States is still, 117 years later, trying to determine which it will be.

Currently, it appears that American Society is for the first time, openly discussing racism on a national level, chaotically at best, but discussions are being had. It also appears that the discussions are in many ways not positive or constructive because of the context in which the discussions are being held. The context of partisan politics has evoked many passionate comments and responses because the stakes are so high— everyone wants their candidate to win at the expense of America winning on a world stage. The stakes are political achievement not diversity integration, valuing all people, or sustaining US unity. Some citizens appear to want to refight the US Civil War.

The biggest concern is that protected class people being ridiculed by politicians and their supporters. This work would be remiss if the reader were left to believe that protected class employees have no role to play in their own success or failure. They have the most important responsibility for their success. They must have DQ even if their leaders and peers do not. They know their protected class status and have no excuse for not understanding the laws, rules, and policies that effect their status. They can help educate leaders and peers and reduce some confusion, chaos, and ignorance by being objective enough to realize that some leaders truly do not understand their situations. They must be cognizant that they are not the only ones in the workplace with problems and their status is not more important than any other protected class employees. Their problems are equally important.

Protected class employees must have DQ so that they do not react solely based on their emotions, fears, and against perceived threats. They must obtain facts that can be substantiated against documented rules, policies, and laws. Everyone is entitled to their own opinions but not their own facts. Undisputed facts can be better documented if emotions are controlled. Protected class employees need to use their EQ, IQ, and DQ to provide evidence of mistreatment and offer solutions to their situation. They must follow organization, local, state, and federal rules, policies, and procedures to file grievances.

This can be difficult if no documented rules, policies, and procedures are available and/or the work environment is not transparent or protective of protected class employees. This should not be however, because it is, many protected class employees hire legal representation to pursue their alleged mistreatment(s). Organization leaders can avoid many issues by educating all employees on what protected class status is and ensuring that all employees know who are protected, who are not, and why. This information should be openly shared and transparent. Individuals need not be personally identified; employees just need to have DQ to understand what criteria need to be met for each protected class status to be valid. Often, there is just a list of protected class groups without definition, criteria, or characteristics provided. Disability issues and LGBTQ status are two examples of cases where protected class status may not be visible; yet leaders must have DQ and not assume someone's status based on stereotypes. If there is a clear concern, the organization must have a way to ensure that leaders are made aware that an individual is in a protected class status without revealing why. This is one reason that all protected class employees should be protected to the same extent. They cannot be protected in the same ways because their statuses are different, but the extent of protection needs to be the same. My suggestion is zero tolerance.

Because of the lack of zero tolerance policies and the negativity associated with being in a protected class in many organizations, many protected class employees face the dilemma of whether or not to even reveal their protected class status to their workplace leaders. For some groups, it is not an option to reveal are not. It can clearly be seen that American Blacks are Black, and they are often the most stereotyped and discriminated against because their status is not hidden—not that it should be.

There are instances where protected class employees intentionally discriminate against other protected class employees. They may or may not be encouraged to do this by majority group employees so that the majority group employees can avoid lawsuits or other punishment. For example, have a Black employee mistreat another Black employee or a woman mistreat another woman. However, there is no law that protects against protected class employees filing claims against other protected class employees. Group norms or solidarity advocated for through CQ leads protected class employees to believe that they are the same despite being mistreated by members of their same group. Group pressure to vote for the woman because she is the woman or for the Black person because she is Black are examples. Discrimination, mistreatment, and violations of the law are wrong regardless of where they originate and by whom.

As society has evolved, manifest destiny has encountered resistance from terrorists and radicals who have the means and the wherewithal to fight back and do not want the United States and other nations to take over their countries for the sake of democracy. Until there is a clear intelligence about how we treat others who are different than ourselves, there will remain votes such as Brexit which was inspired by white identity politics (e.g., vote from Britain to exit the European Union in 2016) that has led to political and social turmoil in England and financial uncertainty within the global economy. Former President George W. Bush, July 12, 2016, made a profound statement that "too often we judge other groups by their worst examples, while judging ourselves by our best intentions." Many leaders stop at their intentions and never follow through with the execution of actions that benefit those who are different than themselves. DQ provides a way for leaders to move from their best intentions to positive actions that value all employees in the workplace and not make decisions based solely on the actions of the worst examples of a group of people.

All humans desire justice and fairness, especially in the workplace where their financial stability is at stake. This project engages nine of the UN's Sustainable Development Goals in the following ways.

UN Sustainable Development Goal	How Diversity Intelligence Engages
1. No Poverty	When all employees are hired and paid what they are due, poverty will be lessened. Many people are discriminated against during the hiring process and pay is a protected class category yet women and minorities, especially Black women are underpaid in the workplace
2. Zero Hunger	Similar to the content from number 1, employees who have a job and are paid well can buy food to feed their family and contribute to feeding others in their communities which will help toward the goal of Zero Hunger
3. Good Health and Well-Being	Similar to the content from number 1, if employees have a job, they can afford health care. If they are not discriminated against on the job, their well-being and mental health tend not to be affected. The ability to have strong physical, mental, and emotional health contributes to overall good health and well-being. When employees are mistreated on the job it reduces physical, mental, and emotional health. Diversity intelligent leaders will not mistreat their employees because they are different

(continued)

(continued)

UN Sustainable Development Goal	How Diversity Intelligence Engages
4. Quality Education	Quality education means different things to different people. This book will contribute to a quality education for those who want and seek to understand how diversity became a part of the workplace. There is no law in American that says an organization has to have diversity—using the word diversity. The laws diverge and evolve toward diversity but does not say diversity. Knowing accurate information about diversity which this book provides will contribute to a quality education. It will also help education leaders not discriminate against individuals at all levels of education and open doors to education for some who have, historically, been denied
5. Gender Equality	Gender is one of the protected class groups and categories that diversity intelligence seeks to explain. Diversity intelligent leaders will not discriminate against employees because of their gender
8. Decent Work and Economic Growth	Decent work and economic group are alluded to in the response to developmental goal 1. Many individuals have been denied decent work because of leaders' lack of diversity intelligence and many communities have not had economic growth because their citizens have been denied decent work and decent pay
9. Industry, Innovation, and Infrastructure	More industries will benefit from better innovation if they use the contributions of all its employees. Infrastructure will expand as business and industry expands. Without innovative employees who are diverse and recognized for their diversity, industry can be weakened
11. Reduced Inequalities	This entire book is about reducing inequalities for all protected class groups and categories in the workplace. With close examination and understanding of the content, readers will learn that every individual in the workplace is in a protected class group or category. Everyone's pay is protected, their religious preference or lack thereof is protected, etc
16. Peace, Justice, and Strong Institutions	Peace, justice, and strong institutions can be had by all if they recognize that diversity just means different, and everyone is different. Different does not mean better; it just means different. Diversity intelligent people learn to value differences and seek peace and justice through moral and ethical behaviors and policies that strengthen institutional values

Yet, some leaders are in denial when they falsely assume that education equals intelligence. Education is obsolete if intelligence is not used to apply the knowledge acquired through education. There are many leaders who are now substituting the term unconventional for bias. They described Donald Trump's vitriol against those who are different, specifically, Mexicans, women, the disabled, and Muslims as unconventional. Many leaders know the difference between unconventional and bias but have chosen not to use their intelligence to state the obvious. DQ may be perceived as an oxymoron by those who choose not to receive DQ as an intelligence, and if so, it is an intentional oxymoron because leaders need to consider DQ as an intelligence. This is especially true when interacting with American Black women. When women's issues are discussed, there is always the assumption that the discussion is about White women and their needs. The intersection between race and gender is rarely discussed. As President Barack Obama stated, "data is not destiny." Perhaps someone has negative data about an individual or group of individuals, what the data represents does not have to become an individual's or the group's destiny. President Bill Clinton said that individuals should not be disempowered, and President John F. Kennedy said that "tolerance implies no lack of commitment to one's own beliefs. Rather it condemns the oppression and persecution of others." Four former US Presidents appeared to have understood and understand how a lack of DQ leads to negative connotations from those who spew negativity. The lack of DQ also allows those who perpetuate ugly, hateful rhetoric and actions to continue in their ignorance. Despite these Presidents' efforts it will take a concerted actionable effort of everyone to use DQ to improve the workplace and society.

All organizations need a DQ standard bearer at the top who understands DQ and knows that exclusion leads to resentment and that assimilation, integration, and inclusion are all needed as appropriate. It needs to be appropriate so that individuals will not feel the need to express sentiments like those of James Baldwin who said that "The American idea of racial progress is measured by how fast I become white (Baldwin, 2010, p.143)." If protected class employees begin to lose hope and are expected to perform the impossible, civility and respect may deteriorate to irreparable levels.

Covey (1991) identified four levels of principle-centered leadership with key principles. They are as follows: Organizational—Alignment; Managerial—Empowerment; Interpersonal—Trust; and Personal—Trustworthiness. He also included a list of eight characteristics that principle-centered leaders should have: (1) They are continually learning; (2) They are service-oriented; (3) They radiate positive energy; (4) They believe in other people; (5) They lead balanced lives; (6) They see life as an adventure; (7) They are synergistic; and (8) They exercise for self-renewal. Despite the development of these characteristics in 1991, they have the potential to be effective when aligned with DQ. Leaders who are principled should want to learn and develop DQ, be seen as a servant leader to all employees, including those in protected class groups and categories, and remain positive throughout diversity initiative transitions.

Researchers and practitioners are tasked with instituting change that will enhance the diversity of their organizations. Integrating DQ with IQ, EQ, and CQ will help them to accomplish this. Table 7.1 suggests that there is still a lot of diversity work needed in society and the workplace. Table 7.1 is by no means all-inclusive but is comprehensive and in many ways rather shocking and very surprising. It is very surprising to those who believed that upon the election of President Barack Hussein Obama in 2008 that the United States of America was post-racial. It is also very surprising for those who were active during the American Civil Rights Movement and believed that more change had occurred than these articles and actions of their fellow Americans reflect. It is not surprising that many of the headlines are about race and the animosity that exists against American Blacks, although Hispanics from Mexico and Muslims are openly discriminated against as well.

Leaders must be pragmatic and recognize that it is difficult for many employees to separate their personal lives from their work lives especially when they spend so much time in the workplace. They must be able to accept differences during those hours without adversely affecting protected class group members who also deal with unacceptance in the general society. There is often no reprieve for protected class group members inside or outside the organization. They face discrimination when they go out to eat, during shopping, and while traveling and still must endure 40–60 hours per week of discomfort on the job. Table 7.1 provides a listing of news headlines that discuss adverse treatment of protected class group and category members in American society and workplaces. There is also a diversity intelligence Facebook group dedicated to sharing information about the continuous news and history related to protected class groups and categories throughout the World. The link to the group is https://www.facebook.com/groups/918339 944894064/. This group requires no activity from members. Members learn at their own pace.

It is astonishing that over the past 59 years, since the passage of the Civil Rights Act of 1964, that diversity, diversity management, or similar

Table 7.1   2015–2023 News headlines related to protected class groups

Protected class category or diversity	News article title	Reference
Diversity	Starbucks ties executive pay to 2025 diversity targets	Haddon, H. (2020). "Starbucks ties executive pay to 2025 diversity targets." https://www.wsj.com/articles/starbucks-ties-executivepay-to-2025-diversity-targets-11602680401?reflink=desktopwebshare_permalink
	Diversity matters	Hunt, V., Layton, D., & Prince, S. (2015). Diversity matters. *McKinsey & Company, 1*(1), 15–29. https://www.mckinsey.com/capabilities/people-and-organizational-performance/our-insights/why-diversity-matters
	Salesforce plans to double its number of Black leaders in the United States by 2023	Zaveri, P. (2020). Salesforce plans to double its number of Black leaders in the United States by 2023. https://www.businessinsider.com/salesforce-double-black-leaders-employees-racial-justice-2020-7
	Academia's Rejection of Diversity	Brooks, Arthur C. Academia's Rejection of Diversity (October 30, 2015). Mobile NY Times
	The Weakening Definition of 'Diversity'	White, Gillian B. (May 13, 2015) retrieved from http://www.theatlantic.com/business/archive/2015/05/the-weakening-definition-of-diversity/393080/
Racism	Companies have a hard time holding on to Black Employees	Pandey, E. (2020, November 17). *Companies have a hard time holding on to Black Employees.* Axios. https://www.axios.com/2020/11/17/corporate-america-black-employee-turnover-rate
	5 Rules for White People with Black Friends	Retrieved October 31, 2015 http://www.atlredline.com/5-rules-for-white-people-with-black-friends-1737903792

Protected class category or diversity	News article title	Reference
	US companies vow to fight racism but face critics on diversity	Kerber, R., Coster, H., & McLymore, A. (2020). US companies vow to fight racism but face critics on diversity. *Reuters*. https://www.reuters.com/article/us-min neapolis-police-companies-insight/u-s-companies-vow-to-fight-racism-but-face-critics-on-diversity-idUSKBN23H1KW
	8 Successful and Thriving Black Communities Destroyed by Racist White Neighbors	
	10 US States that had the most lynchings of Blacks from 1882–1968	KARK Retrieved on October, 30, 2015 from http://www.ark ansasmatters.com/
	AR Student Dresses in Blackface; Causes Controversy	
	Study: Black Girls Are Being Pushed Out of School	Retrieved 10/31/2015 from http://www.npr.org/sections/codeswitch/2015/02/13/384005652/study-black-girls-are-being-pushed-out-of-school Kimberle Williams Crenshaw
	Black Girls Matter: Pushed Out, Overpoliced and Underprotected	
	The hidden racism of school discipline, in 7 charts	Retrieved on 10/31/2015 from http//:www.vox.com/2015/10/31/9646504/discipline-race-charts
	This homework assignment says a lot about how America treats its history of Slavery	Retrieved on 10/30/2015 from http//:www.vox.com/2015/10/30/9640302/homework-family-origin-slavery
	Louisville President Sorry for Posing in Sombrero	Jaschik, Scott. (October 30, 2015) on www.insidehighered.com
	New face of depression: The strong black woman	http://blackdoctor.org/462194/black-women-depression/
	To Prevent Bias, British Applications to be Name Blind	Redden, Elizabeth. (October 27, 2015) on www.insiderhighe red.com

(continued)

Table 7.1 (continued)

Protected class category or diversity	News article title	Reference
	Racial Tensions at Ithaca College	Logue, Josh. (October 30, 2015) on www.insidehighered.com
	Charleston, Dylann Roof and the racism of millennials from The Washington Post	Attiah, Karen, (June18, 2015) retrieved from https://www.washingtonpost.com/blogs/post-partisan/wp/2015/06/18/charleston-racism-and-the-myth-of-tolerant-millennials/
Ableism or Disability	EEOC Issues New Enforcement Guidance on Pregnancy Discrimination	Retrieved from http://www.eeoc.gov/eeoc/newsroom/release/6-25-15.cfm
	Why I Wrote the Americans with Disabilities Act	Burgdorf, Jr., Robert L. (July 29, 2015) Retrieved from http://blog.dol.gov/2015/07/29/why-i-wrote-the-americans-with-disabilities-act/
Genderism or Sexism	The White House Focuses on Women and Girls of Color With a New $118 Million Initiative	McClain, Dani (November 16, 2015) Retrieved from http://www.thenation.com/article/white-house-turns-toward-women-and-girls-of-color-with-new-118-million-initiative/
	Boston is offering free negotiation classes to every woman who works in the city	Paquette, Danielle (November 13, 2015) Retrieved from https://www.washingtonpost.com/news/wonk/wp/2015/11/13/boston-wants-to-teach-every-woman-in-the-city-to-negotiate-better-pay/
	Where are all the women CEOs	Fuhrmans, V. (2020). Where are all the women CEOs. *Wall Street Journal*. https://www.wsj.com/articles/why-so-few-ceos-are-women-you-can-have-a-seat-at-the-table-and-not-be-a-player-11581003276
	Working moms have more successful daughters and more caring sons, Harvard Business School study says	Fisher, Gabriel (June 23, 2015) Retrieved from http://qz.com/434056/working-moms-have-more-successful-daughters-and-more-caring-sons-harvard-business-school-study-says/
	Depression In Black Woman	Gould, P. (August 3, 2015) Retrieved from http://blackdoctor.org/462194/black-women-depression/

Protected class category or diversity	News article title	Reference
	Study Finds Smart Women Scare Men	Johnson, Kimberley (October 21, 2015) Retrieved from http://samuel-warde.com/2015/10/study-finds-smart-women-scare-men/
	Donald Trump just gave a master class on how to get away with sexism	Taub, Amanda (August 7, 2015) Retrieved from http://www.vox.com/2015/8/7/9114943/donald-trump-sexism-debate
LGBT	America might have accidentally banned transgender discrimination in 1964	Guo, Jeff (November 11, 2015) Retrieved from https://www.washingtonpost.com/news/wonk/wp/2015/11/11/america-might-have-accidentally-banned-transgender-discrimination-in-1964/
National Origin	Applebee's attack victim: "I'm scared for my life"	Ibrahim, Mukhtar (November 6, 2015) Retrieved from http://www.mprnews.org/story/2015/11/06/applebees-attack-victim
	International student sues his university for discrimination after dismissal	Redden, Elizabeth (October 28, 2015) Retrieved from https://www.insidehighered.com/news/2015/10/28/international-student-sues-his-university-discrimination-after-dismissal?utm_source=Inside+Higher+Ed&utm_campaign=7377b430ba-DNU20151002&utm_medium=email&utm_term=0_1fcbc04421-7377b430ba-198192909
	The new American slavery: Invited to the US, foreign workers find a nightmare	Garrison, Jessica, Ken Bessinger, and Jeremy Singer-Vine (July 24, 2015) Retrieved from http://www.buzzfeed.com/jessicagarrison/the-new-american-slavery-invited-to-the-us-for-eign-workers-f?utm_term=.wgWQxb8Bo#.qmEzrnB4e
Ageism	Why age discrimination is worse for women	DePillis, Lydia (October 26, 2015) https://www.washingtonpost.com/news/wonk/wp/2015/10/26/why-age-discrimination-is-worse-for-women/

terms are not listed as a leadership competency or characteristic of an effective leader. This leads me to believe that it was never the serious intent of executive leadership in organizations to truly integrate diversity into the workplace environment. Hence, the need for DQ despite all the money, time, and effort spent on diversity initiatives. Table 7.1 provides evidence that there has been limited results from diversity training. Executive leaders need to determine the leadership characteristics a leader who supports diversity efforts should continuously exhibit (Hughes & Brown, 2018; Scott & Klein, 2022). DQ can assist executive leaders in their efforts to determine supportive diversity leadership criteria and characteristics. Do executive leaders care enough about protected class employees enough to help remove institutional barriers to their success and do the executive leaders have the DQ to effect change? Executive leaders in the most powerful positions in organizations should be able to affect, influence, and champion diversity change efforts and still make money for their stakeholders. It should not be an either diversity or diversity for money conundrum.

One would have thought there would have been more improvement since the Civil Rights Movement; however, it appears that discrimination has been passed on from one generation to the next. If discrimination can be taught, then DQ can also be taught to help reduce discrimination. Individuals can learn to change their behavior toward those who are different. The lack of DQ among the younger generations reveals that diversity is not being taught and the ignorance, confusion, and chaos are perpetual.

Hughes (2014) suggested that all diversity training occurs at the same time as all other legally, mandated annual training of employees to help infuse diversity into the culture of the organization like safety training, sexual harassment, and all other forms of training for which organizations have zero tolerance. Harassment prevention training is the most common term used in workplaces to reflect diversity training. Using the term harassment suggests that overt actions of harassment should be reported, thus covert actions, often expressed through passive aggression toward protected class employees, remain unchecked and unaddressed by organization leaders (Hughes & Brown, 2018). Organization leaders must establish a standard of diversity excellence so that they will be able to hold all employees accountable for their behavior and attitudes toward each other. Hughes (2010, 2012) defined maintenance value as the employees' personal development of themselves.

CONCLUSION

DQ is a change process and one more tool to add to a leaders' skill set to enhance their ability to lead all employees.

The following themes have emerged from the content within this book:

> Theme 1: DQ requires organizational support.
> Theme 2: DQ can be used to help establish an organizational climate of trust.
> Theme 3: DQ leaders must be able to manage their personal discomfort and the discomfort of others and resistance to change.
> Theme 4: When teaching DQ educational strategies and processes must be adjusted according to the different developmental levels of leaders.
> Theme 5: DQ education focused on providing knowledge about protected class groups and categories can be used to improve workplace performance.
> Theme 6: DQ leaders must recognize that some leaders will never change their positions, views, or behaviors toward protected class employees. Protected class employees have come to accept that they will never be able to relax, and it is not paranoia, when out amid mainstream society and sometimes within the workplace, because they never know whom they will encounter who is resistant to change.
> Theme 7: DQ needs to become an effective leader characteristic and/or competency because IQ, EQ, and CQ are not being used to help protected class employees advance within organizations.

All these themes covered in this book and are capable of being applied by counselors, educators and trainers who are willing to deal with and accept them as valid and useful to their success at diversity training. Scholars can examine these themes and extend the DQ literature. The addition of DQ to intelligence theories has the potential to transform existing views and alter research practice. DQ also improves the intelligence of individuals. Researchers must consider the following:

1. How can DQ improve current thinking of leaders?
2. How can DQ provide solutions and remedy alleged deficiencies in current diversity theories?
3. How can DQ alter current research practice?
4. In what way(s) does Gestalt psychology relate to DQ?
5. How can DQ help explain philosophical and societal imperfections related to diversity?

DQ can be an introduction to understanding diversity for individuals unfamiliar to why it is important and why it should be implemented. DQ also attempts to advocate for the morality/ethical paradigm that guides diversity management, which seems to be embedded in understanding the sociopolitical, cultural, and historical implications of D & I. DQ requires individuals with diversity expertise to provide train-the-trainer sessions for leaders of diversity efforts who are not yet diversity intelligent. DQ trainers in leadership development programs whose goals are to help leaders become diversity intelligent must understand where diversity originated, where it is currently, and how to move it forward alongside IQ, EQ, and CQ.

Diversity intelligent leaders will have developed the following competencies: diversity expertise, ethics, morals, talent development, talent management, diversity theory, leadership development, career development, cognitive diversity, equity, protected class employee understanding. These competencies align with many of the fundamental leadership competencies so they should not be difficult for leaders to integrate within their daily activities. Knowing what to do without applying what one knows makes one an ineffective diversity leader.

REFERENCES

Covey, S. R. (1991). *Principle-Centered Leadership*. Simon and Schuster.

Du Bois, W. E. B., & Blaisdell, B. (2013). *WEB Du Bois: Selections from His Writings*. Courier Corporation.

Hughes, C. (2010). People as Technology Conceptual Model: Towards a New Value Creation Paradigm for Strategic Human Resource Development. *Human Resource Development Review*, 9(1), 48–71. https://doi.org/10.1177/1534484309353561

Hughes, C. (2012). *Valuing People and Technology in the Workplace: A Competitive Advantage Framework*. IGI Global.

Hughes, C. (2014). *American Black Women and Interpersonal Leadership Styles*. The Netherlands Sense Publishers.

Hughes, C., & Brown, L. M. (2018). Exploring Leaders' Discriminatory, Passive-Aggressive Behavior Toward Protected Class Employees Using Diversity Intelligence. *Advances in Developing Human Resources, 20*(3), 263–284.

Scott, C. L., & Klein, L. B. (2022). Advancing Traditional Leadership Theories by Incorporating Multicultural and Workforce Diversity Leadership Traits, Behaviors, and Supporting practices: Implications for Organizational Leaders. *Journal of Leadership, Accountability and Ethics, 19*(3), 1–11.

Bibliography

Abele, A. E., & Wiese, B. S. (2008). The Nomological Network of Self-Management Strategies and Career Success. *Journal of Occupational and Organizational Psychology, 81*(4), 733–749.

Adams, J. S. (1963). Toward an Understanding of Inequity. *Journal of Abnormal and Social Psychology, 67*(5), 422–436.

Adams, J. S. (1965). Inequity in Social Exchange. *Advances in Experimental Social Psychology, 2*, 267–299.

Adamson, S. J., Doherty, N., & Viney, C. (1998). The Meanings of Career Revisited: Implications for Theory and Practice. *British Journal of Management, 9*(4), 251–259.

Areheart, B. A. (2019). Organizational Justice and Antidiscrimination. *Minnesota Law Review, 104*, 1921–1986.

Age Discrimination in Employment Act of 1967, Pub. L. No. 90-202 Code, 29 U.S.C. § 621.

Agote, L., Aramburu, N., & Lines, R. (2016). Authentic Leadership Perception, Trust in the Leader, and Followers' Emotions in Organizational Change Processes. *The Journal of Applied Behavioral Science, 52*(1), 35–63.

Aguinis, H. (2009). *Performance Management* (2nd ed.). Pearson Prentice Hall.

Aguinis, H., & Kraiger, K. (2009). Benefits of Training and Development for Individuals and Teams, Organizations, and Society. *Annual Review of Psychology, 60*, 451–474.

Aguinis, H., & Pierce, C. A. (2008). Enhancing the Relevance of Organizational Behavior by Embracing Performance Management Research. *Journal of Organizational Behavior, 29*(1), 139–145.

Ahuja, G. (2000). Collaboration Networks, Structural Holes, and Innovation: A Longitudinal Study. *Administrative Science Quarterly, 45*(3), 425–455.

Alavi, M., & Leidner, D. E. (2001). Review: Knowledge Management and Knowledge Management Systems: Conceptual Foundations and Research Issues. *MIS Quarterly, 25*(1), 107–136.

Albelda, R. P. (1986). Occupational Segregation by Race and Gender, 1958–1981. *Industrial and Labor Relations Review, 39*(3), 404–411.

Alderfer, C. P. (2000). National Culture and the New Corporate Language for Race Relations. In R. T. Carter (Ed.), *Addressing Cultural Issues in Organizations Beyond the Corporate Context* (pp. 19–33). Sage.

Alderfer, C. P., Alderfer, C. J., Bell, E. L., & Jones, J. (1992). The Race Relations Competence Workshop: Theory and Results. *Human Relations, 45*(12), 1259–1291. *Business Source Premier*, EBSCO*host* (Accessed 28 Dec 2014).

Alfred, M. (2001). Expanding Theories of Career Developoment: Adding the Voices of African American Women in the White Academy. *Adult Education Quarterly, 51*(2), 108–127.

Allen, Z. (1996). *Black Women Leaders of the Civil Rights Movement*. Franklin Watts.

Alvarado, M., & Lynham, S. (2005). Experiences of Hispanic Executives in the USA Workplace: An Exploratory Overview of Current Knowledge and Understanding. In L. Morris, & F. Nafukho (Eds.), *Proceedings of the Academy of Human Resource Development Annual Research Conference* (pp. 890–897). Academy of Human Resource Development.

Americans with Disabilities Act of 1990 (ADA), 42 U.S.C. §§ 12101–12213 (2000).

Amis, J. M., Mair, J., & Munir, K. A. (2020). The Organizational Reproduction of Inequality. *Academy of Management Annals, 14*(1), 195–230.

Amodio, D. M. (2009). Intergroup Anxiety Effects on the Control of Racial Stereotypes: A Psychoneuroendocrine Analysis. *Journal of Experimental Social Psychology, 45*(1), 60–67.

Anand, R., & Winters, M. F. (2008). A Retrospective View of Corporate Diversity Training from 1964 to the Present. *Academy of Management Learning & Education, 7*(3), 356–372.

Anand, V., Ashforth, B. E., & Joshi, M. (2004). Business as Usual: The Acceptance and Perpetuation of Corruption in Organizations. *The Academy of Management Executive, 18*(2), 39–53.

Anand, V., Glick, W. H., & Manz, C. C. (2002). Thriving on the Knowledge of Outsiders: Tapping Organizational Social Capital. *Academy of Management Executive, 19*(1), 87–101.

Andoh, R. P. K., Owusu, E. A., Annan-Prah, E. C., & Boampong, G. N. (2022). Training Value, Employee Internal States and Training Transfer:

Examining the Web of Relationships. *The Learning Organization, 29*(6), 674–691. https://doi.org/10.1108/tlo-09-2022-0100

Ang, S., & Van Dyne, L. (2015). *Handbook of Cultural Intelligence*. Routledge.

Ang, S., Van Dyne, L., Koh, C., Ng, K. Y., Templer, K. J., Tay, C., & Chandrasekar, N. A. (2007). Cultural Intelligence: Its Measurement and Effects on Cultural Judgment and Decision Making, Cultural Adaptation and Task Performance. *Management and Organization Review, 3*(3), 335–371.

April, K., Dharani, B., & April, A. (2023). Contextualised Discrimination. In *Lived Experiences of Exclusion in the Workplace: Psychological & Behavioural Effects* (pp. 109–153). Emerald Publishing Limited.

Argyris, C. (1985). Making Knowledge More Relevant to Practice: Maps for Action. In E. E. Lawler III, A. M. Mohrman, S. A Mohrman, G. E. Ledford Jr., & T. G. Cummings (Eds.), *Doing Research That Is Useful for Theory and Practice* (pp. 79–125). Jossey-Bass.

Arneson, J., Rothwell, W., & Naughton, J. (2013). Training and Development Competencies Redefined to Create Competitive Advantage. *Training & Development, 67*(1), 42–47.

Arthur, M. B., DeFillippi, R. J., & Jones, C. (2001). Project-Based Learning as the Interplay of Career and Company Non-Financial Capital. *Management Learning, 32*(1), 99–117.

Arthur, M. B., Hall, D. T., & Lawrence, B. S. (Eds.). (1989). *Handbook of Career Theory*. Cambridge University Press.

Arvey, R. D., & Murphy, K. R. (1998). Performance Evaluation in Work Settings. *Annual Review of Psychology, 49*(1), 141–168.

Ashforth, B. E., & Anand, V. (2003). The Normalization of Corruption in Organizations. *Research in Organizational Behavior, 25*, 1–52.

Ausubel, D. P. (1960). The Use of Advance Organizers in the Learning and Retention of Meaningful Verbal Material. *Journal of Educational Psychology, 51*(5), 267–272.

Ausubel, D. P. (1963). *The Psychology of Meaningful Verbal Learning*. Holt, Rinehart & Winston.

Ausubel, D. P., & Youssef, M. (1963). Role of Discriminability in Meaningful Parallel Learning. *Journal of Educational Psychology, 54*(6), 331–336.

Avery, D. R. (2011). Support for Diversity in Organizations: A Theoretical Exploration of Its Origins and Offshoots. *Organizational Psychology Review, 1*(3), 239–256. https://doi.org/10.1177/2041386611402115

Avery, D. R., Dumas, T. L., George, E., Joshi, A., Loyd, D. L., van Knippenberg, D., Wang, M., & Xu, H. (2022). Racial Biases in the Publication Process: Exploring Expressions and Solutions. *Journal of Management, 48*(1), 7–16.

Avery, D. R., Hall, A. V., Preston, M., Ruggs, E. N., & Washington, E. (2023). Is Justice Colorblind? A Review of Workplace Racioethnic Differences

Through the Lens of Organizational Justice. *Annual Review of Organizational Psychology and Organizational Behavior, 10*, 389–412. https://www.annualreviews.org/doi/abs/10.1146/annurev-orgpsych-120920-052627

Bachrach, D. G., Patel, P. C., & Pratto, F. (2022). As Clear as Black and White: Racially Disparate Concerns Over Career Progression for Remote Workers Across Racial Faultlines. *Business & Society*, 1–28. https://doi.org/10.1177/00076503221121823

Badal, S., & Harter, J. K. (2013). Gender Diversity, Business-Unit Engagement, and Performance. *Journal of Leadership & Organizational Studies, 21*(4), 2–12. https://doi.org/10.1177/1548051813504460

Baird, L., & Meshoulam, I. (1988). Managing Two Fits of Strategic Human Resource Management. *Academy of Management Review, 13*(1), 116–128.

Baker, S. (2008a, September 8). Management by the Numbers. *Business Week*, pp. 32–36.

Baker, S. (2008b). *The Numerati*. Houghton Mifflin.

Balan, P., & Lindsay, N. J. (2009). *Innovation Capability and Entrepreneurial Orientation Dimensions for Australian Hotels*. Cooperative Research Centre for Sustainable Tourism.

Bandura, A. (1977). *Social Learning Theory*. Prentice Hall.

Bandura, A. (1986). *Social Foundations of Thought and Action: A Social Cognitive Theory*. Prentice Hall.

Bandura, A. (1997a). *Self-Efficacy: The Exercise of Control*. W. H. Freeman.

Bandura, A. (1997b). Self-Efficacy: Toward a Unifying Theory of Behavioral Change. *Psychological Review, 84*(2), 191–215.

Bandura, A. (2002). Social Cognitive Theory in Cultural Context. *Applied Psychology, 51*(2), 269–290.

Bandura, A., Ross, D., & Ross, S. A. (1961). Transmission of Aggression Through Imitation of Aggressive Models. *Journal of Abnormal and Social Psychology, 63*(3), 575–582.

Banks, C. H. (2002). A Descriptive Analysis of the Perceived Effectiveness of Virginia Tech's Faculty Development Institute. *Dissertation Abstracts International, 64*(8) (UMI No. 3102585).

Banks, C. H. (2006a). Career Planning: Toward an Inclusive Model. In M. Karsten (Ed.), *Gender, Race and Ethnicity in the Workplace* (Vol. III, pp. 99–116). Greenwood Publishing Group.

Banks, C. H. (2006b). Career Planning: Towards a More Inclusive Model for Women and Diverse Individuals. In F. Nafukho & H. Chen (Eds.), *Academy of Human Resource Development International Conference (AHRD) Proceedings. Symp. 31–1* (pp. 640–647). Academy of Human Resource Development.

Banks, J. A. (2008). Diversity, Group Identity, and Citizenship Education in a Global Age. *Educational Researcher, 37*(3), 129–139.

Banks, K. H. (2009). A Qualitative Investigation of White Students' Perceptions of Diversity. *Journal of Diversity in Higher Education, 2*(3), 149–155.

Banks, C. G., & Murphy, K. R. (1985). Toward Narrowing the Research-Practice Gap in Performance Appraisal. *Personnel Psychology, 38*, 335–345.

Banks, C. H., & Nafukho, F. M. (2008). Career Transitions Across and Within Organizations: Implications for Human Resource Development. In T. M. Chermack & J. Storberg-Walker (Eds.), *Academy of Human Resource Development Annual Research Conference Proceedings* (pp. 1096–1102). Academy of Human Resource Development.

Banks, C. H., Collier, M. M., & Preyan, L. M. (2010). Leveraging Diversity Through Faculty Perception of Their Power to Influence Diversity. *International Journal of Human Resource Development and Management, 10*(3), 208–223.

Banks, K. H., Kohn-Wood, L. P., & Spencer, M. (2006). An Examination of the African American Experience of Everyday Discrimination and Symptoms of Psychological Distress. *Community Mental Health Journal, 42*(6), 555–570. https://doi.org/10.1007/s10597-006-9052-9

Bao, P., Xiao, Z., Bao, G., & Noorderhaven, N. (2021). Inclusive Leadership and Employee Work Engagement: A Moderated Mediation Model. *Baltic Journal of Management, 17*(1), 124–139. https://doi.org/10.1108/bjm-06-2021-0219

Barbulescu, R., & Bidwell, M. (2013). Do Women Choose Different Jobs from Men? Mechanisms of Application Segregation in the Market for Managerial Workers. *Organization Science, 24*(3), 737–756.

Barnard, C. I. (1938). *The Functions of the Executive*. Harvard University Press.

Bar-On, R. (2000). Emotional and Social Intelligence: Insights from the Emotional Quotient Inventory (EQ-i). In R. Bar-On & J. D. Parker (Eds.), *Handbook of Emotional Intelligence: Theory, Development, Assessment and Application at Home, School and in the Workplace* (pp. 363–388). Jossey-Bass.

Bar-On, R. (2004). *Bar-On Emotional Quotient Inventory: A Measure of Emotional Intelligence [Technical Manual]*. MHS Systems.

Barrie, C. (2020). Searching Racism After George Floyd. *Socius, 6*. https://doi.org/10.1177/2378023120971507

Barsh, J., & Yee, L. (2011). *Unlocking the Full Potential of Women in the U.S. Economy*. McKinsey & Company.

Barsh, J., & Yee, L. (2012). *Unlocking the Full Potential of Women at Work*. McKinsey & Company/Wall Street Journal.

Baruch, Y., & Jenkins, S. (2007). Swearing at Work and Permissive Leadership Culture: When Anti-Social Becomes Social and Incivility Is Acceptable. *Leadership & Organization Development Journal, 28*(6), 492–507.

Bass, B. M. (1985). *Leadership and Performance Beyond Expectation*. Free Press.

Bass, B. M. (1988). The Inspirational Processes of Leadership. *Journal of Management Development, 7*(5), 21–31.

Bass, B. M. (1999). Two Decades of Research and Development in Transformational Leadership. *European Journal of Work & Organizational Psychology, 8*(1), 9–32.

Bass, B. M., & Leadership, T. (1998). *Industrial, Military, and Educational Impact*. Lawrence Erlbaum Associates.

Bass, B. M., & Riggio, R. E. (2010). The Transformational Model of Leadership. In G. R. Hickman (Ed.), *Leading Organizations: Perspectives for A New Era* (2nd ed.). Sage.

Bassi, L., Cheney, S., & Lewis, E. (1998). Trends in Workplace Learning: Supply and Demand in Interesting Times. *Training and Development, 52*(11), 51–57.

Baumeister, R. F., & Leary, M. R. (1995). The Need to Belong: Desire for Interpersonal Attachments as a Fundamental Human Motivation. *Psychological Bulletin, 117*(3), 497–529. https://doi.org/10.1037/0033-2909.117.3.497

Baumeister, R. F., & Tierney, J. (2011). *Willpower: Rediscovering the Greatest Human Strength*. Penguin Press.

Baumgartel, H., & Jeanpierre, F. (1972). Applying New Knowledge in the Back Home Setting: A Study of Indian Managers' Adoptive Efforts. *Journal of Applied Behavioral Science, 8*(6), 674–694.

Becker, G. S., & Capital, H. (1964). *A Theoretical and Empirical Analysis, with Special Reference to Education*. University of Chicago Press.

Becker, G. S., & Capital, H. (1993). *A Theoretical and Empirical Analysis, with Special Reference to Education* (3rd ed.). University of Chicago Press.

Becker, B. E., Huselid, M. A., & Beatty, R. W. (2009). *The Differentiated Workforce: Transforming Talent into Strategic Impact*. Harvard Business Press.

Beckhard, R., & Harris, R. T. (1987). *Organizational Transitions: Managing Complex Change* (2nd ed.). Addison-Wesley Publishing Company.

Beer, M. (2001). Why Management Research Findings are Unimplementable: An Action Science Perspective. *Reflections: The SoL Journal, 2*(3), 58–65. https://doi.org/10.1162/152417301570383

Belasco, J. A., & Stayer, R. C. (1993). *Flight of the Buffalo: Soaring to Excellence, Learning to Let Employees Lead*. Warner Books.

Bell, D, A. (1980). Brown v. Board of Education and the Interest-Convergence Dilemma. *Harvard Law Review, 93*, 518–533.

Bell, D. A. (1995). Who's Afraid of Critical Race Theory. *University of Illinois Law Review*, 893–910.

Bell, D. (2003). Diversity's Distractions. *Columbia Law Review, 103*, 1622–1633.

Bell, E. L. J. (2002, October). Seven Strategies for Winning at Work. *Essence Magazine*, p. 198.

Bell, E. L. J., & Nkomo, S. M. (1994). *Barriers to Workplace Advancement Experienced by African-Americans.* MIT Press.

Bell, E. L. J., & Nkomo, S. M. (2001). *Our Separate Ways: Black and White Women and the Struggle for Professional Identity.* Harvard University Press.

Bem, D. J. (1972). Self-Perception Theory. In L. Berkowitz (Ed.), *Advances in Experimental and Social Psychology* (Vol. 6, pp. 1–62). Academic Press.

Benard, S., & Correll, S. J. (2010). Normative Discrimination and the Motherhood Penalty. *Gender & Society, 24*(5), 616–646.

Benko, C., & Pelster, B. (2013). How Women Decide: In B2B Selling, It Matters If Your Buyer Is Female. *Harvard Business Review, 91*(9), 78–84.

Berger, N. O., Kehrhahn, M. T., & Summerville, M. (2004). Research to Practice: Throwing a Rope Across the Divide. *Human Resource Development International, 7*(3), 403–409.

Bernardin, H. J., & Buckley, M. R. (1981). Strategies in Rater Training. *Academy of Management Review, 6*(2), 205–212.

Bernardin, H. J., & Villanova, P. (1986). Performance Appraisal. In E. A. Locke (Ed.), *Generalizing from Laboratory to Field Settings* (pp. 43–62). Lexington Books.

Bernardin, H. J., Buckley, M. R., Tyler, C. L., & Wiese, D. S. (2000). A Reconsideration of Strategies in Rater Training. *Research in Personnel and Human Resources Management, 18,* 221–274.

Betz, F. (1993). *Strategic Technology Management.* McGraw-Hill.

Betz, N. E. (2001). Career Self-Efficacy. In F. T. L. Leong & A. Barak (Eds.), *Contemporary Models in Vocational Psychology: A Volume in Honor of Samuel H. Osipow* (pp. 55–77). Lawrence Erlbaum Associates.

Betz, N. E., & Hackett, G. (2006). Career Self-Efficacy Theory: Back to the Future. *Journal of Career Assessment, 14*(1), 3–11.

Bezrukova, K., Jehn, K. A., & Spell, C. S. (2012). Reviewing Diversity Training: Where We Have Been and Where We Should Go. *Academy of Management Learning & Education, 11*(2), 207–227.

Bhattacharyya, B., & Berdahl, J. L. (2023). Do You See Me? An Inductive Examination of Differences Between Women of Color's Experiences of and Responses to Invisibility at Work. *Journal of Applied Psychology.* https://doi.org/10.1037/apl0001072

Bhattacharya, M., & Wright, P. M. (2005). Managing Human Assets in an Uncertain World: Applying Real World Options Theory to HRM. *International Journal of Human Resource Management, 16*(6), 929–948.

Bielaszka-DuVernay, C. (2014). Hiring for Emotional Intelligence. *Harvard Business Review Onpoint* (Summer), 12–16.

Bierema, L. L. (2010). Resisting HRD's Resistance to Diversity. *Journal of European Industrial Training, 34*(6), 565–576.

Biernat, M., Tocci, M. J., & Williams, J. C. (2012). The Language of Performance Evaluations: Gender-Based Shifts in Content and Consistency of Judgment. *Social Psychological and Personality Science, 3*(2), 186–192.

Bigman, Y. E., Yam, K. C., Marciano, D., Reynolds, S. J., & Gray, K. (2021). Threat of Racial and Economic Inequality Increases Preference for Algorithm Decision-Making. *Computers in Human Behavior, 122*, 106859.

Blackmon, D. A. (2008). *Slavery by Another Name: The Re-Enslavement of Black Americans from the Civil War to World War II*. Anchor Books.

Blake, S. (1999). At the Crossroads of Race and Gender: Lessons from the Mentoring Experiences of Professional Black Women. In A. J. Murrell, F. J. Crosby, & R. J. Ely (Eds.), *Mentoring Dilemmas: Developmental Relationships within Multicultural Organizations* (pp. 83–104). Lawrence Erlbaum.

Bloom, B. (1968). Learning for Mastery. *Evaluation Comment, 1*(2), 1–12.

Blustein, D. L., Walbridge, M. M., Friedlander, M. L., & Palladino, D. E. (1991). Contributions of Psychological Separation and Parental Attachment to the Career Development Process. *Journal of Counseling Psychology, 38*(1), 39–50.

Bolman, L. G., & Deal, T. E. (2008). *Reframing Organizations: Artistry, Choice, and Leadership* (4th ed.). Jossey-Bass.

Bolton, R., & Gold, J. (1994). Career Management: Matching the Needs of Individuals with the Needs of Organizations. *Personnel Review, 23*(1), 6–24.

Bossidy, L., Charan, R., & Burck, C. (2002). *Execution: The Discipline of Getting Things Done*. Crown Publishing.

Boudreaux, M. A. (2001). Career Development: What Is Its Role in Human Resource Development? In O. A. Aliaga (Ed.), *Academy of HRD 2001 Conference Proceedings* (pp. 805–812). Academy of Human Resource Development.

Bourdieu, P. (1986). The Forms of Capital. In J. G. Richardson (Ed.), *Handbook of Theory and Research for Sociology of Education* (pp. 241–258). Greenwood Press.

Bova, B. (2000). Mentoring Revisited: The Black Woman's Experience. *Mentoring & Tutoring, 8*(1), 5–16.

Bower, M. (1966). *The Will to Manage: Corporate Success Through Programmed Management*. McGraw-Hill.

Bowleg, L. (2012). The Problem with the Phrase Women and Minorities: Intersectionality—An Important Theoretical Framework for Public Health. *American Journal of Public Health, 102*(7), 1267–1273.

Bradberry, T. (2015). *18 Behaviors of Emotionally Intelligent People: Emotional Intelligence Is a Huge Driver of Success* (pp. ¶ 5–23). Retrieved February 12, 2016, from http://time.com/3838524/emotional-intelligence-signs/

Bradberry, T., & Greaves, J. (2009). *Emotional Intelligence*. TalentSmart.

Brass, D. J., & Burkhardt, M. E. (1993). Potential Power and Power Use: An Investigation of Structure and Behavior. *Academy of Management Journal, 36*(3), 441–470.

Brathwaite, S. T. (2002). Denny's: A Diversity Success Story. *Franchising World, 34*(5), 28–29.

Brault, Matthew W. (2012). *Americans with Disabilities: 2010* (pp. P70–P131) (pp. 1–131). US Department of Commerce, Economics and Statistics Administration, US Census Bureau.

Brennan, J. (2023). *The Diversity, Equity and Inclusion Dilemma: The Wrong Reasons or the Wrong Kind?* (Occasional Paper) Bridwell Institute. https://www.smu.edu/-/media/Site/Cox/CentersAndInstitutes/BridwellInstitute/SMU-Bridwell-Occasional-Paper_Final-web.pdf

Brief, A. P., Buttram, R. T., Reizenstein, R. M., Pugh, S. D., Callahan, J. D., McCline, R. L., & Vaslow, J. B. (2002). Beyond Good Intentions. In P. J. Frost, W. R. Nord, & L. A. Krefting (Eds.), *HRM Reality: Putting Competence in Context* (pp. 187–200). Prentice Hall.

Brinson, H. (2006). *The Effect of Race and Gender in Organizational Leadership Success: A Study of African American Women and Their Challenges to Become Leaders in Corporate America* [Unpublished Doctoral Dissertation]. Capella University, Dissertation Abstracts International.

Brockner, J. (2014, Summer). Why It's So Hard to Be Fair. *Harvard Business Review Onpoint*, pp. 44–51.

Brown, M. T. (1995). The Career Development of African Americans: Theoretical and Empirical Issues. In F. T. Leong (Ed.), *Career Development and Vocational Behavior of Racial and Ethnic Minorities* (pp. 7–36). Erlbaum.

Brown, M. E., & Treviño, L. K. (2006). Ethical Leadership: A Review and Future Directions. *The Leadership Quarterly, 17*(6), 595–616.

Brown, M. E., Treviño, L. K., & Harrison, D. A. (2005). Ethical Leadership: A Social Learning Perspective for Construct Development and Testing. *Organizational Behavior and Human Decision Processes, 97*(2), 117–134.

Browne, I., & Misra, J. (2003). The Intersection of Gender and Race in the Labor Market. *Annual Review of Sociology, 29*, 487–513.

Bruner, J. S., Goodnow, J. J., & Austin, G. A. (1956). *A Study of Thinking*. Wiley.

Bruning, R. H., Schraw, G. J., & Norby, M. M. (2011). *Cognitive Psychology and Instruction* (5th ed.). Pearson.

Buchanan, N. T., & Ormerod, A. J. (2002). Racialized Sexual Harassment in the Lives of African American Women. *Women & Therapy, 25*(3/4), 107–125.

Buchanan, N. T., & Settles, I. H. (2019). Managing (In)Visibility and Hypervisibility in the Workplace. *Journal of Vocational Behavior, 113*, 1–5.

Buckley, M. R., Beu, D. S., Frink, D. D., Howard, J. L., Berkson, H., Mobbs, T. A., & Ferris, G. R. (2001). Ethical Issues in Human Resources Systems. *Human Resource Management Review, 11*(1), 11–29.

Buhai, I. S., & van der Leij, M. J. (2023). A Social Network Analysis of Occupational Segregation. *Journal of Economic Dynamics and Control, 147*, 1–23. https://doi.org/10.1016/j.jedc.2022.104593

Burack, E. H. (1999). Bridging Research to Corporate Application. In L. Larwood & U. E. Gattiker (Eds.), *Impact Analysis: How Reach Can Enter Application and Make a Difference* (pp. 17–46). Erlbaum.

Burgess, D., & Borgida, E. (1999). Who Women Are, Who Women Should Be: Descriptive and Prescriptive Stereotyping in Gender Discrimination. *Psychology, Public Policy and Law, 5*(3), 665–692.

Burke, C. S., Stagl, K. C., Klein, C., Goodwin, G. F., Salas, E., & Halpin, S. M. (2006). What Type of Leadership Behaviors Are Functional in Teams? A Meta-Analysis. *The Leadership Quarterly, 17*(3), 288–307.

Burkhardt, M. E., & Brass, D. J. (1990). Changing Patterns or Patterns of Change: The Effects of a Change in Technology on Social Network Structure and Power. *Administrative Science Quarterly, 35*(1), 104–127.

Burns, J. M. (1978). *Leadership.* Harper & Row.

Burrows, D., Pietri, E. S., Johnson, I. R., & Ashburn-Nardo, L. (2022). Promoting Inclusive Environments: In-Group Organizational Endorsement as a Tool to Increase Feelings of Identity-Safety Among Black Women. *Sex Roles, 86*(1–2), 67–88. https://doi.org/10.1007/s11199-021-01253-2

Burt, R. S. (1997). The Contingent Value of Social Capital. *Administrative Science Quarterly, 42*(2), 339–365.

Burt, R. S., & Holes, S. (1992). *The Social Structure of Competition.* Harvard University Press.

Bush, P. D. (1987). The Theory of Institutional Change. *Journal of Economic Issues, 21*(3), 1075–1116.

Brass, D., & Krackhardt, D. (1999). The Social Captial of Twenty-First Century Leaders. In J. G. Hunt, G. E. Dodge, & L. Wong (Eds.), *Out-of-the-Box Leadership: Transforming the Twenty-First Century Army and Other Top Performing Organizations* (pp. 179–194). JAI Press.

Brown, R., & Harvey, R. (1996). *Job Component Validation Using the Myers-Briggs Type Indicator (MBTI) and the Common-Metric Questionnaire (CMQ).* Paper presented at the Annual Conference of the Society of Industrial and Organizational Psychology (SIOP), San Diego, CA. Retrieved from the Virginia Tech University website: http://harvey.psyc.vt.edu/Documents/BrownHarveySIOP.pdf.

Bruce, A. (2001). *Leaders Start to Finish: A Road Map for Developing Top Performers.* American Society for Training and Development.

Byk, L. (1992). *Professional Black Women's Family Patterns and Career Development: An Exploratory Case Study* [Unpublished doctoral dissertation]. New York University.

Byrd, M. (2007). Educating and Developing Leaders of Racially Diverse Organizations. *Human Resource Development Quarterly, 18*(2), 275–279.

Byrd, M. (2009a). Telling Our Stories: If We Don't Tell Them They Won't Be Told. In M. Byrd & C. A. Stanley (Eds.), *Giving Voice: The Socio-Cultural Realities of African American Women's Leadership Experiences. Advances in Developing Resources, 11*(5), 582–605.

Byrd, M. (2009b). Educating and Developing Leaders of Racially Diverse Organizations. *Human Resource Development Quarterly, 18*(2), 275–279. https://doi.org/10.1002/hrdq.1203

Byrd, M. Y. (2014). Re-Conceptualizing and Re-Visioning Diversity in the Workforce: Toward a Social Justice Paradigm. In M. Y. Byrd & C. L. Scott (Eds.), *Diversity in the Workforce: Current Issues and Emerging Trends* (pp. 334–346). Routledge.

Byrd, M. Y., & Hughes, C. (2021). Re-Conceptualizing Diversity Management: Organization-Serving, Justice-Oriented, or Both? In *Implementation Strategies for Improving Diversity in Organizations* (pp. 39–74). IGI Global.

Byrnes, N., & Crockett, R. O. (2009, May 28). Ursula Burns: An Historic Succession at Xerox. *Business Week.*

Callan, V. J. (1993). Subordinate-Manager Communication in Different Sex Dyads: Consequences for Job Satisfaction. *Journal of Occupational and Organizational Psychology, 66*(1), 13–27.

Campbell, J. P. (1990). Modeling the Performance Prediction Problem in Industrial and Organizational Psychology. In M. D. Dunnette & L. M. Hough (Eds.), *Handbook of Industrial and Organizational Psychology* (2nd ed., Vol. 1, pp. 687–732). Consulting Psychologists Press.

Caplow, T. (1954). *The Sociology of Work.* McGraw-Hill Book Company.

Cappelli, P., & Singh, H. (1992). Integrating Strategic Human Resources and Strategic Management. In D. Lewin, O. S. Mitchell, & P. D. Sherer (Eds.), *Research Frontiers in Industrial Relations and Human Resources* (pp. 165–192). Industrial Relations Research Association.

Carli, L. L. (1999). Gender, Interpersonal Power, and Social Influence. *Journal of Social Issues, 55*(1), 81–99.

Carrell, M. R., Mann, E. E., & Sigler, T. H. (2006). Defining Workforce Diversity Programs and Practices in Organizations: A Longitudinal Study. *Labor Law Journal, 57*(1), 5–12.

Carrig, K., & Wright, P. M. (2006). *Building Profit through Building People: Making Your Workforce the Strongest Link in the Value-Profit Chain.* Society for Human Resource Management.

Carter, E. R. (2020). Restructure Your Organization to Actually Advance Racial Justice. *Harvard Business Review*, 1–5.

Carter, R. T., & Cook, D. A. (1992). A Culturally Relevant Perspective for Understanding the Career Paths of Visible Racial/Ethnic Group People. In H. D. Lea & Z. B. Leibowitz (Eds.), *Adult Career Development: Concepts, Issues, and Practices* (pp. 192–217). The National Career Development Association.

Carter, E., Kepner, E., Shaw, M., & Woodson, W. B. (1982). The Effective Management of Diversity. *Advanced Management Journal, 47*, 49–53.

Cartwright, B. Y., Washington, R. D., & McConnell, L. R. (2009). Examining Racial Microaggressions in Rehabilitation Counselor Education. *Rehabilitation Education, 23*(2), 171–182.

Cascio, W. F. (2019). Training Trends: Macro, Micro, and Policy Issues. *Human Resource Management Review, 29*(2), 284–297. https://doi.org/10.1016/j.hrmr.2017.11.001

Cascio, W. F., & Aguinis, H. (2005). *Applied Psychology in Human Resource Management* (6th ed.). Pearson Education.

Cascio, W. F., & Collings, D. G. (2022), Potential: The Forgotten Factor in Talent Management Research. In D. Collings, V. Vaiman, & H. Scullion (Eds.), *Talent Management: A Decade of Developments (Talent Management)* (pp. 65–84). Emerald Publishing Limited. https://doi.org/10.1108/978-1-80117-834-120221004

Catalyst. (1999). *Women of Color in Corporate Management: Opportunities and Barriers*. Catalyst.

Catalyst, Inc. (2008). *2008 Catalyst Census of Women Corporate Officers and Top Earners of the Fortune 500*. Catalyst.

Catalyst. (2014). *Women CEOs of the Fortune 1000*. http://www.catalyst.org/knowledge/women-ceos-fortune-1000

Caudron, S., & Hayes, C. (1997). Are Diversity Programs Benefiting African Americans? *Black Enterprise, 27*(7), 121–136.

Champy, J., & Hammer, M. (1993). *Reengineering the Corporation*. HarperBusiness.

Chandler, J. A., Johnson, N. E., Jordan, S. L., & Short, J. C. (2022). A Meta-Analysis of Humble Leadership: Reviewing Individual, Team, and Organizational Outcomes of Leader Humility. *The Leadership Quarterly*, 101660. https://doi.org/10.1016/j.leaqua.2022.101660

Charan, R., Drotter, S., & Noel, J. (2001). *The Leadership Pipeline: How to Build the Leadership Powered Company*. Jossey-Bass.

Chaudhry, S. (2023). Measuring Diversity, Equity and Inclusion: A Holistic Approach. *Development and Learning in Organizations: An International Journal, 37*(2), 4–6.

Cheatham, H. E. (1990). Africentricity and Career Development of African Americans. *Career Development Quarterly, 38*(4), 334–346.

Chemers, M. M., Zurbriggen, E. L., Syed, M., Goza, B. K., & Bearman, S. (2011). The Role of Efficacy and Identity in Science Career Commitment Among Underrepresented Minority Students. *Journal of Social Issues, 67*(3), 469–491.

Chen, G., Gully, S. M., & Eden, D. (2001). Validation of a New General Self-Efficacy Scale. *Organizational Research Methods, 4*(1), 62–83.

Cheung, H. K., King, E., Lindsey, A., Membere, A., Markell, H. M., & Kilcullen, M. (2016). Understanding and Reducing Workplace Discrimination. *Research in Personnel and Human Resources Management, 34*, 101–152.

Chomsky, N. (1959). A Review of B. F. Skinner's Verbal Behavior. *Language, 35*(1), 26–58.

Chow, R. M., Phillips, L. T., Lowery, B. S., & Unzueta, M. M. (2021). Fighting Backlash to Racial Equity Efforts. *MIT Sloan Management Review, 62*(4), 25–31.

Christiansen, B., & Sezerel, H. (2013). Diversity Management in Transcultural Organizations. *Global Business Perspectives, 1*(2), 132–143.

Chua, A., & Rubenfeld, J. (2014). *The Triple Package: How Three Unlikely Traits Explain the Rise and Fall of Cultural Groups in America.* The Penguin Press.

Civil Rights Act of 1964, 42 U.S.C. § 2000, P.L. 88–352 (1964).

Civil Rights Act of 1991, P.L. 102–166 (1991).

Clark, C. M., Olender, L., Kenski, D., & Cardoni, C. (2013). Exploring and Addressing Faculty-To-Faculty Incivility: A National Perspective and Literature Review. *Journal of Nursing Education, 52*(4), 211–218.

Clement, S. (2015). *Millennials are Just About as Racist as Their Parents.* Retrieved July 28, 2015, from https://www.washingtonpost.com/blogs/wonkblog/wp/2015/04/07/white-millennials-are-just-about-as-racist-as-their-parents/

Cleveland, J. N., & Murphy, K. R. (1992). Analyzing Performance Appraisal as Goal-Directed Behavior. *Research in Personnel and Human Resources Management, 10*(2), 121–185.

Coates, T.-N. (2014, June). The Case for Reparations. *The Atlantic, 313*(5), 54–71.

Cocchiara, F. K., Connerley, M. L., & Bell, M. P. (2010). 'A GEM' for Increasing the Effectiveness of Diversity Training. *Human Resource Management, 49*(6), 1089–1106.

Cohen, R. J. (1994). *Psychology and Adjustment: Values, Culture, and Change.* Allyn & Bacon.

Cohen, C. F. (2002). Glass Ceilings and Glass Slippers: Still Stereotyping After All These Years? In P. J. Frost, W. R. Nord, & L. A. Krefting (Eds.), *HRM Reality: Putting Competence in Context* (pp. 205–213). Prentice Hall.

Cohen, W. M., & Levinthal, D. A. (1990). Absorptive Capacity: A New Perspective on Learning and Innovation. *Administrative Science Quarterly, 35*(1), 128–152.

Coleman, J. S. (1988). Social Capital in the Creation of Human Capital. *American Journal of Sociology, 94*, S95–S120.

Collier, M. J. (2003). *Intercultural Alliances: Critical Transformation.* Sage.

Collins, P. H. (1990). *Black Feminist Thought: Knowledge, Consciousness, and the Politics of Empowerment.* Routledge.

Collins, J. C., & Porras, J. I. (1994). *Built to Last: Successful Habits of Visionary Companies.* HarperBusiness.

Combs, G. M. (2002). Meeting the Leadership Challenge of a Diverse and Pluralistic Workplace: Implications of Self-Efficacy for Diversity Training. *Journal of Leadership & Organizational Studies, 8*(4), 1–16.

Combs, G. M. (2003). The Duality of Race and Gender for Managerial African American Women: Implications of Informal Social Networks on Career Advancement. *Human Resource Development Review, 2*(4), 385–405.

Combs, G. M., & Luthans, F. (2007). Diversity Training: Analysis of the Impact of Self-Efficacy. *Human Resource Development Quarterly, 18*(1), 91–120.

Combs, G., Nadkarni, S., & Combs, M. W. (2005). Implementing Affirmative Action Plans in Multi-National Corporations. *Organizational Dynamics, 34*(4), 346–360.

Connley, C. (2021, January 12). *How Corporate America's Diversity Initiatives Continue to Fail Black Women.* CNBC. https://www.cnbc.com/2020/07/01/how-corporate-americas-diversity-initiatives-continue-to-fail-black-women.html

Cook, E. P., Heppner, M. J., & O'Brien, K. M. (2002). Career Development of Women of Color and White Women: Assumptions, Conceptualization, and Interventions from an Ecological Perspective. *The Career Development Quarterly, 50*(4), 291–305.

Cook, E. P., Heppner, M. J., & O'Brien, K. M. (2005). Multicultural and Gender Influences in Women's Career Development: An Ecological Perspective. *Journal of Multicultural Counseling and Development, 33*(3), 165–179.

Copeland, L. (1988). Valuing Diversity: Part 1; Making the Most of Cultural Differences in the Workplace. *Personnel, 65*(6), 52–60.

Correll, S. J. (2013). Minimizing the Motherhood Penalty: What Works, What Doesn't and Why. In *Research Symposium: Gender & Work: Challenging Conventional Wisdom* (pp. 80–86). Harvard Business School.

Correll, S. J., Benard, S., & Paik, I. (2007). Getting a Job: Is There a Motherhood Penalty? *American Journal of Sociology, 112*(5), 1297–1339.

Cose, E. (1993). *The Rage of a Privileged Class.* HarperCollins.

Covey, S. R. (1991). *Principle-Centered Leadership.* Simon and Schuster.

Covey, S. R. (2006). Leading in the Knowledge Worker Age. *The Leader of the Future, 2*, 215–225.

Covey, S. R. (2013). *The 8th Habit: From Effectiveness to Greatness.* Simon and Schuster.

Cox, T., Jr. (1991). The Multicultural Organization. *The Academy of Management Executive, 5*(2), 43–47.

Cox, T., Jr. (2001). *Creating the Multicultural Organization: A Strategy for Capturing the Power of Diversity.* Jossey-Bass.

Cox, T. H., & Blake, S. (1991). Managing Cultural Diversity: Implications for Organizational Competitiveness. *Academy of Management Executive, 5*(3), 45–56.

Cox, T. H., Lobel, S. A., & McLeod, P. L. (1991). Effects of Ethnic Group Cultural Differences on Cooperative and Competitive Behavior on a Group Task. *Academy of Management Journal, 34*(4), 827–847.

Cramer, S. H. (1999). Overview of Career Development Theory. In J. A. Paulter (Eds.), *Workforce Education: Issues for the New Century* (pp. 77–86). Prakken Publications.

Crenshaw, K. (1989). Demarginalizing the Intersection of Race and Sex: A Black Feminist Critique of Antidiscrimination Doctrine, Feminist Theory and Antiracist Politics. *University of Chicago Legal Forum, 1989*, 139–167.

Crenshaw, K. W. (2010). Twenty Years of Critical Race Theory: Looking Back to Move Forward. *Connecticut Law Review, 43*, 1253–1353.

Crenshaw, K. W. (2016, March 14). *On Intersectionality.* Youtube Video, 30:46. https://Www.Youtube.Com/Watch?V=-Dw4hlgypla

Crites, J. O. (1978). *Career Maturity Inventory* (Rev. ed.). CTB/McGraw-Hill.

Crites, J. O., & Savickas, M. L. (1996). Revision of the Career Maturity Inventory. *Journal of Career Assessment, 4*(2), 131–138.

Cropanzano, R., Bowen, D. E., & Gilliland, S. W. (2007). The Management of Organizational Justice. *Academy of Management Perspectives, 21*(4), 34–48.

Cross, K. P. (1981). *Adults as Learners: Increasing Participation and Facilitating Learning.* Jossey-Bass.

Cummings, T. G., & Worley, C. G. (2005). Human Resources Management Interventions: Developing and Assisting Members. In *Organization Development and Change* (8th ed., pp. 396–433). South-Western, Thomson Corporation.

Daire, A. P., LaMothe, S., & Fuller, D. P. (2007, March). Differences Between Black/African American and White College Students Regarding Influences on High School Completion, College Attendance and Career Choice. *The Career Development Quarterly, 55*, 275–279.

Dasgupta, P. (2005). Economics of Social Capital. *The Economic Record, 81*(s1), S2–S21.

Dass, P., & Parker, B. (1999). Strategies for Managing Human Resource Diversity: From Resistance to Learning. *Academy of Management Executive, 13*(2), 68–80.

David, S., & Congleton, C. (2014, Summer). Emotional Agility: How Effective Leaderrs Manage Their Negative Thoughts and Feelings. *Harvard Business Review Onpoint*, 88–92.

Davis, L., & North, D. (1970). Institutional Change and American Economic Growth: A First Step Towards a Theory of Institutional Innovation. *The Journal of Economic History, 30*(01), 131–149.

Davis, P., Naughton, J., & Rothwell, W. (2004). New Roles and New Competencies for the Profession. *Training and Development Journal, 58*(4), 26–36.

Dawis, R., England, G. W., & Lofquist, L. H. (1964). *A Theory of Work Adjustment. Minnesota Studies in Vocational Rehabilitation, XV* (pp. 1–27). University of Minnesota, Industrial Relations Center.

Day, D. V., & Sulsky, L. M. (1995). Effects of Frame-of-Reference Training and Information Configuration on Memory Organization and Rating Accuracy. *Journal of Applied Psychology, 80*(1), 158–167.

Day, L. E. (1995). The Pitfalls of Diversity Training. *Training & Development, 49*(12), 24–30.

Day, N. E., & Schoenrade, P. (2000). The Relationship Among Reported Disclosure of Sexual Orientation, Anti-Discrimination Policies, Top Management Support and Work Attitudes of Gay and Lesbian Employees. *Personnel Review, 29*(3), 346–363.

Deal, T., & Kennedy, A. A. (1984). *Corporate Cultures*. Addison-Wesley.

Dearborn, K. (2002). Studies in Emotional Intelligence Redefine our Approach to Leadership Development. *Public Personnel Management, 31*(4), 523–530.

Deci, E. L., & Ryan, R. M. (1985). *Intrinsic Motivation and Self-Determination in Human Behavior*. Springer Science & Business Media.

DeFillippi, R. J., & Arthur, M. B. (1994). The Boundaryless Career: A Competency-Based Perspective. *Journal of Organizational Behavior, 15*(4), 307–324.

Deitch, E. A., Barsky, A., Butz, R. M., Chan, S., Brief, A. P., & Bradley, J. C. (2003). Subtle Yet Significant: The Existence and Impact of Everyday Racial Discrimination in the Workplace. *Human Relations, 56*(11), 1299–1324. *Business Source Premier*, EBSCO*host* (Accessed 28 Dec 2014).

Delery, J. E. (1998). Issues of Fit in Strategic Human Resource Management: Implications for Research. *Human Resource Management Review, 8*(3), 289–309.

de Leon, R. P., & Rosette, A. S. (2022). "Invisible" Discrimination: Divergent Outcomes for the Nonprototypicality of Black Women. *Academy of Management Journal, 65*(3), 784–812.

Deming, W. E. (1982). *Out of the Crisis*. MIT Center for Advanced Engineering Study.

Dewey, J. (1910). *How We Think*. D. C. Heath & Co.

D'Netto, B., & Sohal, A. S. (1999). Human Resource Practices and Workforce Diversity: An Empirical Assessment. *International Journal of Manpower, 20*(8), 530–547.

Dias, F. A. (2023). The (In) Flexibility of Racial Discrimination: Labor Market Context and the Racial Wage Gap in the United States, 2000 to 2021. *Socius, 9*. https://doi.org/10.1177/23780231221148932

Dickens, D. D., & Chavez, E. L. (2018). Navigating the Workplace: The Costs and Benefits of Shifting Identities at Work Among Early Career U.S. Black Women. *Sex Roles, 78*(11–12), 760–774. https://doi.org/10.1007/s11199-017-0844-x

Dickens, F., & Dickens, J. B. (1982). *The Black Manager:Making It in the Corporate World*. Amacom.

Dickens, D. D., Womack, V. Y., & Dimes, T. (2019). Managing Hypervisibility: An Exploration of Theory and Research on Identity Shifting Strategies in the Workplace Among Black Women. *Journal of Vocational Behavior, 113*, 153–163.

Dillard, J. M., & Campbell, N. J. (1981). Influences of Puerto Rican, Black, and Anglo Parents' Career Behavior on Their Adolescent Children's Career Development. *Vocational Guidance Quarterly, 30*(2), 139–148.

DiPadova, L. N., & Faerman, S. R. (1993). Using the Competing Values Framework to Facilitate Managerial Understanding Across Levels of Organizational Hierarchy. *Human Resource Management, 32*(1), 143–174.

Di Vesta, F. (1974). Cognitive Structures and Symbolic Processes. *Teachers College Record, 75*(3), 357–370.

Doane, A. W., & Bonilla-Silva, E. (Eds.). (2003). *White Out: The Continuing Significance of Racism*. Psychology Press.

Dobbin, F., & Kalev, A. (2016). Why Diversity Programs Fail. *Harvard Business Review, 94*(7), 14.

Dobbin, F., & Kalev, A. (2022). *Getting to Diversity: What Works and What Doesn't*. Harvard University Press.

Dobbin, F., Kalev, A., & Kelly, E. (2007). Diversity Management in Corporate America. *American Sociological Association, 6*(4), 21–27.

Doverspike, D., Taylor, M. A., Shultz, K. S., & McKay, P. F. (2000). Responding to the Challenge of a Changing Workforce: Recruiting Nontraditional Demographic Groups. *Public Personnel Management, 29*(4), 445–459.

Dovidio, J. F., Gaertner, S. E., Kawakami, K., & Hodson, G. (2002). Why Can't We Just Get Along? Interpersonal Biases and Interracial Distrust. *Cultural Diversity and Ethnic Minority Psychology, 8*(2), 88–102.

Downton, J. V. (1973). *Rebel Leadership: Commitment and Charisma in the Revolutionary Process*. Free Press.

Doyle, A. (2011). *Powering Up: How America's Women Achievers Become Leaders*. Xlibris Corporation.

Drosou, M., Jagadish, H. V., Pitoura, E., & Stoyanovich, J. (2017). Diversity in Big Data: A Review. *Big Data, 5*(2), 73–84.

Drucker, P. F. (1954). *The Practice of Management*. Harper.

Drucker, P. F. (1969). *The Age of Discontinuity*. Butterworth-Heinemann.

Drucker, P. F. (1992). *Managing for the Future*. Butterworth Heinemann.

Drucker, P. F. (1994). The Age of Social Transformation. *The Atlantic Monthly, 274*(5), 53–80.

Drucker, P. F. (1999). Knowledge-Worker Productivity: The Biggest Challenge. *California Management Review, 41*(2), 79–94.

Drucker, P. F. (2004). What Makes an Effective Executive? *Harvard Business Review, 86*(2), 58–63.

Drucker, P. F. (2008). *Management* (Rev. ed.). HarperCollins.

Dubin, R. (1976). Theory Building in Applied Areas. In M. Dunnette (Ed.), *Handbook of Industrial and Organizational Psychology* (pp. 17–26). Rand McNally.

Dubois, D., & Rothwell, W. (2004). *Competency-Based Human Resource Management: Discover a New System for Unleashing the Productive Power of Exemplary Performers*. Davies-Black.

Du Bois, W. E. B., & Blaisdell, B. (2013). *WEB Du Bois: Selections from His Writings*. Courier Corporation.

Duckworth, A. L., Peterson, C., Matthews, M. D., & Kelly, D. R. (2007). Grit: Perseverance and Passion for Long-Term Goals. *Journal of Personality & Social Psychology, 92*(6),1087–1101.

Dwivedi, P., Gee, I. H., Withers, M. C., & Boivie, S. (2022). No Reason to Leave: The Effects of CEO Diversity-Valuing Behavior on Psychological Safety and Turnover for Female Executives. *Journal of Applied Psychology*. Advance online publication. https://doi.org/10.1037/apl0001071

Dweck, C. S. (2006). *Mindset: The New Psychology of Success*. Random House.

Eagly, A. H., & Karau, S. J. (2002). Role Congruity Theory of Prejudice Toward Female Leaders. *Psychological Review, 109*(3), 573–598.

Earley, P. C., & Ang, S. (2003). *Cultural Intelligence: Individual Interactions across Cultures*. Stanford University Press.

Earley, P. C., & Mosakowski, E. (2004). Cultural Intelligence. *Harvard Business Review, 82*(10), 139–146.

EEOC. *Harassment*. http://www.eeoc.gov/laws/types/harassment.cfm

EEOC. (2023). *Laws & Guidance*. U.S. Equal Employment Opportunity Commission (eeoc.gov). https://www.eeoc.gov/laws-guidance

Egan, T. M. (2002). Organization Development: An Examination of Definitions and Dependent Variables. *Organization Development Journal, 20*(2), 59–70.

Elias, A. (2023). Racism as Neglect and Denial. *Ethnic and Racial Studies*, 1–23.

Elsass, P. M., & Graves, L. M. (1997, October). Demographic Diversity in Decision-Making Groups: The Experiences of Women and People of Color. *Academy of Management Review, 22*(4), 946–973.

Ely, R. J., & Thomas, D. A. (2001). Cultural Diversity at Work: The Effects of Diversity Perspectives on Work Group Processes and Outcomes. *Administrative Science Quarterly, 46*(2), 229–273.

Ertug, G., Brennecke, J., Kovacs, B., & Zou, T. (2022). What Does Homophily Do? A Review of the Consequences of Homophily. *Academy of Management Annals, 16*(1), 38–69. https://doi.org/10.5465/annals.2020.0230

Espedal, B. (2005). Management Development: Using Internal or External Resources in Developing Core Competence. *Human Resource Development Review, 4*(2), 136–158.

Etsy, K. (1988). Diversity Is Good for Business. *Executive Excellence, 5*(1), 5–6.

Ettorre, B. (1992, March). Women at Work: Breaking the Glass … or Just Window Dressing? *Management Review, 81*(3), 16–22.

Evans, K. M., & Herr, E. L. (1994). The Influence of Racial Identity and the Perception of Discrimination on the Career Aspirations of African American Men and Women. *Journal of Vocational Behavior, 44*(2), 173–184.

Farley, J. E. (1987). Disproportionate Black and Hispanic Unemployment in US Metropolitan Areas: The Roles of Racial Inequality, Segregation and Discrimination in Male Joblessness. *American Journal of Economics and Sociology, 46*(2), 129–150.

Fassinger, R. E. (2008). Workplace Diversity and Public Policy: Challenges and Opportunities for Psychology. *American Psychologist, 63*(4), 252–268.

Fassinger, R. E., & Richie, B. S. (1994). Being the Best: Preliminary Results from a National Study of the Achievements of Prominent Black and White Women. *Journal of Counseling Psychology, 41*(2), 191–204.

Feagin, J. R., & Sikes, M. P. (1994). *Living with Racism: The Black Middle-Class Experience*. Beacon.

Federal Glass Ceiling Commission. (1995). *Good for Business: Making Full Use of the Nation's Human Capital*. Retrieved April 7, 2012, from http://www.dol.gov/oasam/programs/history/reich/reports/ceiling.pdf

Federman, B. (2009). *Employee Engagement: A Roadmap for Creating Profits, Optimizing Performance, and Increasing Loyalty*. Jossey-Bass.

Feldman, S., & Huddy, L. (2005). Racial Resentment and White Opposition to Race-Conscious Programs: Principles or Prejudice? *American Journal of Political Science, 49*(1), 168–183.

Ferdman, B. M. (1999). The Color and Culture of Gender in Organizations: Attending to Race and Ethnicity. In G. N. Powell (Ed.), *The Handbook of Gender and Work* (pp. 17–34). Sage.

Fernandez, J. P. (1991). *Managing a Diverse Workforce: Regaining the Competitive Edge*. Lexington Books.

Feyerabend, P. (1955). Wittgenstein's Philosophical Investigations. *The Philosophical Review, 64*, 449–483.

Fischer, T., & Sitkin, S. B. (2023). Leadership Styles: A Comprehensive Assessment and Way Forward. *Academy of Management Annals, 17*(1), 331–372.

Fitzgerald, L. F., & Betz, N. E. (1994). Career Development in Cultural Contexts: The Role of Gender, Race, Class and Sexual Orientation. In M. L. Savickas & R. W. Lent (Eds.), *Convergence in Career Development Theories* (pp. 103–117). CPP Books.

Fleming, J. H., Coffman, C., & Harter, J. K. (2005, July–August). Manage Your Human Sigma. *Harvard Business Review, 83*(7), 106–114.

Folger, R., & Greenberg, J. (1985). Procedural Justice: An Interpretive Analysis of Personnel Systems. *Research in Personnel and Human Resource Management, 3*(1), 141–183.

Foster, S. (1993). Difference and Equality: A Critical Assessment of the Concept of Diversity. *Wisconsin Law Review*, 105–161.

Fox, R. (2001). Constructivism Examined. *Oxford Review of Education, 27*(1), 23–35.

Fox, S., & Stallworth, L. E. (2005). Racial/Ethnic Bullying: Exploring Links Between Bullying and Racism in the US Workplace. *Journal of Vocational Behavior, 66*(3), 438–456.

Franklin, J. H. (1947). *From Slavery to Freedom: A History of American Negroes*. Knopf.

Freedman, S. M. (1978). Some Determinants of Compensation Decisions. *Academy of Management Journal, 21*(3), 397–409.

Freeman, S. J. M. (1990). *Managing Lives: Corporate Women and Social Change*. The University of Massachusetts Press.

French, J. R. P., Raven, B., & Cartwright, D. (1959). The Bases of Social Power. In D. Cartwright (Ed.), *Classics of Organization Theory* (pp. 311–320). Dynamics, Institute of Social Research, University of Minnesota.

Friedman, M. (1970, September 13). The Social Responsibility of Business Is to Increase Its Profits. *The New York Times Magazine*, pp. 32–33.

Friedman, M. (1994). *Money Mischief: Episodes in Monetary History*. Harcourt Brace.

Friedman, R. A., & Krackhardt, D. (1997). Social Capital and Career Mobility: A Structural Theory of Lower Returns to Education for Asians. *Journal of Applied Behavioral Science, 33*(3), 316–334.

Friedman, T. L., & Mandelbaum, M. (2011). *That Used to Be Us: How America Fell Behind in the World It Invented and How We Can Come Back*. Farrar, Strauss, and Giroux.

Frieze, C., Hazzan, O., Blum, L., & Dias, M. B. (2006). Culture and Environments as Determinants of Women's Participation in Computing: Revealing the "Women-CS" Fit. In *Proceedings of the ACM SIGCSE Conference* (pp. 22–26). ACM Press.

Fulkerson, J. R., & Schuler, R. S. (1992). Managing Worldwide Diversity at Pepsi-Cola International. In S. E. Jackson (Ed.), *Diversity in the Workplace: Human Resources Initiatives, Society for Industrial and Organisational Psychology* (The Professional Practice Series). Guildford Press.

Gabriel, A. *MSNBC Has Been Whitewashed: Melissa Harris-Perry Exits, Buffoonish White Pundits Rule Once More*. Retrieved March 1, 2016, from http://www.salon.com/2016/03/01/msnbc_has_been_whitewashed_melissa_harris_perry_exits_buffoonish_white_pundits_rule_once_more/

Gailbraith-Jones, M. K. (1989). *A Study of Factors That Influence the Career Decisions of Black Writers* [Unpublished dissertation]. Stores, CT, University of Connecticut.

Galbraith, J. R., Lawler, E. E., & Associates. (1993). *Organizing for the Future: The New Logic for Managing Complex Organizations*. Jossey-Bass.

Gale, B. T. (1980). Can More Capital Buy Higher Productivity? *Harvard Business Review, 58*(4), 78–86.

Galea, N., Powell, A., & Salignac, F. (2023). The Role of Homosociality in Maintaining Men's Powerfulness in Construction Companies. *Construction Management and Economics, 41*(2), 172–182.

Gall, M. D., Gall, J. P., & Borg, W. R. (2007). *Educational Research: An Introduction* (8th ed.). Pearson.

Galloway, R. F. (1997). Community Leadership Programs: New Implications for Local Leadership Enhancement, Economic Development, and Benefits for Regional Industries. *Economic Development Quarterly, 15*(2), 6–9.

Gandhi, Mahatma. (2016). BrainyQuote.com, Xplore Inc. http://www.brainyquote.com/quotes/quotes/m/mahatmagan150718.html. Accessed 21 Feb 2016.

Gates, H. L., Jr., & Curran, A. S. (Eds.). (2022). *Who's Black and Why? A Hidden Chapter from the Eighteenth-Century Invention of Race*. Harvard University Press.

Gelfand, M. J., Imai, L., & Fehr, R. (2008). Thinking Intelligently About Cultural Intelligence. In S. Ang & L. Van Dyne (Eds.), *Handbook on Cultural Intelligence: Theory, Measurement and Applications* (pp. 375–388). ME Sharpe.

Gelfand, M. J., Nishii, L. H., Raver, J. L., & Schneider, B. (2005). Discrimination in Organizations: An Organizational-Level Systems Perspective. *Discrimination at Work: Psychological and Organizational Bases, 104,* 117–144. Psychology Press.

Gephart, M. A., Marsick, V. J., Van Buren, M. E., Spiro, M. S., & Senge, P. (1996). Learning Organizations Come Alive. *Training and Development, 50*(12), 34–46.

Ghiselli, E. E., & Brown, C. W. (1948). *Personnel and Industrial Psychology.* McGraw-Hill.

Gilley, A. M., Callahan, J., & Bierema, L. (2002). *Critical Issues in HRD: A New Agenda for the Twenty-first Century.* Perseus Books Group.

Ginzberg, E., Ginsburg, S. W., Alexrad, S., & Herma, J. L. (1951). *Occupational Choice.* Columbia University Press.

Giscombe, K., & Mattis, M. C. (2002). Leveling the Playing Field for Women of Color in Corporate Management: Is the Business Case Enough? *Journal of Business Ethics, 37*(1), 103–119.

Glaser, R. (1984). Education and Thinking: The Role of Knowledge. *American Psychologist, 39*(2), 93–104.

Glass, J. (1990). The Impact of Occupational Segregation on Working Conditions. *Social Forces, 68*(3), 779–796. https://doi.org/10.1093/sf/68.3.779

Glick, W. H., Chet Miller, C., & Huber, G. P. (1993). The Impact of Upper-Echelon Diversity on Organizational Performance. In G. P. Huber & W. H. Glick (Eds.), *Organizational Change and Redesign: Ideas and Insights for Improving Performance* (pp. 176–214). Oxford University Press.

Glymph, T. (2008). *Out of the House of Bondage: The Transformation of the Plantation Household.* Cambridge University Press.

Glynn, M. A., & DeJordy, R. (2010). Leadership Through an Organization Behavior Lens: A Look at the Last Half-Century of Research. In N. Nohria & R. Khurana (Eds.), *Handbook of Leadership Theory and Practice* (pp. 119–157). Harvard Business School Press.

Goldstein, I. L. (1974). *Training: Program Development and Evaluation.* Brooks/Cole.

Goleman, D. (1995). *Emotional Intelligence.* Bantam Books.

Goleman, D. (1996). *Emotional Intelligence: Why It Can Matter More Than IQ.* Bantam Books.

Goleman, D. (1998a). *Working with Emotional Intelligence.* Bantam Books.

Goleman, D. (1998b). What Makes a Leader? *Harvard Business Review, 76*(1998), 93–102.

Goleman, D. (2000). Leadership That Gets Results. *Harvard Business Review, 78*(2), 78–93.

Goleman, D. (2013). Leadership That Gets Results. *Harvard Business Review, 78*(2), 26–38.

Gómez, L. E., & Destinies, M. (2007). *The Making of the Mexican American Race*. New York University Press.

Gotanda, N. (1996). Failure of the Color-Blind Vision: Race, Ethnicity, and the California Civil Rights Initiative. *Ethnicity, and the California Civil Rights Initiative, 23*, 1135–1151.

Gotsis, G., & Grimani, K. (2016). Diversity as an Aspect of Effective Leadership: Integrating and Moving Forward. *Leadership & Organization Development Journal, 37*(2), 241–264. https://doi.org/10.1108/lodj-06-2014-0107

Graham, J. W. (1991). Servant-Leadership in Organizations: Inspirational and Moral. *The Leadership Quarterly, 2*(2), 105–119. https://doi.org/10.1016/1048-9843(91)90025-W

Gray, E. (2015). How High Is Your XQ? Your Next Job Might Depend on It. *Time Magazine, 185*(23), 40–46.

Gray, K. C., & Herr, E. L. (1998). *Workforce Education: The Basics*. Allyn & Bacon.

Gredler, M. E. (2009). *Learning and Instruction: Theory into Practice* (6th ed.). Pearson Education.

Greenhalgh, T., & Peacock, R. (2005). Effectiveness and Efficiency of Search Methods in Systematic Reviews of Complex Evidence: Audit of Primary Sources. *British Medical Journal, 331*(7524), 1064–1065.

Greenhaus, J. H., Callanan, G. A., & Godshalk, V. M. (2009). *Career Management* (4th ed.). Sage.

Greenhaus, J. H., Parasuraman, S., & Wormley, W. M. (1990). Effects of Race on Organizational Experiences, Job Performance Evaluations, and Career Outcomes. *Academy of Management Journal, 33*(1), 74–86.

Greer, T. W., & Peters, A. L. (2022). Understanding and Reducing Negative Interpersonal Behaviors: A Critical HRD Approach to Improve Workplace Inclusion. *The Palgrave Handbook of Critical Human Resource Development* (pp. 325–345). Springer International Publishing.

Grossman, R. J. (2000, March). Race in the Workplace. *HR Magazine*, pp. 41–45.

Groysberg, B., & Connolly, K. (2013). Great Leaders Who Make the Mix Work: Twenty-Four CEOS on Creating Diverse and Inclusive Organizations. *Harvard Business Review, 91*(9), 68–76.

Gutierrez, L. M. (1990). Working with Women of Color: An Empowerment Perspective. *Social Work, 35*(2), 149–153.

Gutiérrez y Muhs, G., Niemann, Y. F., Gonzalez, C. G., & Harris, A. P. (2012). *Presumed Incompetent: The Intersections of Race and Class for Women in Academia*. University Press of Colorado.

Gutman, A., Koppes, L. L., & Vodanovich, S. J. (2011). *EEO Law and Personnel Practices* (3rd ed.). Psychology Press.

Hackett, G., & Betz, N. E. (1981). A Self-Efficacy Approach to the Career Development of Women. *Journal of Vocational Behavior, 18*(3), 326–339.

Hackett, G., & Betz, N. E. (1989). An Exploration of the Mathematics Self-Efficacy/Mathematics Performance Correspondence. *Journal for Research in Mathematics Education, 20*(3), 261–273.

Hackett, G., & Byars, A. M. (1996). Social Cognitive Theory and the Career Development of African American Women. *The Career Development Quarterly, 44*(4), 322–340.

Hall, D. T. (1996). *The Career Is Dead—Long Live the Career: A Relational Approach to Careers.* Jossey-Bass.

Hall, D. T., Briscoe, J. P., Dickmann, M., & Mayrhofer, W. (2012). Implications of the Management of People and Organizations. In J. P. Briscoe, D. T. Hall, & W. Mayrhofer (Eds.), *Careers Around the World: Individual and Contextual Perspectives* (pp. 166–186). Routledge.

Hall, J. C., Everett, J. E., & Hamilton-Mason, J. (2012). Black Women Talk About Workplace Stress and How They Cope. *Journal of Black Studies, 43*(2), 207–226.

Hamel, G., & Prahalad, C. K. (1994). *Competing for the Future.* Harvard Business School Press.

Hansen, F. (2003). Diversity's Business Case Doesn't Add Up. *Workforce, 82*(4), 28–32.

Hansen, J.-I. (1974). Book Review of J.O. Crites Career Maturity Inventory. *Journal of Counseling Psychology, 21*(2), 168–172.

Harley, S. (1997). Speaking Up: The Politics of Black Women's Labor History. In E. Higginbotham & K. Romero (Eds.), *Women and Work: Exploring Race, Gender and Class* (pp. 28–51). Sage.

Harris, M. M. (1994). Rater Motivation in the Performance Appraisal Context: A Theoretical Framework. *Journal of Management, 20*(4), 737–756.

Harrison, D. A., & Klein, K. J. (2007). What's the Difference? Diversity Constructs as Separation, Variety, or Disparity in Organizations. *Academy of Management Review, 32*(4), 1199–1228.

Hatala, J. P. (2006). Social Network Analysis in Human Resource Development: A New Methodology. *Human Resource Development Review, 5*(1), 45–71.

Hax, A. C., & Majluf, N. S. (1996). *The Strategy Concept and Process: A Pragmatic Approach* (2nd ed.). Prentice Hall.

Hayes, K. H. (2000). *Managing Career Transitions: Your Career as a Work in Progress* (2nd ed.). Prentice Hall.

Hecht, B. (2020). Moving Beyond Diversity Toward Racial Equity. *Harvard Business Review*, 2–7. https://hbr.org/2020/06/moving-beyond-diversity-toward-racial-equity

Heffernan, T. (2022). Sexism, Racism, Prejudice, and Bias: A Literature Review and Synthesis of Research Surrounding Student Evaluations of Courses and Teaching. *Assessment & Evaluation in Higher Education, 47*(1), 144–154.

Heifetz, R. A. (1994). *Leadership Without Easy Answers*. Belkap Press of Harvard University Press.

Heilman, M. E. (2001). Description and Prescription: How Gender Stereotypes Prevent Women's Ascent Up the Organizational Ladder. *Journal of Social Issues, 57*(4), 657–674.

Heilman, M. E., Block, C. J., & Lucas, J. A. (1992). Presumed Incompetent? Stigmatization and Affirmative Action Efforts. *Journal of Applied Psychology, 77*(4), 536–544.

Heilman, M. E., Wallen, A. S., Fuchs, D., & Tamkins, M. M. (2004). Penalties for Success: Reactions to Women Who Succeed at Male Gender Typed Tasks. *Journal of Applied Psychology, 89*(3), 416–427.

Hekman, D. R., Johnson, S. K., Foo, M.-D., & Yang, W. (2017). Does Diversity-Valuing Behavior Result in Diminished Performance Ratings for Non-White and Female Leaders? *Academy of Management Journal, 60*(2), 771–797.

Helgesen, S. (1990). *The Female Advantage: Women's Ways of Leadership*. Doubleday Currency.

Hellerstedt, K., Uman, T., & Wennberg, K. (2022). Fooled By Diversity? When Diversity Initiatives Exacerbate Rather Than Mitigate Inequality. *Academy of Management Perspectives*. https://doi.org/10.5465/amp.2021.0206

Helm, R., Wallace, G., & Hunt, L. (2009). An Examination of a Diversity Concentration for a Graduate Level Business Degree Program. *Business Education & Accreditation, 1*(1), 15–28.

Hemphill, H., & Haines, R. (1997). *Discrimination, Harassment, and the Failure of Diversity Training: What to Do Now*. Greenwood Publishing Group.

Herr, E. L., & Lear, P. B. (1984). The Family as an Influence on the Career Development. In J. C. Hansen & S. H. Cramer (Eds.), *Perspectives on Work and the Family* (pp. 1–13). Aspen System Cooperation.

Herring, C. (2009). Does Diversity Pay? Race, Gender, and the Business Case for Diversity. *American Sociological Review, 74*(2), 208–224.

Herrnstein, R. J., & Murray, C. (1994). *The Bell Curve: Intelligence and Class Structure in American Life*. Free Press Enterprise.

Herzberg, F. I. (1966). *Work and the Nature of Man*. World.

Hill, M. S., & Ragland, J. C. (1995). *Women as Educational Leaders: Opening Windows, Pushing Ceilings*. Corwin Press.

Hinings, C. R., & Greenwood, R. (2002). Disconnects and Consequences in Organization Theory? *Administrative Science Quarterly, 47*, 411–421.

Hirsh, C. E. (2009). The Strength of Weak Enforcement: The Impact of Discrimination Charges, Legal Environments, and Organizational Conditions on Workplace Segregation. *American Sociological Review, 74*(2), 245–271.

Hirsh, C. E., & Kornrich, S. (2008). The Context of Discrimination: Workplace Conditions, Institutional Environments, and Sex and Race Discrimination Charges. *American Journal of Sociology, 113*(5), 1394–1432.

Hoang, T., Suh, J., & Sabharwal, M. (2022). Beyond a Numbers Game? Impact of Diversity and Inclusion on the Perception of Organizational Justice. *Public Administration Review, 82*(3), 537–555.

Hofacker, S. A. (2014). Diversity and Inclusion in the Engineering Workplace: A Call for Majority Intentionality to Increase Career Self-Efficacy. In *American Society for Engineering Education: 2014 ASEE Southeast Section Conference*.

Hogan, R., & Kaiser, R. B. (2005). What We Know About Leadership. *Review of General Psychology, 9*(2), 169–180.

Holladay, C. L., & Quinones, M. A. (2003). Practice Variability and Transfer of Training: The Role of Self-Efficacy Generality. *Journal of Applied Psychology, 88*(6), 1094–1103.

Holladay, C. L., & Quinones, M. A. (2008). The Influence of Training Focus and Trainer Characteristics on Diversity Training Effectiveness. *Academy of Management Learning & Education, 7*(3), 343–354.

Holladay, C. L., Knight, J. L., Paige, D. L., & Quiñones, M. A. (2003). The Influence of Framing on Attitudes Toward Diversity Training. *Human Resource Development Quarterly, 14*(3), 245–263.

Holland, J. L. (1959). A Theory of Vocational Choice. *Journal of Counseling Psychology, 6*(1), 35–45.

Holland, J. L. (1973). *Making Vocational Choices: A Theory of Careers*. Prentice-Hall.

Holland, J. L. (1997). *Making Vocational Choices: A Theory of Vocational Personalities and Work Environment* (3rd ed.). Psychological Assessment Resources.

Holton, E. F., & Lowe, J. S. (2007). Toward a General Research Process for Using Dubin's Theory Building Model. *Human Resource Development Review, 6*(3), 297–320.

Hong, L., & Page, S. E. (2004). Groups of Diverse Problem Solvers Can Outperform Groups of High-Ability Problem Solvers. *Proceedings of the National Academy of Sciences, 101*(46), 16385–16389.

Horniman, A. B. (2004). Leading: A Performing Learning Art. In M. Goldsmith, H. J. Morgan, & A. J. Ogg (Eds.), *Leading Organizational Learning: Harnessing the Power of Knowledge* (pp. 185–194). Jossey-Bass.

Horsman, R. (1981). *Race and Manifest Destiny*. Harvard University Press.

Hoskisson, R., Hitt, M., Ireland, R. D., & Harrison, J. (2008). *Competing for Advantage* (2nd ed.). South-Western.

Hotchkiss, L., & Borrow, H. (1984). Sociological Perspectives on Career Choice and Attainment. In D. Brown & L. Brooks (Eds.), *Career Choice and Development* (pp. 137–168). Jossey-Bass.

Hounshell, D. (1984). *From the American System to Mass Production, 1800–1932: The Development of Manufacturing Technology in the United States*. Johns Hopkins University Press.

Houser, K. A. (2019). Can AI Solve the Diversity Problem in the Tech Industry: Mitigating Noise and Bias in Employment Decision-Making. *Stanford Technology Law Review, 22*, 290–354.

Hoynes, H. W., Miller, D. L., & Schaller, J. (2012). *Who Suffers During Recessions?* (No. w17951). National Bureau of Economic Research.

HRfocus. (2003, October). Getting Results from Diversity Training—In Dollars and Cents. 80(10), 3–4.

Hudson, M., Netto, G., Noon, M., Sosenko, F., De Lima, P., & Kamenou-Aigbekaen, N. (2017). Ethnicity and Low Wage Traps: Favouritism, Homosocial Reproduction and Economic Marginalization. *Work, Employment and Society, 31*(6), 992–1009.

Hughes, C. (2010). People as Technology Conceptual Model: Towards a New Value Creation Paradigm for Strategic Human Resource Development. *Human Resource Development Review, 9*(1), 48–71. https://doi.org/10.1177/1534484309353561

Hughes, C. (2012). *Valuing People and Technology in the Workplace: A Competitive Advantage Framework*. IGI Global.

Hughes, C. (2014). *American Black Women and Interpersonal Leadership Styles*. The Netherlands Sense Publishers.

Hughes, C. (Ed.). (2015a). *The Impact of Diversity on Organization and Career Development*. IGI Global.

Hughes, C. (2015b). Valuing Diversity Through a Career Development Paradigm Shift. *Academy of Business Research Journal, 2*, 40–67.

Hughes, C. (2016). *Diversity Intelligence: Integrating Diversity Intelligence Alongside Intellectual, Emotional, and Cultural Intelligence for Leadership and Career Development*. Palgrave Macmillan.

Hughes, C. (2018a). Conclusion: Diversity Intelligence as a Core of Diversity Training and Leadership Development. *Advances in Developing Human Resources, 20*(3), 370–378.

Hughes, C. (2018b). *Workforce Inter-Personnel Diversity: The Power to Influence Human Productivity and Career Development*. Springer International Publishing.

Hughes, C. (2023, in press-a). The Intersection of Diversity, Equity, and Inclusion (DEI), Diversity Intelligence, and Ethics with the Role of HRD Scholars, Professionals, and Practitioners. In D. Russ-Eft & A. Alizadeh (Eds.), *Ethics in Human Resource Development*. Palgrave Macmillan.

Hughes, C. (in press-b). *Valuing People and Technology in the Workplace: Ethical Implications and Imperatives for Success*. IGI Global.

Hughes, C., & Brown, L. M. (2018). Exploring Leaders' Discriminatory, Passive-Aggressive Behavior Toward Protected Class Employees Using Diversity Intelligence. *Advances in Developing Human Resources, 20*(3), 263–284.

Hughes, C., & Bryd, M. (2015). *Managing HRD Programs: Current Issues and Evolving Trends.* Palgrave Macmillan.

Hughes, C., & DeVaughn, S. (2012). Leveraging Workforce Diversity Through a Career Development Paradigm Shift. In C. L. Scott & M. Y. Byrd (Eds.), *Handbook of Research on Workforce Diversity in a Global Society: Technologies and Concepts* (pp. 262–272). IGI Global.

Hughes, C., & Liang, X. (2020). *Hughes and Liang Diversity Intelligence®(DQ) Scale© 2020.* https://www.diversityintelligencellc.com

Hughes, C., & Mamiseishvili, K. (2014). Linguistic Profiling in the Workforce. In M. Byrd & C. Scott (Eds.), *Diversity in the Workforce: Current Issues and Emerging Trends* (pp. 249–265). Routledge.

Hughes, C., & Niu, Y. (2021a). Preface: Shifting Career Realities and Navigating Career Journeys. *Advances in Developing Human Resources, 23*(3), 195–202.

Hughes, C., & Niu, Y. (2021b). Responding to Career Development Uncertainties and Successfully Navigating Career Journeys. *Advances in Developing Human Resources, 23*(3), 267–272.

Hughes, C., Lusk, S., & Strause, S. (2016). Recognizing and Accommodating Employees with PTSD: Intersection of Human Resource Development, Rehabilitation, and Psychology. In *New Horizons in Adult Education and Human Resource Development.*

Hughes, C., Robert, L., Frady, K., & Arroyos, A. (2019). *Managing Technology and Middle and Low Skilled Employees: Advances for Economic Regeneration.* Emerald Publishing.

Hughes, D., & Dodge, M. A. (1997). African American Women in the Workplace: Relationships Between Job Conditions, Racial Bias at Work, and Perceived Job Quality. *American Journal of Community Psychology, 25*(5), 581–599.

Hughes, J. L. (1936, July). Let America Be America Again. In *Esquire* (p. 92). https://classic.esquire.com/article/1936/7/1/let-america-be-america-again

Huselid, M. A. (1995). The Impact of Human Resource Management Practices on Turnover, Productivity, and Corporate Financial Performance. *Academy of Management Journal, 38*(3), 635–872.

Ibarra, H. (1993). Personal Networks of Women and Minorities in Management: A Conceptual Framework. *Academy of Management Review, 18*(1), 56–87.

Ibarra, H. (1995). Race, Opportunity, and Diversity of Social Circles in Managerial Networks. *Academy of Management Journal, 38*, 673–703.

Igbaria, M., & Guimaraes, T. (1993). Antecedents and Consequences of Job Satisfaction Among Information Center Employees. *Journal of Management Information Systems, 9*(4), 145–175. https://doi.org/10.1145/144 001.372749

Inkson, K., & Arthur, M. B. (2001). How to Be a Successful Career Capitalist. *Organizational Dynamics, 30*(1), 48–61.

Ireland, R. D., & Hitt, M. A. (1999). Achieving and Maintaining Strategic Competitiveness in the 21st Century: The Role of Strategic Leadership. *The Academy of Management Executive, 13*(1), 43–57.

Irving, P. G., & Meyer, J. P. (1995). On Using Direct Measures of Met Expectations: A Methological Note. *Journal of Management, 21*, 1159–1176.

Isaacson, L. E., & Brown, D. (1997). *Career Information, Career Counseling, and Career Development* (6th ed.). Allyn & Bacon.

Ivancevich, J. M., & Gilbert, J. A. (2000). Diversity Management-Time for a New Approach. *Public Personnel Management, 29*(1), 75–92.

Jackson, L. R. (2012). *The Self-Efficacy Beliefs of Black Women Leaders in Fortune 500 Companies* (Unpublished doctoral dissertation). University of Arkansas, Fayetteville, AR.

Jackson, P. B., Thoits, P. A., & Taylor, H. F. (1995). Composition of the Workplace and Psychological Well-Being: The Effects of Tokenism on America's Black Elite. *Social Forces, 74*(2), 530–557.

Jackson, R. L. (2000). So Real Illusions of Black Intellectualism: Exploring Race, Roles, and Gender in the Academy. *Communication Theory, 10*(1), 48–63.

Jackson, S. E. (1992). Team Composition in Organizational Settings: Issues in Managing an Increasingly Diverse Workforce. In S. Worchel, W. Wood, & J. Simpson (Eds.), *Group Process and Productivity* (pp. 138–173). Sage.

Jacobs, R. L. (1989). Systems Theory Applied to Human Resource Development. In D. B. Gradous (Ed.), *Systems Theory Applied to Human Resource Development* (pp. 27–60). American Society for Training and Development.

Jago, A. G., & Vroom, V. H. (1978). Predicting Leader Behavior from a Measure of Behavioral Intent. *Academy of Management Journal, 21*(4), 715–721.

Janssens, M., & Steyaert, C. (2003). *Theories of Diversity within Organisation Studies: Debates and Future Trajectories*. Fondazione Eni Enrico Mattei Note di Lavoro Series (Working Paper 14).

Jayne, M. E. A., & Dipboye, R. L. (2004). Leveraging Diversity to Improve Business Performance: Research Findings and Recommendations for Organizations. *Human Resource Management, 43*(4), 409–424.

Jenkins, J. J. (1974). Remember That Old Theory of Memory? Well, Forget It! *American Psychologist, 25*(11), 785–795.

Jiang, Z., DeHart-Davis, L., & Borry, E. L. (2022). Managerial Practice and Diversity Climate: The Roles of Workplace Voice, Centralization, and Teamwork. *Public Administration Review, 82*(3), 459–472. https://doi.org/10.1111/puar.13494

Johlke, M. C., & Duhan, D. F. (2001). Testing Competing Models of Sales Force Communication. *The Journal of Personal Selling and Sales Management, 21*(4), 265–277.

John J. Heldrich Center for Workforce Development. (2002). *Work Trends Survey Report. A Workplace Divided: How Americans View Discrimination and Race on the Job.* Rutgers University.

Johnson, I. R., & Pietri, E. S. (2022). An Ally You Say? Endorsing White Women as Allies to Encourage Perceptions of Allyship and Organizational Identity-Safety Among Black Women. *Group Processes & Intergroup Relations, 25*(2), 453–473.

Johnson, R. E. (1975). Meaning in Complex Learning. *Review of Educational Research, 45*(3), 425–459.

Johnson, V. E., Nadal, K. L., Sissoko, D. R. G., & King, R. (2021). "It's Not in Your Head": Gaslighting, 'Splaining, Victim Blaming, and Other Harmful Reactions to Microaggressions. *Perspectives on Psychological Science, 16*(5), 1024–1036.

Johnson-Bailey, J., & Cervero, R. (2008). Different Worlds and Divergent Paths: Academic Careers Defined by Race and Gender. *Harvard Educational Review, 78*, 311–332.

Johnston, P. C., Schimmel, T., & O'Hara, H. (2010). Revisiting the AAUP Recommendation: Initial Validation of a University Faculty Model of Collegiality. *College Quarterly, 13*(2), 1–13.

Johnston, S., & Teicher, J. (2010). Is Diversity Management Past Its 'Use-By Date' for Professional and Managerial Women? *International Journal of Employment Studies, 18*(1, Special Edition), 34–62.

Jones, D. (1999). The Definition of Diversity: Two Views: A More Inclusive Definition. *Journal of Library Administration, 27*(1–2), 5–15.

Jones, G. (2008). How the Best of the Best get Better and Better. *Harvard Business Review, 86*(6), 123–127.

Jones, J. M., & Carter, R. T. (1996). Racism and White Racial Identity: Merging Realities. In B. P. Bowser & R. G. Hunt (Eds.), *Impacts of Racism on White Americans* (pp. 1–23). Sage.

Jones, J. R., & Harter, J. K. (2005). Race Effects on the Employee Engagement-Turnover Intention Relationship. *Journal of Leadership & Organizational Studies, 11*(2), 78–88.

Jones, K. P., King, E. B., Nelson, J., Geller, D. S., & Bowes-Sperry, L. (2013). Beyond the Business Case: An Ethical Perspective of Diversity Training. *Human Resource Management, 52*(1), 55–74.

Joshi, A., Son, J., & Roh, H. (2015). When Can Women Close the Gap? A Meta-Analytic Test of Sex Differences in Performance and Rewards. *Academy of Management Journal, 58*(5), 1516–1545.

Jost, J. T., Rudman, L. A., Blair, I. V., Carney, D. R., Dasgupta, N., Glaser, J., & Hardin, C. D. (2009). The Existence of Implicit Bias Is Beyond Reasonable Doubt: A Refutation of Ideological and Methodological Objections and Executive Summary of Ten Studies that No Manager Should Ignore. *Research in Organizational Behavior, 29*, 39–69.

Judge, T. A., Colbert, A. E., & Ilies, R. (2004). Intelligence and Leadership: A Quantitative Review and Test of Theoretical Propositions. *Journal of Applied Psychology, 89*(3), 542–552.

Judge, T. A., Livingston, B. A., & Hurst, C. (2012). Do Nice Guys—and Gals—Really Finish Last? The Joint Effects of Sex and Agreeableness on Income. *Journal of Personality and Social Psychology, 102*(2), 390–407.

Jun, S., Phillips, L. T., & Foster-Gimbel, O. A. (2023). The Missing Middle: Asian Employees' Experience of Workplace Discrimination and Pro-Black Allyship. *Journal of Applied Psychology, 108*(2), 225–248. https://doi.org/10.1037/apl0001068.supp

Jung, H., & Welch, E. W. (2022). The Impact of Demographic Composition of Social Networks on Perceived Inclusion in the Workplace. *Public Administration Review, 82*(3), 522–536. https://doi.org/10.1111/puar.13470

Juran, J. M. (1989). *Juran on Leadership for Quality*. The Free Press.

Kahn, W. A. (1990). Psychological Conditions of Personal Engagement and Disengagement at Work. *Academy of Management Journal, 33*(4), 692–724. https://doi.org/10.2307/256287

Kaida, L., & Boyd, M. (2022). Revisiting Gender Occupational Segregation Trends in Canada: 1991–2016. *Canadian Review of Sociology/Revue Canadienne de Sociologie, 59*(S1), 4–25.

Kalev, A. (2009). Cracking the Glass Cages? Restructuring and Ascriptive Inequality at Work. *American Journal of Sociology, 114*(6), 1591–1643.

Kaliannan, M., Darmalinggam, D., Dorasamy, M., & Abraham, M. (2022). Inclusive Talent Development as a Key Talent Management Approach: A Systematic Literature Review. *Human Resource Management Review, 33*(1), 100926. https://doi.org/10.1016/j.hrmr.2022.100926

Kane, G. (2019). The Technology Fallacy: People Are the Real Key to Digital Transformation. *Research-Technology Management, 62*(6), 44–49.

Kane, G. C., Phillips, A. N., Copulsky, J. R., & Andrus, G. R. (2019). *The Technology Fallacy: How People Are the Real Key to Digital Transformation*. MIT Press.

Kanter, R. M. (1977). *Men and Women of the Corporation*. Basic Books.

Kaptein, M., & Van Helvoort, M. (2019). A Model of Neutralization Techniques. *Deviant Behavior, 40*(10), 1260–1285. https://doi.org/10.1080/01639625.2018.1491696

Karsten, M. F. (Ed.). (2006). *Gender, Race, and Ethnicity in the Workplace: Management, Gender, and Ethnicity in the United States* (Vol. 1). Greenwood Publishing Group.

Karsten, M. F., & Igou, F. (2005). Career Planning: A Model for a Diverse Workforce. In *Refereed Proceedings of the North American Management Society Track at the 2005 Midwest Business Administration Association Conference.* MBAA.

Katz, J. H., & Moore, K. R. (2004). Racism in the Workplace: OD Practitioners' Role in Change. *OD Practitioner, 36*(1), 13–16.

Katz, J. H., & Moore, K. R. (2012). Racism in the Workplace. In J. Vogelsang (Ed.), *Handbook for Strategic HR: Best Practices in Organization Development from the OD Network* (pp. 177–181). AMACON.

Kaye, B. (1997). *Up Is Not the Only Way: A Guide to Developing Workforce Talent.* Davies-Black.

Kegan, R., & Lahey, L. L. (2001, November). The Real Reason People Won't Change. *Harvard Business Review*, 85–92.

Kelly, E., & Dobbin, F. (1998). How Affirmative Action Became Diversity Management: Employer Response to Antidiscrimination Laws, 1961 to 1996. *American Behavioral Scientist, 41*(7), 960–984.

Kelly, E., & Dobbin, F. (1999). Civil Rights Law at Work: Sex Discrimination and the Rise of Maternity Leave Policies. *American Journal of Sociology, 105*(2), 455–492.

Kenning, C. (2015). *College President's Sombrero Photo Sparks Outcry, Apology.* http://www.usatoday.com/story/news/nation-now/2015/10/29/college-presidents-sombrero-photo-sparks-outcry-apology/74848118/

Kenny, M. E., & Donaldson, G. A. (1991). Contributions of Parental Attachment and Family Structure to the Social and Psychological Functioning of First-Year College Students. *Journal of Counseling Psychology, 38*(4), 479–486.

Kerno, S., & Kuznia, K. (2007). Modern Career Navigation: Preparing for Success Despite Uncertainties. *Industrial Engineer, 39*(10), 31–33.

Kick, E. L., Fraser, J. C., & Davis, B. L. (2006, February). Performance Management, Managerial Citizenship and Worker Commitment: A Study of the United States Postal Service with Some Global Implications. *Economic and Industrial Democracy, 27*(1), 137–172.

Kidder, D. L., Lankau, M. J., Chrobot-Mason, D., Mollica, K. A., & Friedman, R. A. (2004). Backlash Toward Diversity Initiatives: Examining the Impact of Diversity Program Justification, Personal and Group Outcomes. *International Journal of Conflict Management, 15*(1), 77–102.

Kim, W. C., & Mauborgne, R. (2003, January). Fair Process: Managing the Knowledge Economy. *Harvard Business Review Classics, 81*(1), 127–136.

King, D. D., Fattoracci, E. S. M., Hollingsworth, D. W., Stahr, E., & Nelson, M. (2022). When Thriving Requires Effortful Surviving: Delineating Manifestations and Resource Expenditure Outcomes of Microaggressions for Black Employees. *Journal of Applied Psychology, 108*(2), 183–207.

King, E. B., Botsford, W., Hebl, M. R., Kazama, S., Dawson, J. F., & Perkins, A. (2012). Benevolent Sexism at Work: Gender Differences in the Distribution of Challenging Developmental Experiences. *Journal of Management, 38*(6), 1835–1866.

King, E. B., Gulick, L. M. V., & Avery, D. R. (2010). The Divide Between Diversity Training and Diversity Education: Integrating Best Practices. *Journal of Management Education, 34*(6), 891–906.

Kincheloe, J. L. (1999). *How Do We Tell the Workers? The Socioeconomic Foundations of Work and Vocational Education.* Westview Press.

Kincheloe, J. L., Steinberg, S. R., & Gresson III, A. D. (1997). *Measured Lies: The Bell Curve Examined.* St. Martin's Press, Scholarly and Reference Division.

Kinnier, R. T., Brigman, S. L., & Noble, F. C. (1990). Career Indecision and Family Enmeshment. *Journal of Counseling and Development, 68*(3), 309–312.

Kiselica, M. S. (1999). *Confronting Prejudice and Racism During Multicultural Training.* American Counseling Association.

Kivel, P. (2002). *Uprooting Racism: How White People Can Work for Racial Justice.* New Society Publishers.

Knowlton, K., Carton, A. M., & Grant, A. M. (2022). Help (Un) Wanted: Why the Most Powerful Allies Are the Most Likely to Stumble—And When They Fulfill Their Potential. *Research in Organizational Behavior*, 100180.

Koblin, J. (2016). *Melissa Harris-Perry Walks Off Her MSNBC Show After Pre-emptions.* Retrieved February 26, 2016, from http://www.nytimes.com/2016/02/27/business/media/melissa-harris-perry-walks-off-her-msnbc-show-after-pre-emptions.html?_r=0

Konrad, A. M. (2006). Leveraging Workplace Diversity in Organizations. *Organization Management Journal, 3*(3), 194–189.

Kontoghiorghes, C. (2004). Reconceptualizing the Learning Transfer Conceptual Framework: Empirical Validation of a New Systemic Model. *International Journal of Training and Development, 8*(3), 210–221.

Konyu-Fogel, G. (2011). *Exploring the Effect of Global Mindset on Leadership Behavior: An Empirical Study of Business Leaders in Global Organizations.* Lap Lambert Academic Publishing GMBH & Co.

Konyu-Fogel, G. (2015). Career Management and Human Resource Development of a Global, Diverse Workforce. In C. Hughes (Ed.), *The Impact of Diversity on Organization and Career Development* (pp. 80–104). IGI Global.

Kossek, E. E., Buzzanell, P. M., Wright, B. J., Batz-Barbarich, C., Moors, A. C., Sullivan, C., Kokini, K., Hirsch, A. S., Maxey, K., & Nikalje, A. (2022). Implementing Diversity Training Targeting Faculty Microaggressions and Inclusion: Practical Insights and Initial Findings. *The Journal of Applied Behavioral Science*, 1–27. https://doi.org/10.1177/00218863221132321

Kotter, J. P. (1996). *Leading Change*. Harvard University Press.

Kotter, J. P., & Cohen, D. S. (2002). *The Heart of Change: Real-Life Stories of How People Change Their Organizations*. Harvard University Press.

Kouzes, J. M., & Posner, B. Z. (1995). *The Leadership Challenge: How to Keep Getting Extraordinary Things Done in Organizations*. Jossey-Bass.

Kouzes, J. M., & Posner, B. Z. (1997). *Leadership Practices Inventory Workbook*. Jossey-Bass/Pfeiffer.

Kouzes, J. M., & Posner, B. Z. (2000). *Leadership Practices Inventory: Psychometric Properties*. Wiley.

Kouzes, J. M., & Posner, B. Z. (2003). *The Leadership Practices Inventory (LPI): Participant's Workbook* (Vol. 47). Wiley.

Kozlowski, S. W. J., & Salas, E. (Eds.). (2010). *Learning, Training, and Development in Organizations*. Routledge.

Kraiger, K., & Ford, J. K. (2007). The Expanding Role of Workplace Training: Themes and Trends Influencing Training Research and Practice. In L. L. Koppes (Ed.), *Historical Perspectives in Industrial and Organizational Psychology* (pp. 281–309). Psychology Press.

Kranz, G. (2007). A Higher Standard for Managers: Spending on Managerial Training Initiatives Is Soaring as Employers Wake Up to Profound Skills Gaps. *Workforce Management*, 86(11), 21–25.

Kraus, M. W., Torrez, B., & Hollie, LaStarr. (2022). How Narratives of Racial Progress Create Barriers to Diversity, Equity, and Inclusion in Organizations. *Current Opinion in Psychology*, 43, 108–113. https://doi.org/10.1016/j.copsyc.2021.06.022

Kulik, C. (1998). Managing Diversity in Organizations. An Exercise Based on Racial Awareness Training. *Journal of Management Education*, 22(2), 193–204.

Kulik, C. T., & Roberson, L. (2008). 8 Diversity Initiative Effectiveness: What Organizations Can (and Cannot) Expect from Diversity Recruitment, Diversity Training, and Formal Mentoring Programs. In A. Brief (Ed.), *Diversity at Work* (pp. 265–317). Cambridge University Press.

Kummerow, J. (2009). Uses of Type in Career Counseling. In I. B. Myers, M. H. McCaulley, N. L. Quenk, & A. L. Hammer (Eds.), *MBTI Manual: A Guide to the Development and use of the Myers-Briggs Type Indicator Instrument* (3rd ed., pp. 285–324). CPP.

Kupritz, V. W. (2002). The Relative Impact of Workplace Design on Training Transfer. *Human Resource Development Quarterly, 13*(4), 427–447.

Lach, J. (1999). Minority Women Hit a "Concrete Ceiling." *American Demographics, 21*(9), 18–21.

Lalonde, D. (2021). Does Cultural Appropriation Cause Harm? *Politics, Groups, and Identities, 9*(2), 329–346.

Lamb, M., & Sutherland, M. (2010). The Components of Career Capital for Knowledge Workers in the Global Economy. *The International Journal of Human Resource Management, 21*(3), 295–312.

Latham, G. P., Fay, C. H., & Saari, L. M. (1979). The Development of Behavioral Observation Scales for Appraising the Performance of Foremen. *Personnel Psychology, 32*(2), 299–311.

Latham, G. P., & Locke, E. A. (1991). Self-Regulation Through Goal Setting. *Organizational Behavior and Human Decision Processes, 50*(2), 212–247.

Laud, R. L., & Johnson, M. (2013). Journey to the Top: Are There Really Gender Differences in the Selection and Utilization of Career Tactics? *Journal of Organizational Culture, Communications and Conflict, 17*(1), 51–68.

Lawler III, E. E. (1986). *High Involvement Management.* Jossey-Bass.

Lawler III, E. E. (2000). *Rewarding Excellence: Pay Strategies for the New Economy.* Jossey-Bass Publishers.

Lawler III, E. E. (2003). *Treat People Right! How Organizations and Individuals can Propel Each Other into a Virtuous Spiral of Success.* Jossey-Bass.

Lawrence, C. R. (1987). The Id, the Ego, and Equal Protection: Reckoning with Unconscious Racism. *Stanford Law Review, 39*, 317–388.

Lawrence III, C. (2007). Unconscious Racism Revisited: Reflections on the Impact and Origins of the Id, the Ego, and Equal Protection. *Connecticut Law Review, 40*, 931–977.

Le Deist, F. D., & Winterton, J. (2005). What Is Competence? *Human Resource Development International, 8*(1), 27–46.

Lee, D. M. S., & Allen, T. J. (1982). Integrating New Technical Staff: Implications for Acquiring New Technology. *Management Science, 28*(12), 1405–1420.

Lee, J. (2022). A Critical Review and Theorization of Workplace Backlash: Looking Back and Moving Forward Through the Lens of Social Dominance Theory. *Human Resource Management Review*, 100900.

Lee, M. R., & Lan, Y.-C. (2007). From Web 2.0 to Conversational Knowledge Management: Towards Collaborative Intelligence. *Journal of Entrepreneurship Research, 2*(2), 47–62.

Legood, A., van der Werff, L., Lee, A., & Den Hartog, D. (2021). A Meta-Analysis of the Role of Trust in the Leadership-Performance Relationship. *European Journal of Work and Organizational Psychology, 30*(1), 1–22.

Leifer, M. S., & Newstrom, J. W. (1980). Solving the Transfer of Training Problems. *Training and Development Journal, 34*(8), 42–46.

Leiter, M. P., & Bakker, A. B. (2010). Work Engagement: Introduction. In A. B. Bakker & M. P. Leiter (Eds.), *Work Engagement: A Handbook of Essential Theory and Research* (pp. 1–9). Psychology Press.

Lenard, P. T., & Balint, P. (2020). What Is (the Wrong of) Cultural Appropriation? *Ethnicities, 20*(2), 331–352.

Lent, R. W., Brown, S. D., & Hackett, G. (1994). Toward A Unifying Social Cognitive Theory of Career and Academic Interest, Choice, and Performance. *Journal of Vocational Behavior, 45*(1), 79–122.

Lent, R. W., Brown, S. D., & Hackett, G. (1996). Career Development from a Social Cognitive Perspective. In D. Brown & L. Brooks (Eds.), *Career Choice and Development* (3rd ed., pp. 373–422). Jossey-Bass.

Lent, R. W., Brown, S. D., & Hackett, G. (2002). Social Cognitive Career Theory. In D. Brown & Associates (Eds.), *Career Choice and Development* (4th ed., pp. 255–311). Jossey-Bass.

Leonard-Barton, D. (1985). Experts as Negative Opinion Leaders in the Diffusion of a Technological Innovation. *Journal of Consumer Research, 11*(4), 914–926.

Lepper, M. R., Greene, D., & Nisbett, R. E. (1973). Undermining Children's Intrinsic Interest with Extrinsic Reward: A Test of the "Overjustification" Hypothesis. *Journal of Personality and Social Psychology, 28*(1), 129–137.

Leventhal, G. S., & Whiteside, H. D. (1973). Equity and the Use of Reward to Elicit High Performance. *Journal of Personality and Social Psychology, 25*(1), 75–83.

Levinson, H. (1970). Management by Whose Objectives? *Harvard Business Review, 48*(4), 125–134.

Levitt, B., & March, J. G. (1988). Organizational Learning. *Annual Review of Sociology, 14*, 319–340.

Lewin, K. (1946). Action Research and Minority Problems. *Journal of Social Issues, 2*(4), 34–46.

Lewis, C. M., & Lewis, J. R. (2011). *Women and Slavery in America.* University of Arkansas Press.

Libbrecht, N., Lievens, F., & Schollaert, E. (2010). Measurement Equivalence of the Wong and Law Emotional Intelligence Scale Across Self and Other Ratings. *Educational and Psychological Measurement, 70*(6), 1007–1020.

Likert, R. (1961). *New Patterns of Management.* McGraw-Hill.

Likert, R. (1967). *The Human Organization.* McGraw-Hill.

Lin, S.-C., & Huang, Y.-M. (2005). The Role of Social Capital in the Relationship Between Human Capital and Career Mobility: Moderator or Mediator? *Journal of Intellectual Capital, 6*(2), 191–205.

Lincoln, J. R., & Miller, J. (1979). Work and Friendship Ties in Organizations: A Comparative Analysis of Relational Networks. *Administrative Science Quarterly, 24*(2), 181–199.

Lindsay, N. J., & Balan, P. (2005). Entrepreneurial Self-Efficacy and Personal Entrepreneur Success. In *AGSE International Entrepreneurship Research Exchange (2nd: 2005: Melbourne, VIC).*

Lipman-Blumen, J. (1992). Connective Leadership: Female Leadership Styles in the 21st Century Workplace. *Sociological Perspectives, 35*(1), 183–203.

Lipshitz, R., Friedman, V., & Popper, M. (2006). *Demystifying Organizational Learning.* Sage.

Litwin, G. H., & Stringer, R. A., Jr. (1968). *Motivation and Organizational Climate.* Division of Research, Harvard Business School.

Livingston, R. (2020). How to Promote Racial Equity in the Workplace. *Harvard Business Review, 98*(5), 64–72.

Locke, E. A. (1969). Purpose Without Consciousness: A Contradiction. *Psychological Reports, 25*(3), 991–1009.

Locke, S. S. (1997). Incredible Shrinking Protected Class: Redefining the Scope of Disability Under the Americans with Disabilities Act. *The University of Colorado Law Review, 68,* 107–127.

Loden, M. (1996). *Implementing Diversity.* Irwin Professional Publishing.

Loden, M., & Rosener, J. B. (1991). *Workforce America! Managing Employee Diversity as a Vital Resource.* Business One Irwin.

London, M., & Diamante, T. (2002). Technology-Focused Expansive Professionals: Developing Continuous Learning in the High-Technology Sector. *Human Resource Development Review, 1*(4), 500–524.

Lopes, P. N., Brackett, M. A., Nezlek, J. B., Schütz, A., Sellin, I., & Salovey, P. (2004). Emotional Intelligence and Social Interaction. *Personality and Social Psychology, 30*(8), 1018–1034.

Lopez, F. G., Campbell, V. L., & Watkins, C. E. (1988). Family Structure, Psychological Separations, and College Adjustment: A Canonical Analysis and Cross-Validation. *Journal of Counseling Psychology, 35*(4), 402–409.

Lovallo, D., & Kahneman, D. (2003). Delusions of Success: How Optimism Undermines Executives' Decision. *Harvard Business Review, 81*(7), 56–63.

Mac Kay, W. R., & Miller, C. A. (1982). Relations of Socioeconomic Status and Sex Variables to the Complexity of Worker Functions in the Occupational Choices of Elementary School Children. *Journal of Vocational Behavior, 20*(1), 31–39.

Mackey, J. D., Ellen III, B. P., McAllister, C. P., & Alexander, K. C. (2021). The Dark Side of Leadership: A Systematic Literature Review and Meta-Analysis of Destructive Leadership Research. *Journal of Business Research, 132*, 705–718.

Madden, J. F. (2012). Performance-Support Bias and the Gender Pay Gap Among Stockbrokers. *Gender & Society, 26*(3), 488–518.

Maghbouleh, N., Schachter, A., & Flores, R. D. (2022). Middle Eastern and North African Americans May Not Be Perceived, Nor Perceive Themselves, to Be White. *Proceedings of the National Academy of Sciences, 119*(7). https://doi.org/10.1073/pnas.2117940119

Maidique, M. A., & Hayes, R. H. (1984). The Art of High-Technology Management. *Sloan Management Review, 25*(2), 17–31.

Mallick, M. (2020). Do You Know Why Your Company Needs a Chief Diversity Officer. *Harvard Business Review*, 1–5.

Manville, B. (2001). Learning in the New Economy. *Leader to Leader, 20*, 36–45.

Manz, C. C. (1986). Self-Leadership: Toward an Expanded Theory of Self-Influence Processes in Organizations. *The Academy of Management Review, 11*(3), 585–600.

March, J. G., & Simon, H. A. (1958). *Organizations*. Wiley.

Marini, M. M., & Greenberger, E. (1978). Sex Differences in Occupational Aspirations and Expectations. *Sociology of Work and Occupations, 5*(2), 147–178.

Marquardt, M. J. (2002). *Building the Learning Organization: Mastering the 5 Elements for Corporate Learning*. Davies-Black Publishing.

Marques, J. (2007). Diversity as a Win-Win Strategy. *Management Services, 51*(1), 22–24.

Martelli, J. T. (1998). Training for New Technology: Midwest Steel Company. In W. Rothwell (Ed.), *Linking HRD Programs with Organizational Strategy* (pp. 85–96). ASTD.

Martin, P. Y., Harrison, D., & Dinitto, D. (1983). Advancement for Women in Hierarchical Organizations: A Multilevel Analysis of Problems and Prospects. *Journal of Applied Behavioral Science, 19*(1), 19–33.

Martinez, M. E. (2010). *Learning and Cognition: The Design of the Mind*. Pearson.

Martocchio, J. J., & Judge, T. A. (1997). Relationship Between Conscientiousness and Learning in Employee Training: Mediating Influences of Self-Deception and Self-Efficacy. *Journal of Applied Psychology, 82*(5), 764–773. https://doi.org/10.1037/0021-9010.82.5.764

Marx, K. (1906). *Capital* (Vol. 1). Kerr.

Maslow, A. H. (1987). *Motivation and Personality* (3rd ed.). Harper & Row.

Mattingly, M. J., & Smith, K. E. (2010). Changes in Wives' Employment when Husbands Stop Working: A Recession-Prosperity Comparison. *Family Relations, 59*(4), 343–357.

Maume, D. J. (1999). Glass Ceilings and Glass Escalators Occupational Segregation and Race and Sex Differences in Managerial Promotions. *Work and Occupations, 26*(4), 483–509. https://doi.org/10.1177/073088849902600 4005

Mayer, J. D., & Salovey, P. (1997). What Is Emotional Intelligence? In P. Salovey & D. Sluyter (Eds.), *Emotional Development and Emotional Intelligence: Educational Implications* (pp. 3–34). Basic Books.

Mayer, J. D., Salovey, P., & Caruso, D. R. (2000). Models of Emotional Intelligence. In R. J. Sternberg (Ed.), *Handbook of Human Intelligence* (2nd ed., pp. 396–422). Cambridge University Press.

McClelland, D. C. (1961). *The Achieving Society*. Free Press.

McCloskey, F., & Barber, J. (2005). Georgia Power Turns a Crisis into a Diversity Journey. *Diversity Factor, 13*(4), 16–22. *MasterFILE Premier*, EBSCO*host* (Accessed 27 Dec 2014).

McCluney, C. L., & Rabelo, V. C. (2019). Conditions of Visibility: An Intersectional Examination of Black Women's Belongingness and Distinctiveness at Work. *Journal of Vocational Behavior, 113*, 143–152.

McCollum, V. J. C. (1998). Career Development Issues and Strategies for Counseling African Americans. *Journal of Career Development, 25*(1), 41–52.

McDonnell, M., & Baxter, D. (2019). Chatbots and Gender Stereotyping. *Interacting with Computers, 31*(2), 116–121.

McGonigal, K. (2012). *The Will Power Instinct: How Self-Control Works, Why It Matters, and What You Can Do To Get More of It*. Avery.

McGregor, D. (2006). *The Human Side of Enterprise* (Annotated). The McGraw-Hill Companies.

McKinney, J. C. (1966). *Constructive Typology and Social Theory*. Appleton-Century-Crofts.

McLagan, P. A. (1989). *Models for HRD Practice*. American Society for Training and Development.

McLaughlin, G. W., Hunt, W. K., & Montgomery, J. R. (1976). Socioeconomic Status and Career Aspirations and Perceptions of Women Seniors in High School. *Vocational Guidance Quarterly, 25*(2), 155–162.

McLean, G. N. (2006). *Organization Development*. Berrett-Koehler.

McLean, G. N. (2014). National HRD. In N. Chalofsky, T. S. Rocco, & M. L. Morris (Eds.), *Handbook of Human Resource Development* (pp. 643–661). Sage.

McLean, G. N., & McLean, L. (2001). If We Can't Define HRD in One Country, How Can We Define It in an International Context? *Human Resource Development International, 4*(3), 313–326.

McLean, G. N., Osman-Gani, A. M., & Cho, E. (2004). Human Resource Development as National Policy. *Advances in Developing Human Resources, 6*(3), 269–293.

McLean, L. D. (2005). Organizational Culture's Influence on Creativity and Innovation: A Review of the Literature and Implications for Human Resource Development. *Advances in Developing Human Resources, 7*(2), 226–246. https://doi.org/10.1177/1523422305274528

McLeod, P. L., Lobel, S. A., & Cox, T. H. (1996). Ethnic Diversity and Creativity in Small Groups. *Small Group Research, 27*(2), 248–264.

McPherson, M., Smith-Lovin, L., & Cook, J. M. (2001). Birds of a Feather: Homophily in Social Networks. *Annual Review of Sociology, 27*, 415–444.

Medina, F. J., Munduate, L., & Guerra, J. M. (2008). Power and Conflict in Cooperative and Competitive Contexts. *European Journal of Work and Organizational Psychology, 17*(3), 349–362.

Mehan, H. (1996). Constitutive Processes of Race and Exclusion. *Anthropology & Education Quarterly, 27*(2), 270–278.

Mehra, A., Kilduff, M., & Brass, D. J. (1998). At the Margins: A Distinctiveness Approach to Social Identity and Social Networks of Underrepresented Groups. *Academy of Management Journal, 41*(4), 441–452.

Mehra, R., Alspaugh, A., Dunn, J. T., Franck, L. S., McLemore, M. R., Keene, D. E., Kershaw, T. S., & Ickovics, J. R. (2023). "'Oh Gosh, Why Go?' Cause They Are Going to Look at Me and Not Hire": Intersectional Experiences of Black Women Navigating Employment During Pregnancy and Parenting. *BMC Pregnancy and Childbirth, 23*(1), 1–13.

Meredith, J. (1993). Theory Building Through Conceptual Methods. *International Journal of Operations & Production Management, 13*(5), 3–11.

Mero, N. P., & Motowidlo, S. J. (1995). Effects of Rater Accountability on the Accuracy and the Favorability of Performance Ratings. *Journal of Applied Psychology, 80*(4), 517–524.

Metcalfe, B. A. (1987). Male and Female Managers: An Analysis of Biographical and Self-Concept Data. *Work & Stress, 1*(3), 207–219.

Milem, J. F., Chang, M. J., & Antonio, A. L. (2005). *Making Diversity Work on Campus: A Research-Based Perspective.* Association American Colleges and Universities.

Miller, C. C. (1990). *Cognitive Diversity Within Management Teams: Implications for Strategic Decision Processes and Organizational Performance* [Unpublished doctoral dissertation]. Graduate School of Business, University of Texas.

Miller, C. C., Burke, L. M., & Glick, W. H. (1998). Cognitive Diversity Among Upper-Echelon Executives: Implications for Strategic Decision Processes. *Strategic Management Journal, 19*(1), 39–58.

Miller, C. C., Chiu, S., Wesley II, C. L., Vera, D., & Avery, D. R. (2022). Cognitive Diversity at the Strategic Apex: Assessing Evidence on the Value of Different Perspectives and Ideas among Senior Leaders. *Academy of Management Annals, 16*(2), 806–852.

Miller, G. A. (1956). The Magical Number Seven, Plus-Or-Minus Two: Some Limits on Our Capacity for Processing Information. *Psychological Review, 63*(2), 81–97.

Milliken, F. J., Morrison, E. W., & Hewlin, P. F. (2003). An Exploratory Study of Employee Silence: Issues That Employees Don't Communicate Upward and Why. *Journal of Management Studies, 40*(6), 1453–1476.

Mintzberg, H. (1998). Covert Leadership: Notes on Managing Professionals. Knowledge Workers Respond to Inspiration, Not Supervision. *Harvard Business Review, 76*(6), 140–147.

Mitchell, M. S., Rivera, G., & Treviño, L. K. (2023). Unethical Leadership: A Review, Analysis, and Research Agenda. *Personnel Psychology, 76*, 1–37. Advance online publication. https://doi.org/10.1111/peps.12574

Mitchell, T. (1974). Expectancy Models of Job Satisfaction, Occupational Preference and Effort: A Theoretical, Methodological, and Empirical Appraisal. *Psychological Bulletin, 81*(12), 1053–1077.

Mizell, C. A. (1999). African American Men's Personal Sense of Mastery: The Consequences of the Adolescent Environment, Self-Concept, and Adult Achievement. *Journal of Black Psychology, 25*(2), 210–230.

Mor Barak, M. E. (2015). Inclusion Is the Key to Diversity Management, but What Is Inclusion? *Human Service Organizations: Management, Leadership & Governance, 39*(2), 83–88.

Mor Barak, M. E. (2017). *Managing Diversity: Toward a Globally Inclusive Workplace* (4th ed.). Sage.

Moore, S. (1999). Understanding and Managing Diversity Among Groups at Work: Key Issues for Organisational Training and Development. *Journal of European Industrial Training, 23*(4/5), 208–218.

Moran, J. W., & Brightman, B. K. (2000). Leading Organizational Change. *Journal of Workplace Learning: Employee Counseling Today, 12*(2), 66–74.

Morrison, A. M. (1992). *The New Leaders: Guidelines on Leadership Diversity in America*. Jossey-Bass Publishers.

Morrison, E. W. (2023). Employee Voice and Silence: Taking Stock a Decade Later. *Annual Review of Organizational Psychology and Organizational Behavior, 10*(1), 79–107. https://doi.org/10.1146/annurev-orgpsych-120920-054654

Mosley, A. J., & Biernat, M. (2021). The New Identity Theft: Perceptions of Cultural Appropriation in Intergroup Contexts. *Journal of Personality and Social Psychology, 121*(2), 308.

Muchinsky, P. M. (2004). When the Psychometrics of Test Development Meets Organizational Realities: A Conceptual Framework for Organizational Change, Examples and Recommendations. *Personnel Psychology, 57*(1), 179–205. https://doi.org/10.1111/j.1744-6570.2004.tb02488.x

Münsterberg, H. (1913). *Psychology and Industrial Efficiency*. Houghton Mifflin.

Murphy, K. R. (1989). Is the Relationship Between Cognitive Ability and Job Performance Stable Over Time? *Human Performance, 2*(3), 183–200.

Murphy, K. R. (2008). Explaining the Weak Relationship between Job Performance and Ratings of Job Performance. *Industrial and Organizational Psychology: Perspectives on Science and Practice, 1*(2), 148–160.

Murphy, K. R., & Cleveland, J. N. (1991). *Performance Appraisal: Organizational Perspective*. Allyn & Bacon.

Murphy, S. E., & Ensher, E. A. (2001). The Role of Mentoring Support and Self-Management Strategies on Reported Career Outcomes. *Journal of Career Development, 27*(4), 229–246.

Myers, C. S. (1925). *Industrial Psychology*. The People's Institute Publishing Company.

Myrdal, G. (1944). *An American Dilemma*. Harper & Row.

Nagda, B. A., Spearmon, M. L., Holley, L. C., Harding, S., Balassone, M. L., Motse-Swanson, D., & de Mello, S. (1999). Intergroup Dialogues: An Innovative Approach to Teaching about Diversity and Justice in Social Work Programs. *Journal of Social Work Education, 35*(3), 433–449.

Nahapiet, J., & Ghoshal, S. (1998). Social Capital, Intellectual Capital, and the Organizational Advantage. *Academy of Management Review, 23*(2), 242–266.

Naidoo, A. V. (1990). *Factors Affecting the Career Maturity of African American Undergraduate Students: A Causal Model* [Unpublished doctoral dissertation]. Ball State University, Muncie, IN.

National Academies of Sciences, Engineering, and Medicine. (2023). *Advancing Antiracism, Diversity, Equity, and Inclusion in STEMM Organizations: Beyond Broadening Participation*. The National Academies Press. https://doi.org/10.17226/26803

Nauta, M. M., Epperson, D. L., & Kahn, J. H. (1998). A Multiple-Groups Analysis of Predictors of Higher Level Career Aspirations Among Women in Mathematics, Science, and Engineering. *Journal of Counseling Psychology, 45*(4), 483–496.

Near, J. P., Dworkin, T. M., & Miceli, M. P. (1993). Explaining the Whistle-Blowing Process: Suggestions from Power Theory and Justice Theory. *Organization Science, 4*(3), 393–411.

Neisser, U. (1967). *Cognitive Psychology*. Appleton-Century-Crofts.

Ng, E. S., & Sears, G. J. (2020). Walking the Talk on Diversity: CEO Beliefs, Moral Values, and the Implementation of Workplace Diversity Practices. *Journal of Business Ethics, 164*(3), 437–450. https://doi.org/10.1007/s10551-018-4051-7

Nishii, L. H., Khattab, J., Shemla, M., & Paluch, R. M. (2018). A Multi-Level Process Model for Understanding Diversity Practice Effectiveness. *Academy of Management Annals, 12*(1), 37–82.

Nkomo, S. M. (1992). The Emperor Has No Clothes: Rewriting "Race in Organizations." *Academy of Management Review, 17*(3), 487–513.

Nkomo, S. M., & Cox, T., Jr. (1989). Gender Differences in the Upward Mobility of Black Managers: Double Whammy or Double Advantage? *Sex Roles, 21*(11/12), 825–839.

Nkomo, S. M., Bell, M. P., Roberts, L. M., Joshi, A., & Thatcher, S. M. B. (2019). Diversity at a Critical Juncture: New Theories for a Complex Phenomenon. *Academy of Management Review, 44*(3), 498–517.

North, C. S., Gordon, M., Kim, Y.-S., Wallace, N. E., Smith, R. P., Pfefferbaum, B., Hong, B. A., Ali, O., Wang, C., & Pollio, D. E. (2014). Expression of Ethnic Prejudice in Focus Groups from Agencies Affected by the 9/11 Attacks on the World Trade Center. *Journal of Ethnic and Cultural Diversity in Social Work, 23*(2), 93–109.

Obasi, C. (2022). Black Social Workers: Identity, Racism, Invisibility/ Hypervisibility at Work. *Journal of Social Work, 22*(2), 479–497.

Odiorne, G. S. (1965). *Management by Objectives: A System of Managerial Leadership*. Pitman Publishing.

Office of Federal Contract Compliance Programs (OFCCP). (2014). *Executive Order 11246: EEO and Affirmative Action Guidelines for Federal Contractors Regarding Race, Color, Gender, Religion, and National Origin*. http://www.dol.gov/ofccp/regs/compliance/fs11246.htm

Ogbu, J. U. (1988). Black Education: A Cultural-Ecological Perspective. In H. P. McAdoo (Ed.), *Black Families* (pp. 79–94). Sage.

Okpokiri, C. (2022). We Are Never Going Back—Social Workers Should Be Proud 'Woke Champions.' *British Journal of Social Work, 52*(7), 3777–3782.

O'Leary, B. J., & Weathington, B. L. (2006). Beyond the Business Case for Diversity in Organizations. *Employee Responsibilities & Rights Journal, 18*(4), 1–10. https://doi.org/10.1007/s10672-006-9024-9

O'Leary-Kelly, A. M., & Newman, J. L. (2004). The Implications of Performance Feedback Research for Understanding Antisocial Work Behavior. *Human Resource Management Review, 13*(4), 605–629.

Olson, S. J. (1999). Gender Equity in Workforce Education. In A. J. Paulter Jr. (Ed.), *Workforce Education: Issues for the New Century* (pp. 223–239). Prakken Publications.

Ormrod, J. E. (1999). *Human Learning* (3rd ed.). Prentice-Hall.

Orpen, C. (1994). The Effects of Organizational and Individual Career Management on Career Success. *International Journal of Manpower, 15*(1), 27–37.

Orr, J. E. (1996). *Talking About Machines. An Ethnography of a Modern Job*. ILR Press/Cornell University Press.

Osland, J., Mendenhall, M. E., Bird, A., Oddou, G. R., Maznevski, M. L., Stevens, M., & Stahl, G. K. (2013). *Global Leadership: Research, Practice and Development* (2nd ed.). Routledge Global Human Resource Management Series, Taylor & Francis Publishing.

Page, S. E., & Difference, T. (2007). *How the Power of Diversity Creates Better Groups, Firms, Schools, and Societies.* Princeton University Press.

Paglis, L. L. (1999). *Searching for the Wellspring of Leading Change: Leader Self-Efficacy in Organizations* [Unpublished doctoral dissertation]. Purdue University, West Lafayette, IN.

Paglis, L. L., & Green, S. G. (2002). Leadership Self-Efficacy and Managers' Motivation for Leading Change. *Journal of Organizational Behavior, 23*(2), 215–235.

Pajares, F. (1996). Self-Efficacy Beliefs in Academic Settings. *Review of Educational Research, 66*(4), 543–578.

Paradies, Y. (2006). A Systematic Review of Empirical Research on Self-Reported Racism and Health. *International Journal of Epidemiology, 35*(4), 888–901.

Pareek, U. (1989). Motivational Analysis of Organizations-Climate (MAO-C). In J. W. Pfeiffer (Ed.), *The 1989 Annual: Developing Human Resources* (pp. 161–180). Pfeiffer & Company.

Parham, T. A., & Austin, N. L. (1994). Career Development and African Americans: A Contextual Reappraisal Using the Nigrescence Construct. *Journal of Vocational Behavior, 44*(2), 139–154.

Park, S., Park, S., & Shryack, J. (2022). Measures of Climate for Inclusion and Diversity: Review and Summary. *Human Resource Development Quarterly,* 1–18. https://doi.org/10.1002/hrdq.21493

Parker, P. S. (2001). African American Women Executives' Leadership Communication within Dominant-Culture Organizations: (Re) Conceptualizing Notions of Collaboration and Instrumentality. *Management Communication Quarterly, 15*(1), 42–82.

Parker, P. S. (2005). *Race, Gender, and Leadership: Re-Envisioning Organizational Leadership from the Perspectives of African American Women Executives.* Lawrence Erlbaum Associates, Publishers.

Parker, P. S., & dt olgivie. (1996). Gender, Culture, and Leadership: Toward a Culturally Distinct Model of African-American Women Executives' Leadership Strategies. *The Leadership Quarterly, 7*(2), 189–214.

Patterson, O. (1982). *Slavery and Social Death: A Comparative Study.* Harvard University Press.

Patton, W., & McMahon, M. (2006). *Career Development and Systems Theory: Connecting Theory and Practice* (2nd ed., Vol. 1). Sense Publishers.

Paulsen, A. M., & Betz, N. E. (2004). Basic Confidence Predictors of Career Decision-Making Self-Efficacy. *The Career Development Quarterly, 52*(4), 354–362.

Pavlov, I. P. (1927). *Conditioned Reflexes.* Routledge and Kegan Paul.

Pearson, S. M., & Bieschke, K. J. (2001). Succeeding Against the Odds: An Examination of Familial Influences on the Career Development of Professional African American Women. *Journal of Counseling Psychology, 48*(3), 301–309.

Pendry, L. F., Driscoll, D. M., & Susannah, C. T. F. (2007). Diversity Training: Putting Theory into Practice. *Journal of Occupational & Organizational Psychology, 80*(1), 27–50. *Academic Search Elite*, EBSCO*host* (Accessed 18 Dec 2014).

Penrose, E. T. (1959). *The Theory of the Growth of the Firm*. Wiley.

Perna, L., Lundy-Wagner, V., Drezner, N. D., Gasman, M., Yoon, S., Bose, E., & Gary, S. (2009). The Contribution of HBCUs to the Preparation of African American Women for STEM Careers: A Case Study. *Research in Higher Education, 50*(1), 1–23.

Perry, B. (2000). Button-Down Terror: The Metamorphosis of the Hate Movement. *Sociological Focus, 33*(2), 113–131.

Petersen, R. D. (2002). *Understanding Ethnic Violence: Fear, Hatred, and Resentment in Twentieth-Century Eastern Europe*. Cambridge University Press.

Peterson, L. (1999). The Definition of Diversity: Two Views. A More Specific Definition. *Journal of Library Administration, 27*(1–2), 17–26. https://doi.org/10.1300/J111v27n01_03

Petrides, K. V., & Furnham, A. (2000, March). Gender Differences in Measured and Self-Estimated Trait Emotional Intelligence. *Sex Roles, 42*(5–6), 449–461.

Pettigrew, A. M. (1979). On Studying Organizational Culture. *Administrative Science Quarterly, 24*(4), 570–581.

Pfeffer, J. (1992). *Managing with Power: Politics and Influence in Organizations*. Harvard Business School Press.

Pfeffer, J. (1994). *Competitive Advantage Through People: Unleashing the Power of the Work Force*. Harvard Business School Press.

Pfeffer, J. (1998). *The Human Equation. Building Profits by Putting People First*. Harvard Business School.

Pfeffer, J., & Sutton, R. I. (2006). Evidence-Based Management. *Harvard Business Review, 84*(1), 62–75.

Phillips, J. J. (2003). *Return on Investment in Training and Performance Improvement Programs* (2nd ed.). Elsevier Science.

Phillips, U. B. (1918). *American Negro Slavery: A Survey of the Supply, Employment and Control of Negro Labor as Determined by the Plantation Regime*. D. Appleton.

Phillips, T., & Smith, P. (2003). Everyday Incivility: Towards a Benchmark. *The Sociological Review, 51*(1), 85–108.

Piaget, J. (1959). *The Language and Thought of the Child*. Routledge.

Piaget, J. (1970). *Structuralism*. Basic Books.

Pierce, C. (1995). Stress Analogs of Racism and Sexism: Terrorism, Torture, and Disaster. *Mental Health, Racism, and Sexism, 33*, 277–293.

Pierce, C. M. (1970, November). Black Psychiatry One Year After Miami. *Journal of the National Medical Association, 62*(6), 471–473. PMID: 5493608; PMCID: PMC2611929.

Pine II, B. J. (1992). *Mass Customization: The New Frontier in Business Competition*. Harvard Business School.

Pitts, D. W. (2006). Modeling the Impact of Diversity Management. *Review of Public Personnel Administration, 26*(3), 245–268.

Plitmann, Y. (2022). Authentic Compliance with a Symbolic Legal Standard? How Critical Race Theory Can Change Institutionalist Studies on Diversity in the Workplace. *Law & Social Inquiry, 47*(1), 331–346. https://doi.org/10.1017/lsi.2021.38

Plummer, D. L. (2003). *Handbook of Diversity Management: Beyond Awareness to Competency Based Learning*. University Press of America.

Polanyi, M. (1966). *Tacit Dimension*. Doubleday Publishing.

Pope Francis. (2014). *The Joy of the Gospel* (p. 21). BookBaby.

Portocarrero, S., & Carter, J. T. (2022). Diversity Initiatives in the US Workplace: A Brief History, Their Intended and Unintended Consequences. *Sociology Compass, 16*(7), e13001. https://doi.org/10.1111/soc4.13001

Porter, M. W. (1980). *Competitive Strategy*. Free Press.

Porter, L. W., & Lawler, E. E. (1968). *Managerial Attitudes and Performance*. Richard D. Irwin.

Porter, L. W., & Steers, R. M. (1973). Organizational, Work, and Personal Factors in Employee Turnover and Absenteeism. *Journal of Management, 80*(2), 151–176.

Posner, B. Z., & Kouzes, J. M. (1988). Development and Validation of the Leadership Practices Inventory. *Educational and Psychological Measurement, 48*(2), 483–496.

Posner, B. Z., & Kouzes, J. M. (1993). Psychometric Properties of the Leadership Practices Inventory-Updated. *Educational and Psychological Measurement, 53*(1), 191–199.

Post, C., Muzio, D., Sarala, R., Wei, L., & Faems, D. (2021). Theorizing Diversity in Management Studies: New Perspectives and Future Directions. *Journal of Management Studies, 58*(8), 2003–2023.

Powell, G. N. (1999). *Handbook of Gender and Work*. Sage.

Powell, G. N., & Butterfield, D. A. (1994). Race, Gender and the Glass Ceiling: Empirical Study of Actual Promotions to Top Management. In *Annual Meeting of the Academy of Management*, Dallas, TX.

Prasad, A. (2022). The Model Minority and the Limits of Workplace Inclusion. *Academy of Management Review*. https://doi.org/10.5465/amr.2021.0352

Pratt, J. W. (1927). The Origin of "Manifest Destiny". *The American Historical Review, 32*(4), 795–798.

Pred, A. R. (2004). *The Past Is Not Dead: Facts, Fictions, and Enduring Racial Stereotypes.* University of Minnesota Press.

Prime, J. L. (2005). *Women "Take Care", Men "Take Charge".* Catalyst Inc.

Pullen, E., Fischer, M. W., Morse, G., Garabrant, J., Salyers, M. P., & Rollins, A. L. (2023). Racial Disparities in the Workplace: The Impact of Isolation on Perceived Organizational Support and Job Satisfaction. *Psychiatric Rehabilitation Journal, 46*(1), 45–52. https://doi.org/10.1037/prj0000543

Pyant, C. T., & Yanico, B. J. (1991). Relationship of Racial Identity and Gender Role Attitudes to Black Women's Psychological Well-Being. *Journal of Counseling Psychology, 38*(3), 315–322.

Qin, J., Muenjohn, N., & Chhetri, P. (2014). A Review of Diversity Conceptualizations: Variety, Trends, and a Framework. *Human Resource Development Review, 13*(2), 133–157.

Quillian, L., Pager, D., Hexel, O., & Midtbøen, A. H. (2017). Meta-Analysis of Field Experiments Shows No Change in Racial Discrimination in Hiring Over Time. *Proceedings of the National Academy of Sciences, 114*(41), 10870–10875. https://doi.org/10.1073/pnas.1706255114

Raghavan, M., Barocas, S., Kleinberg, J., & Levy, K. (2020). Mitigating Bias in Algorithmic Hiring: Evaluating Claims and Practices. In *Proceedings of the 2020 Conference on Fairness, Accountability, and Transparency* (pp. 469–481).

Ragins, B. R., & Sundstrom, E. (1989). Gender and Power in Organizations: A Longitudinal Perspective. *Psychological Bulletin, 105*(1), 51–88.

Rajesh, S. (2023, March 19). *Being a Diversity Ally—How Much Is Too Much? Allies at Workplaces Must Champion Their Marginalised Colleagues' Voices Without Being Patronising Towards Them.* https://www.thehindubusinessline.com/opinion/being-a-diversity-ally-how-much-is-too-much/article66639186.ece

Ramlall, S. (2004). A Review of Employee Motivation Theories and Their Implications for Employee Retention within Organizations. *Journal of American Academy of Business, Cambridge, 5*(1/2), 52–63.

Ramsey, M. (1986). *The Super Supervisor.* Positive Presentations.

Randel, A. E., Galvin, B. M., Shore, L. M., Ehrhart, K. H., Chung, B. G., Dean, M. A., & Kedharnath, U. (2018). Inclusive Leadership: Realizing Positive Outcomes Through Belongingness and Being Valued for Uniqueness. *Human Resource Management Review, 28*(2), 190–203.

Ray, V. (2019). A Theory of Racialized Organizations. *American Sociological Review, 84*(1), 26–53.

Redding, G. (2007). The Chess Master and the 10 Simultaneous Opponents: But What If the Game Is Poker? Implications for the Global Mindset. In M.

Javidan, R. M. Steers, & M. A. Hitt (Eds.), *The Global Mindset* (Vol. 19, pp. 49–73). Elsevier.

Redmond, M. V. (2000). Cultural Distance as a Mediating Factor Between Stress and Intercultural Communication Competence. *International Journal of Intercultural Relations, 24*(1), 151–159.

Reich, R. B. (1992). *The Work of Nations: Preparing Ourselves for 21st Century Capitalism* (Rev. ed.). Vintage Books.

Reich, R. B. (2010). *Aftershock: The Next Economy and America's Future*. Alfred A. Knopf.

Resnicow, K., Stiffler, M. J., & Ajrouch, K. J. (2022). Looking Back: The Contested Whiteness of Arab Identity. *American Journal of Public Health, 112*(8), 1092–1096.

Reynolds-Dobbs, W., Thomas, K. M., & Harrison, M. S. (2008, January). From Mammy to Superwoman: Images That Hinder Black Women's Career Development. *Journal of Career Development, 35*(2), 129–150.

Richie, B. S., Fassinger, R. E., Linn, S. G., Johnson, J., Prosser, J., & Robinson. S. (1997). Persistence, Connection, and Passion: A Qualitative Study of the Career Development of Highly Achieving African American-Black and White Women. *Journal of Counseling Psychology, 44*(2), 133–148.

Ridgeway, C. L. (1982). Status in Groups: The Importance of Motivation. *American Sociological Review, 47*(1), 76–88.

Reynolds, D., Rahman, I., & Bradetich, S. (2014). Hotel Managers' Perceptions of the Value of Diversity Training: An Empirical Investigation. *International Journal of Contemporary Hospitality Management, 26*(3), 426–446.

Roberson, L., Kulik, C. T., & Pepper, M. B. (2001). Designing Effective Diversity Training: Influence of Group Composition and Trainee Experience. *Journal of Organizational Behavior, 22*(8), 871–885.

Roberson, L., Kulik, C. T., & Pepper, M. B. (2003). Using Needs Assessment to Resolve Controversies in Diversity Training Design. *Group & Organization Management, 28*(1), 148–174.

Roberson, Q. M. (2019). Diversity in the Workplace: A Review, Synthesis, and Future Research Agenda. *Annual Review of Organizational Psychology and Organizational Behavior, 6*, 69–88.

Roberson, Q., Moore, O. A., & Bell, B. S. (2022). An Active Learning Approach to Diversity Training. *Academy of Management Review*.

Roberts, S. O., & Rizzo, M. T. (2021). The Psychology of American Racism. *American Psychologist, 76*(3), 475–487.

Robinson, E. (2010). *Disintegration: The Splintering of Black America*. Doubleday.

Robbins, S. (2013, Fall). Culture as Communication. *Harvard Business Review Onpoint*, 18–20.

Robbins, S. P. (2005). *Organizational Behavior* (11th ed.). Pearson Prentice Hall.

Robbins, S. P., & Judge, T. (2011). *Organizational Behavior* (14th ed.). Prentice Hall.

Robnett, B. (1996). African American Women in the Civil Rights Movement, 1954–1965: Gender, Leadership, and Micro-Mobilization. *The American Journal of Sociology, 101*(6), 1661–1693.

Rocco, T. S., & Plakhotnik, M. S. (2009). Literature Reviews, Conceptual Frameworks, and Theoretical Frameworks: Terms, Functions, and Distinctions. *Human Resource Development Review, 8*, 120–130.

Roe, A., & Lunneborg, P. W. (1990). Personality Development and Career Choice. In D. Brown & L. Brooks (Eds.), *Career Choice and Development: Applying Contemporary Theories and Practice* (pp. 68–101). Jossey-Bass.

Rogers, E. M. (1983). *Diffusion of Innovations* (3rd ed.). Free Press.

Ross, E. (2005, April). Find Talent and Use It. *Business Review Weekly, 27*(4), 66–68.

Ross-Gordon, J. M., & Brooks, A. K. (2004). Diversity in Human Resource Development and Continuing Professional Education: What Does It Mean for the Workforce, Clients, and Professionals? *Advances in Developing Human Resources, 6*(1), 69–85.

Rothwell, W. J., Jackson, R. D., Knight, S. C., & Lindholm, J. E. (2005). *Career Planning and Succession Management: Developing Your Organization's Talent—For Today and Tomorrow.* Praeger Publishers.

Rouiller, J. Z., & Goldstein, I. L. (1993). The Relationship Between Organizational Transfer Climate and Positive Transfer of Training. *Human Resource Development Quarterly, 4*(4), 377–390.

Rubin, P. J. (1998). Equal Rights, Special Rights, and the Nature of Antidiscrimination Law. *Michigan Law Review, 97*(2), 564–598.

Rudman, L. A. (1998). Self-Promotion as a Risk Factor for Women: The Costs and Benefits of Counter Stereotypical Impression Management. *Journal of Personality and Social Psychology, 74*(3), 629–645.

Ruggs, E. N., Hebl, M., & Shockley, K. M. (2023). Fighting the 400-Year Pandemic: Racism Against Black People in Organizations. *Journal of Business and Psychology, 38*(1), 1–5.

Rynes, S., & Rosen, B. (1995). A Field Survey of Factors Affecting the Adoption and Perceived Success of Diversity Training. *Personnel Psychology, 48*(2), 247–271.

Sakr, N., Son Hing, L. S., & González-Morales, M. G. (2023). Development and Validation of the Marginalized-Group-Focused Diversity Climate Scale: Group Differences and Outcomes. *Journal of Business Psychology.* https://doi.org/10.1007/s10869-022-09859-3

Salcedo, A., Williams, P., Elias, S., Valencia, M., & Perez, J. (2022). Future Direction in HRD: The Potential of Testimonio as an Approach to Perturb the Dominant Practices in the Workplace. *European Journal of Training and Development, 46*(7/8), 727–739. https://doi.org/10.1108/ejtd-07-2021-0109.

Salovey, P., & Mayer, J. D. (1990). Emotional Intelligence. *Imagination, Cognition and Personality, 9*(3), 185–211.

Sandberg, S. (2013). *Lean In: Women, Work, and the Will to Lead.* Alfred Knopf.

Sanders, J. (2004). *Understand Behavioral Style Differences.* Get GenderSmart! Empowerment Enterprises.

Savickas, M., & Lent, R. W. (1994). *Convergence in Career Development Theories.* Consulting Psychologists Press.

Schein, E. H. (1975). How Career Anchors Hold Executives to Their Career Paths. *Personnel, 52*(3), 11–24.

Schein, E. H. (1983). The Role of the Founder in Creating Organizational Culture. *Organizational Dynamics, 12*(1), 13–28.

Schein, E. H. (1984). Coming to a New Awareness of Organizational Culture. *Sloan Management Review, 25*(2), 3–16.

Schein, E. H. (1988). Organizational Socialization and the Profession of Management. *The Sloan Management Review, 30*(1), 53–65.

Schein, E. H. (1990). Organizational Culture. *American Psychologist, 43*(2), 109–119.

Schlesinger, A. J. (2005). The American Empire? Not so Fast. *World Policy Journal, 22*(1), 43–46.

Scholz, U., Doña, B. G., Sud, S., & Schwarzer, R. (2002). Is General Self-Efficacy a Universal Construct? Psychometric Findings from 25 Countries. *European Journal of Psychological Assessment, 18*(3), 242–251.

Schmader, T., Johns, M., & Forbes, C. (2008). An Integrated Process Model of Stereotype Threat Effects on Performance. *Psychological Review, 115*(2), 336–356.

Schmidt, F. L., & Hunter, J. E. (2000). Select on Intelligence. In E. A. Locke (Ed.), *The Blackwell Handbook of Organizational Principles* (pp. 3–14). Blackwell.

Schmidt, F. L., Hunter, J. E., & Outerbridge, A. N. (1986). Impact of Job Experience and Ability on Job Knowledge, Work Sample Performance, and Supervisory Ratings of Job Performance. *Journal of Applied Psychology, 71*(3), 432–439.

Schneider, D. J. (2005). *The Psychology of Stereotyping.* Guilford Press.

Schreiber, C. T., Price, K. F., & Morrison, A. (1993). Workplace Diversity and the Glass Ceiling: Practices, Barriers, Possibilities. *Human Resource Planning, 16*(2), 51–69.

Schuler, R. S., Dowling, P. J., Smart, J. P., & Huber, V. L. (1992). *Human Resource Management in Australia* (2nd ed.). Harper Educational Publishers.

Schunk, D. H., & Pajares, F. (2002). The Development of Academic Self-Efficacy. In A. Wigfield & J. S. Eccles (Eds.), *Development of Achievement Motivation* (pp. 15–31). Academic Press. https://doi.org/10.1016/B978-012750053-9/50003-6

Schwartz, T. (2014, Summer). What Women Know About Leadership That Men Don't. *Harvard Business Review Onpoint, 16–17*.

Schwarzer, R., & Jerusalem, M. (1995). Generalized Self-Efficacy Scale. In J. Weinman, S. Wright, & M. Johnston (Eds.), *Measures in Health Psychology: A User's Portfolio. Causal and Control Beliefs* (pp. 35–37). NFER-NELSON.

Scott, C. L. (2014). Historical Perspectives. In M. Y. Byrd & C. L. Scott (Eds.), *Diversity in the Workforce: Current Issues and Emerging Trends* (pp. 3–33). Routledge.

Scott, C. L., & Klein, L. B. (2022). Advancing Traditional Leadership Theories by Incorporating Multicultural and Workforce Diversity Leadership Traits, Behaviors, and Supporting practices: Implications for Organizational Leaders. *Journal of Leadership, Accountability and Ethics, 19*(3), 1–11.

Scott, W. R. (1987). The Adolescence of Institutional Theory. *Administrative Science Quarterly, 32*(4), 493–511.

Scott, W. R. (2004). Institutional Theory. In G. Ritzer (Eds.), *Encyclopedia of Social Theory* (pp. 408–414). Sage.

Seales, D. J. (1987). *Factors Which Influence The Professional Success of Black Women: Implications For Career Development*. UMI.

Seigel, M. L. (2004). On Collegiality. *Journal of Legal Education, 54*, 406–441.

Selznick, P. (1949). *TVA and the Grass Roots: A Study of Politics and Organization*. University of California Press.

Senge, P. M. (1990). *The Fifth Discipline: The Art and Practice of the Learning Organization*. Doubleday.

Servan-Schreiber, J.-J. (1967). *The American Challenge*. Atheneum Publishers.

Sesko, A. K., & Biernat, M. (2010). Prototypes of Race and Gender: The Invisibility of Black Women. *Journal of Experimental Social Psychology, 46*(2), 356–360.

Shaw, J., Wickenden, M., Thompson, S., & Mader, P. (2022). Achieving Disability Inclusive Employment—Are the Current Approaches Deep Enough? *Journal of International Development, 34*(5), 942–963.

Shen, J., Chanda, A., D'netto, B., & Monga, M. (2009). Managing Diversity Through Human Resource Management: An International Perspective and Conceptual Framework. *The International Journal of Human Resource Management, 20*(2), 235–251.

Shore, L. M., & Chung, B. G. (2023). Enhancing Leader Inclusion While Preventing Social Exclusion in the Work Group. *Human Resource Management Review, 33*(1), 100902.

Shorter-Gooden, K. (2004). Multiple Resistance Strategies: How African American Women Cope with Racism and Sexism. *Journal of Black Psychology, 30*(3), 406–425.

Shin, H., & Kim, S. (2022). Overcoming Women's Isolation at Work: The Effect of Organizational Structure and Practices on Female Managers' Workplace Relationships. *International Sociology, 37*(3), 330–354. https://doi.org/10.1177/02685809211051282

Shipman, C., & Kay, K. (2009). *Womenomics: Write Your Own Rules for Success.* HarperCollins.

Siegel, R. B. (1985). Employment Equality Under the Pregnancy Discrimination Act of 1978. *Yale Law Journal, 94*(4), 929–956.

Siems, M. (2019). The Law and Ethics of 'Cultural Appropriation.' *International Journal of Law in Context, 15*(4), 408–423.

Silberman, M. L. (1998). *Active Training* (2nd ed.). Jossey-Bass/Pfeiffer.

Silva, C., Carter, N. M., & Beninger, A. (2012). Good Intentions, Imperfect Execution: Women Get Fewer of the "Hot Jobs" Needed to Advance. *Catalyst*, 15–17.

Sims, C. (2010). The Impact of African American Skin Tone Bias in the Workplace: Implications for Critical Human Resource Development. *Online Journal for Workforce Education and Development, 3*(4), 1–17.

Sims, C. M., & Carter, A. D. (2019). Revisiting Parker & ogilvie's African American Women Executive Leadership Model. *The Journal of Business Diversity, 19*(2), 99–112.

Simpson, G. (1984). The Daughters of Charlotte Ray: The Career Development Process During the Exploratory and Establishment Stages of Black Women Attorneys. *Sex Roles, 2*(1/2), 113–139.

Sinclair, A. (2000). Teaching Managers About Masculinities: Are You Kidding? *Management Learning, 31*(1), 83–101.

Singh, R., Ragins, B. R., & Tharenou, P. (2009). What Matters Most? The Relative Role of Mentoring and Career Capital in Career Success. *Journal of Vocational Behavior, 75*(1), 56–67.

Sissoko, D. R. G., Lewis, J. A., & Nadal, K. L. (2023). It's More Than Skin-Deep: Gendered Racial Microaggressions, Skin Tone Satisfaction, and Traumatic Stress Symptoms Among Black Women. *Journal of Black Psychology, 49*(2), 127–152.

Sitzmann, T., Brown, K. G., Casper, W. J., Ely, K., & Zimmerman, R. D. (2008). A Review and Meta-Analysis of the Nomological Network of Trainee Reactions. *Journal of Applied Psychology, 93*(2), 280–295.

Skinner, B. F. (1953). *Science and Human Behavior*. Macmillan.

Skinner, B. F. (1957). *Verbal Learning*. Appleton-Century-Crofts.

Slepian, M. L., & Jacoby-Senghor, D. S. (2021). Identity Threats in Everyday Life: Distinguishing Belonging from Inclusion. *Social Psychological and Personality Science, 12*(3), 392–406.

Smith, A. N., Watkins, M. B., Ladge, J. J., & Carlton, P. (2019). Making the Invisible Visible: Paradoxical Effects of Intersectional Invisibility on the Career Experiences of Executive Black Women. *Academy of Management Journal, 62*(6), 1705–1734.

Smith, I. A., & Griffiths, A. (2022). Microaggressions, Everyday Discrimination, Workplace Incivilities, and Other Subtle Slights at Work: A Meta-Synthesis. *Human Resource Development Review, 21*(3), 275–299.

Smith, F. (1975). *Comprehension and Learning*. Holt, Rinehart & Winston.

Smith, I. A., & Griffiths, A. (2022). Microaggressions, Everyday Discrimination, Workplace Incivilities, and Other Subtle Slights at Work: A Meta-Synthesis. *Human Resource Development Review, 21*(3), 275–299.

Smith, R. A. (2002). Race, Gender, and Authority in the Workplace: Theory and Research. *Annual Review of Sociology, 28*(1), 509–542. https://doi.org/10.1146/annurev.soc.28.110601.141048

Smithey, P. N., & Lewis, G. B. (1998). Gender, Race and Training in the Federal Civil Service. *Public Administration Quarterly, 22*(2), 204–228.

Snell, S. A., & Dean, J. W. (1992). Integrated Manufacturing and Human Resource Management: A Human Capital Perspective. *Academy of Management Journal, 35*(3), 467–504.

Sodano, A. G., & Baler, S. G. (1983). Accommodation to Contrast: Being Different in the Organization. *New Directions for Mental Health Services, 20*(December), 25–36.

Sokoloff, N. J. (1992). *Black Women and White Women in the Professions: Occupational Segregation by Race and Gender, 1960–1980*. Routledge.

Sonnemaker, T. (2021). 2020 Brought a Wave of Discrimination and Harassment Allegations Against Major Companies Like Amazon, McDonald's, and Pinterest. These Are Some of the Year's High-Profile Legal Battles. *Business Insider*. https://www.businessinsider.com/every-company-that-was-sued-discrimination-and-harassment-lawsuits-2020-2021-1

Stata, R. (1989). Organizational Learning: The Key to Management Innovation. *Sloan Management Review, 30*(3), 63–74.

Stefancic, J. (2011). Terrace v. Thompson and the Legacy of Manifest Destiny. *Nevada Law Journal, 12*, 532–548.

Stephenson, K., & Lewin, D. (1996). Managing Workforce Diversity: Macro and Micro Level HR Implications of Network Analysis. *International Journal of Manpower, 17*(4/5), 168–196.

Stern, W. (1912). *The Psychological Methods of Intelligence Testing* (G. Whipple, Trans.). Warwick and York.

Sternberg, R. J. (1986). A Framework for Understanding Conceptions of Intelligence. In R. J. Sternberg & D. K. Detterman (Eds.), *What Is Intelligence? Contemporary Viewpoints on Its Nature and Definition* (pp. 3–15). Able.

Sternberg, R. J. (1997). *Successful Intelligence.* Plume.

Sternberg, R. J. (1999). The Theory of Successful Intelligence. *Review of General Psychology, 3*(4), 292–316. https://doi.org/10.1037/1089-2680.3.4.292

Sternberg, R. J. (2002). Successful Intelligence: A New Approach to Leadership. In R. E. Riggio, S. E. Murphy, & F.J. Pirozzolo (Eds.), *Multiple Intelligences and Leadership,* (pp. 9–28). Erlbaum.

Sternberg, R. J., & Vroom, V. H. (2002). The Person Versus the Situation in Leadership. *The Leadership Quarterly, 13*(3), 301–323.

Stevens, F. G., Plaut, V. C., & Sanchez-Burks, J. (2008). Unlocking the Benefits of Diversity: All-Inclusive Multiculturalism and Positive Organizational Change. *Journal of Applied Behavioral Science, 44*(1), 116–133.

Stewart, T. A. (1999). *Intellectual Capital: The New Wealth of Organizations.* Doubleday.

Stone, P. (2013). Opting Out: Challenging Stereotypes and Creating Real Options for Women in the Professions. In *Research Symposium: Gender & Work: Challenging Conventional Wisdom* (Vol. 28). Harvard Business School.

Stoner-Zemel, M. J. (1988). *Visionary Leadership, Management, and High Performing Work Units: An Analysis of Workers' Perceptions* [Unpublished Doctoral Dissertation]. University of Massachusetts, Amherst, Amherst, MA.

Storberg-Walker, J. (2005). Towards a Theory of Human Capital Transformation Through Human Resource Development. In M. L. Morris & F. M. Nafukho (Eds.), *2005 Academy of Human Resource Development Annual Research Conference Proceeding* (pp. 323–330). Academy of Human Resource Development.

Strach, L., & Wicander, L. (1993). Fitting In: Issues of Tokenism and Conformity for Minority Women. *S.A.M. Advanced Management Journal, 59*(3), 22–25.

Sue, D. W. (2004). Whiteness and Ethnocentric Monoculturalism: Making the "Invisible" Visible. *American Psychologist, 59*(8), 759–769.

Sun, T., Schilpzand, P., & Liu, Y. (2023). Workplace Gossip: An Integrative Review of Its Antecedents, Functions, and Consequences. *Journal of Organizational Behavior, 44*(2), 311–334. https://doi.org/10.1002/job.2653

Sum, A., & Khatiwada, I. (2010). The Nation's Underemployed in the 'Great Recession' of 2007–09. *Monthly Labor Review, 133*(11), 3–15.

Super, D. E. (1953). A Theory of Vocational Development. *American Psychologist, 30*(5), 88–92.

Super, D. E. (1980). A Life-Span, Life-Space Approach to Career Development. *Journal of Vocational Behavior, 16*(3), 229–298.

Super, D. E. (1990). A Life-Span, Life-Space Approach to Career Development. In D. Brown, L. Brooks, & Associates (Eds.), *Career Choice Development* (2nd ed., pp. 197–261). Jossey-Bass.

Stainback, K., Tomaskovic-Devey, D., & Skaggs, S. (2010). Organizational Approaches to Inequality: Inertia, Relative Power, and Environments. *Annual Review of Sociology, 36*, 225–247. https://www.annualreviews.org/doi/pdf/10.1146/annurev-soc-070308-120014

Stitt-Gohdes, W. L. (1997). *Career Development: Issues of Gender, Race, and Class* (Information Series No. 371). ERIC Clearinghous on Adult, Career and Vocational Education.

Sue, D. W., Capodilupo, C. M., Torino, G. C., Bucceri, J. M., Holder, A., Nadal, K. L., & Esquilin, M. (2007). Racial Microaggressions in Everyday Life: Implications for Clinical Practice. *American Psychologist, 62*(4), 271–286.

Susskind, A. M., Brymer, R. A., Kim, W. G., Lee, H. Y., & Way, S. A. (2014). Attitudes and Perceptions Toward Affirmative Action Programs: An Application of Institutional Theory. *International Journal of Hospitality Management, 41*, 38–48.

Swanson, D. (2002). Diversity Programs: Attitudes and Realities in the Contemporary Corporate Environment. *Corporate Communications, 7*(4), 257–269.

Swanson, J. L., & Fouad, N. A. (2010). *Career Theory and Practice: Learning Through Case Studies* (2nd ed.). Sage.

Swanson, R. A. (2007). Theory Framework for Applied Disciplines: Boundaries, Contributing, Core, Useful, Novel, and Irrelevant Components. *Human Resource Development Review, 6*(3), 321–339.

Swanson, R. A., & Holton, E. F. (2001). *Foundation of Human Resource Development*. Berrett-Koehler Publishers.

Swanson, R. A., & Holton, E. F. (2009). *Foundations of Human Resource Development* (2nd ed.). Berrett-Koehler Publishers.

Swart, J. (2006). Intellectual Capital: Disentangling an Enigmatic Concept. *Journal of Intellectual Capital, 7*(2), 136–159.

Swim, J. K., & Cohen, L. L. (1997). Overt, Covert, and Subtle Sexism a Comparison Between the Attitudes Toward Women and Modern Sexism Scales. *Psychology of Women Quarterly, 21*(1), 103–118.

Swim, J. K., Hyers, L. L., Cohen, L. L., & Ferguson, M. J. (2001). Everyday Sexism: Evidence for Its Incidence, Nature, and Psychological Impact from Three Daily Diary Studies. *Journal of Social Issues, 57*(1), 31–53.

Tabassum, N., & Nayak, B. S. (2021). Gender Stereotypes and Their Impact on Women's Career Progressions from a Managerial Perspective. *IIM Kozhikode Society & Management Review, 10*(2), 192–208.

Talat, A., Khan, S. N., Chaudary, S., & Neale, N. R. (2023). Investigating the ICT for Team Creativity: A Team Sensemaking Perspective. *IIMB Management Review*, 1–31. https://doi.org/10.1016/j.iimb.2023.03.004

Talley-Ross, N. C. (1995). *Jagged Edges: Black Professional Women in White Male Worlds*. Peter Lang.

Tallarigo, R. (1998). Discrimination, Harassment, and the Failure of Diversity Training: What to Do Now. *Personnel Psychology, 51*(3), 749–752.

Tambe, P., Cappelli, P., & Yakubovich, V. (2019). Artificial Intelligence in Human Resources Management: Challenges and a Path Forward. *California Management Review, 61*(4), 15–42.

Tan, D., Morris, L., & Romero, J. (1996). Changes in Attitude After Diversity Training. *Training & Development, 50*(9), 54–56.

Tang, J. (2000). *Doing Engineering: The Career Attainment and Mobility of Caucasian, Black, and Asian-American Engineers*. Rowman & Littlefield.

Tarique, I., & Schuler, R. S. (2010). Global Talent Management: Literature Review, Integrative Framework, and Suggestions for Further Research. *Journal of World Business, 45*(2), 122–133.

Tatum, B. D. (1999). *Why Are All the Black Kids Sitting Together in the Cafeteria?* Basic Books.

Taylor, F. W. (1911). *The Principles of Scientific Management*. Harper & Row.

Taylor, P., Kochhar, R., Fry, R., Velasco, G., & Motel, S. (2011, July). *Wealth Gaps Rise to Record Highs Between Whites, Blacks, and Hispanics* (Vol. 26). Pew Research Center.

Tedam, P., & Cane, T. (2022). "We Started Talking About Race and Racism After George Floyd": Insights from Research into Practitioner Preparedness for Anti-Racist Social Work Practice in England. *Critical and Radical Social Work, 10*(2), 260–279.

Templer, K. J., Tay, C., & Chandrasekar, N. A. (2006). Motivational Cultural Intelligence, Realistic Job Preview, Realistic Living Conditions Preview, and Cross-Cultural Adjustment. *Group & Organization Management, 31*(1), 154–173.

Tetlock, P. E., & Mitchell, G. (2009). Implicit Bias and Accountability Systems: What Must Organizations Do to Prevent Discrimination? *Research in Organizational Behavior, 29*, 3–38.

Tharenou, P., Latimer, S., & Conroy, D. (1994). How Do You Make It to the Top? An Examination of Influences on Women's and Men's Managerial Advancement. *Academy of Management Journal, 37*(4), 899–931.

Thiederman, S. (2003). *Making Diversity Work: Seven Steps for Defeating Bias in the Workplace*. Dearborn Trade.

Thomas, D. A. (1990). *Strategies for Managing Racial Differences in Work-Centered Develop-Mental Relationships* (Working paper). Wharton School of Business, University of Pennsylvania.

Thomas, D. A. (1993). Racial Dynamics in Cross-Race Developmental Relationships. *Administrative Science Quarterly, 38*(2), 169–194.

Thomas, D. A. (2001). The Truth About Mentoring Minorities: Race Matters. *Harvard Business Review, 79*(4), 98–112.

Thomas, D. A., & Alderfer, C. P. (1989). The Influence of Race on Career Dynamics: Theory and Research on Minority Career Experience. In M. B. Arthur, D. T. Hall, & B. S. Lawrence (Eds.), *Handbook of Career Theory* (pp. 133–158). Cambridge University Press.

Thomas, D. A., & Ely, R. J. (1996). Making Differences Matter: A New Paradigm for Managing Diversity. *Harvard Business Review, 74*(5), 79–90.

Thomas, D. C., & Lazarova, M. B. (2006). Expatriate Adjustment and Performance: Critical Review. In G. K. Stahl & I. Bjorkman (Eds.), *Handbook of Research in International Human Resource Management* (pp. 247–264). Edward Elgar Publishing.

Thomas, G. D., & Hollenshead, C. (2001). Resisting from the Margins: The Coping Strategies of Black Women and Other Women of Color Faculty Members at a Research University. *Journal of Negro Education, 70*(3), 166–175.

Thomas, K. M. (2005). *Diversity Dynamics in the Workplace.* Wadsworth.

Thomas, K. M. (2008). *Diversity Resistance in Organizations.* Lawrence Erlbaum.

Thomas, K. M., Hu, C., Gewin, A. G., Bingham, K., & Yanchus, N. (2005). The Roles of Protégé Race, Gender, and Proactive Socialization Attempts on Peer Monitoring. *Advances in Developing Human Resources, 7*(4), 540–555.

Thomas, R. R. (1991). *Beyond Race and Gender: Unleashing the Power of Your Total Work Force by Managing Diversity.* American Management Association.

Thomas, R. R., Jr. (1990, March/April). From Affirmative Action to Affirming Diversity. *Harvard Business Review, 68*(2), 107–117.

Thomas, R. R., Jr. (2006). *Building on the Promise of Diversity: How Can We Move to the Next Level in Our Workplaces, Our Communities and Our Society.* American Management Association.

Thomason, B., Opie, T., Livingston, B., & Sitzmann, T. (2023). "Woke" Diversity Strategies: Science or Sensationalism? *Academy of Management Perspectives.*

Thompson, M. S., & Keith, V. M. (2001). The Blacker the Berry: Gender, Skin Tone, Self-Esteem, and Self-Efficacy. *Gender and Society, 15*(3), 336–357.

Thorndike, E. L. (1898). Animal Intelligence: An Experimental Study of the Associate Processes in Animals. *Psychological Review Monograph Supplement, 2*(4), 1–8.

Thorndike, E. L. (1911). *Animal Intelligence: Experiment Studies.* Macmillan.

Tolman, E. C. (1932). *Purposive Behavior in Animals and Men.* Century.

Tolman, E. C. (1938). The Determiners of Behavior at a Choice Point. *Psychological Review, 45*(1), 1–41.

Tomaskovic-Devey, D. (1993). *Gender & Racial Inequality at Work: The Sources and Consequences of Job Segregation*. Cornell University ILR Press.

Tomaskovic-Devey, D., & Stainback, K. (2007). Discrimination and Desegregation: Equal Opportunity Progress in US Private Sector Workplaces Since the Civil Rights Act. *The Annals of the American Academy of Political and Social Science, 609*(1), 49–84.

Tomaskovic-Devey, D., Zimmer, C., Stainback, K., Robinson, C., Taylor, T., & McTague, T. (2006). Documenting Desegregation: Segregation in American Workplaces by Race, Ethnicity, and Sex, 1966–2003. *American Sociological Review, 71*(4), 565–588.

Tourangeau, A. E., & McGilton, K. (2004). Measuring Leadership Practices of Nurses Using the Leadership Practices Inventory. *Nursing Research, 53*(3), 182–189.

Treviño, L. K., Weaver, G. R., & Reynolds, S. J. (2006). Behavioral Ethics in Organizations: A Review. *Journal of Management, 32*(6), 951–990.

Trevino, L. K., & M. E. Brown. (2004). Managing to Be Ethical: Debunking Five Business Ethics Myths. *The Academy of Management Executive, 18*(2), 69–81.

Triana, M. D., Carmen, P. G., Chapa, O., Richard, O., & Colella, A. (2021). Sixty Years of Discrimination and Diversity Research in Human Resource Management: A Review with Suggestions for Future Research Directions. *Human Resource Management, 60*(1), 145–204. https://doi.org/10.1002/hrm.22052

Tushman, M. L., & Anderson, P. (1986). Technological Discontinuities and Organizational Environments. *Administrative Science Quarterly, 31*(3), 439–465.

Tversky, A., & Kahneman, D. (1983). Judgment Under Uncertainty: Heuristics and Biases. In D. Kahneman, P. Slovic, & A. Tversky (Eds.), *Judgement Under Uncertainty* (pp. 3–22). Cambridge University Press.

Tziner, A., Murphy, K. R., Cleveland, J. N., & Roberts-Thompson, G. P. (2001). Relationships Between Attitudes Toward Organizations and Performance Appraisal Systems and Rating Behavior. *International Journal of Selection and Assessment, 9*(3), 226–239.

Ulrich, D., & Smallwood, N. (2007). *Leadership Brand: Developing Customer-Focused Leaders to Drive Performance and Build Lasting Value*. Harvard Business School Press.

U.S. Department of Labor. (1997). *Women's Bureau. Update*. U.S. Department of Labor.

U.S. Department of Labor. (2011). *Equal Pay Act of 1963, as Amended*. Retrieved October 19, 2011, from United States Department of Labor http://www.dol.gov/oasam/regs/statutes/equal_pay_act.htm

U.S. Equal Employment Opportunity Commission. (2013). *Fiscal Year 2013: Performance and Accountability Report.* http://www.eeoc.gov/eeoc/plan/upload/2013par.pdf

Vallas, S. P. (2003). Rediscovering the Color Line with Work Organizations: The 'Knitting of Racial Groups' Revisited. *Work and Occupations, 30*(4), 379–400.

Van Der Roest, D., Kleiner, K., & Kleiner, B. (2011). Self-Efficacy: The Biology of Confidence. *Culture & Religion Review Journal, 2011*(1), 26–35.

Van Ewijk, A. R. (2011). Diversity and Diversity Policy: Diving into Fundamental Differences. *Journal of Organizational Change Management, 24*(5), 680–694.

Van Laer, K., & Janssens, M. (2011). Ethnic Minority Professionals' Experiences with Subtle Discrimination in the Workplace. *Human Relations, 64*(9), 1203–1227.

Van Landingham, H., Ellison, R. L., Laique, A., Cladek, A., Khan, H., Gonzalez, C., & Dunn, M. R. (2022). A Scoping Review of Stereotype Threat for BIPOC: Cognitive Effects and Intervention Strategies for the Field of Neuropsychology. *The Clinical Neuropsychologist, 36*(2), 503–522.

Vardi, Y. (1980). Organizational Career Mobility: An Integrative Model. *Academy of Management Review, 5*(3), 341–355.

Van de Ven, A. H., & P. E. Johnson. (2006). Knowledge for Theory and Practice. *Academy of Management Review, 31*(4), 802–821.

Vaughn, B. (2014). *Diversity Training.* CDP Exam Study Guide. The Institute for Diversity Certification. Lulu.com

Vergano, D. (2011, February 17). Watson Dominated at 'Jeopardy!—But What Else Can It Do? *USA Today*, p. 2D.

Viswesvaran, C. (2001). Assessment of Individual Job Performance: A Review of the Past Century and a Look Ahead. In N. Anderson, D. S. Ones, H. K. Sinangil, & C. Viswesvaran (Eds.), *Handbook of Industrial, Work and Organizational Psychology* (Vol. 1, pp. 110–126). Sage.

Vogel, B., Reichard, R. J., Batistič, S., & Černe, M. (2021). A Bibliometric Review of the Leadership Development Field: How We Got Here, Where We Are, and Where We Are Headed. *The Leadership Quarterly, 32*(5), 101381.

Von Bergen, C. W., Soper, B., & Foster, T. (2002). Unintended Negative Effects of Diversity Management. *Public Personnel Management, 31*(2), 239–252.

Voss, J. F. (1978). Cognition and Instruction: Toward a Cognitive Theory of Learning. In A. Lesgold, J. Pellegrino, S. Fokkema, & R. Glaser (Eds.), *Cognitive Psychology and Instruction* (pp. 13–26). Plenum.

Vroom, V. H. (1964). *Work and Motivation.* Wiley.

Vroom, V. H. (1973). A New Look at Managerial Decision Making. *Organizational Dynamics, 1*(4), 66–80.

Vroom, V. H. (1995). *Work and Motivation.* Jossey-Bass.

Vroom, V. H. (2003). Educating Managers for Decision Making and Leadership. *Management Decision, 41*(10), 968–978.

Vroom, V. H., & Maier, N. R. F. (1961). Industrial Social Psychology. *Annual Review of Psychology, 12*(1), 413–446.

Vroom, V. H., & MacCrimmon, K. R. (1968). Toward A Stochastic Model of Managerial Careers. *Administrative Science Quarterly, 13*(1), 26–46.

Vygotsky, L. S. (1979). Consciousness as a Problem in the Psychology of Behavior. *Soviet Psychology, 176*(4), 3–35. (Original work published 1924). http://www.eeoc.gov/eeoc/plan/upload/2013par.pdf

Vygotsky, L. S. (1987). *The Collected Works of L.S. Vygotsky, Vol. 1* (R. W. Rieber & A. S. Carton, Eds.). Plenum Press.

Wajcman, J. (2013). *Managing Like a Man: Women and Men in Corporate Management*. Wiley.

Waldman, D. A., & Sparr, J. L. (2022). Rethinking Diversity Strategies: An Application of Paradox and Positive Organization Behavior Theories. *Academy of Management Perspectives*. https://doi.org/10.5465/amp.2021.0183

Walker, B. A., & Hanson, W. C. (1992). Valuing Differences at Digital Equipment Corporation. In S. E. Jackson (Ed.), *Diversity in the Workplace: Human Resources Initiatives* (pp. 119–137). Guilford.

Wallace, H., Hoover, K. F., & Pepper, M. B. (2014). Multicultural Ethics and Diversity Discourse. *Equality, Diversity and Inclusion: An International Journal, 33*(4), 318–333.

Walton, M. (1986). *The Deming Management Method*. Perigee.

Walton, R. E. (1985). From Control to Commitment in the Workplace. *Harvard Business Review, 63*(2), 77–84.

Wang, H. L. (2022). *The U.S. Census Sees Middle Eastern and North African People as White: Many don't*. https://www.npr.org/2022/02/17/107918 1478/us-census-middle-eastern-white-north-african-mena

Wang, M. (2011). Integrating Organizational, Social, and Individual Perspectives in Web 2.0-Based Workplace E-Learning. *Information Systems Frontiers, 13*(2), 191–205. https://doi.org/10.1007/s10796-009-9191-y

Warren, A. K. (2009). *Cascading Gender Biases, Compounding Effects: An Assessment of Talent Management Systems*. Catalyst.

Watson, J. B. (1913). Psychology as the Behaviorist Sees It. *Psychological Review, 20*(2), 157–177.

Watson, L. B., & Henderson, J. (2023). The Relation Between Gendered Racial Microaggressions and Traumatic Stress Among Highly Educated Black Women. *The Counseling Psychologist, 51*(2), 210–241.

Watson, W. E., Kumar, K., & Michaelsen, L. K. (1993). Cultural Diversity's Impact on Interaction Process and Performance: Comparing Homogeneous and Diverse Task Groups. *Academy of Management Journal, 36*(3), 590–602.

Waytz, A. (2016). The Limits of Empathy. (Cover Story). *Harvard Business Review, 94*(1), 68–73.

Weber, M. (1964). *The Theory of Social and Economic Organization*. Free Press.

Weinberg, A. K., & Destiny, M. (1935). *A Study of Nationalist Expansionism in American History.* The Johns Hopkins Press.

Weiner, B. (1985). An Attributional Theory of Achievement Motivation and Emotion. *Psychological Review, 92*(4), 548–573.

Welch, J. (2005). *Winning.* HarperCollins.

Wellner, A. (2000). How Do YOU Spell Diversity? *Training, 37*(4), 34–38.

Wenstop, F., & Myrmel, A. (2006). Structuring Organizational Value Statements. *Management Research News, 29*(11), 673–683.

Wentling, R. M., & Palma-Rivas, N. (1998). Current Status and Future Trends of Diversity Initiatives in the Workplace: Diversity Experts' Perspective. *Human Resource Development Quarterly, 9*(3), 235–253.

Werner, J. M., & DeSimone, R. L. (2012). *Human Resource Development* (6th ed.). South-Western.

Wesley, Y., & Scoloveno, M. A. (2005). Perception of Self, Motherhood, and Gender Attitudes Among Black Women. In J. Lee (Ed.), *Gender Roles* (pp. 33–52). Nova Science Publishers.

Wheeler, S. C., Jarvis, W. B. G., & Petty, R. E. (2001). Think Unto Others: The Self-Destructive Impact of Negative Racial Stereotypes. *Journal of Experimental Social Psychology, 37*(2), 173–180.

Whitlock, J. (2013, November 8). *Martin Walked into Twisted World: He Confronted an Unrelenting, Prison Yard Mentality in the Miami Locker Room.* ESPN. http://espn.go.com/nfl/story/_/id/9941696/jonathan-martin-wal ked-twisted-world-led-incognito

Whitman, M., & Hamilton, J. O. C. (2010). *The Power of Many: Values for Success in Business and in Life.* Three Rivers Press.

Whitmarsh, L., Brown, D., Cooper, J., Hawkins-Rodgers, Y., & Wentworth, D. K. (2007, March). Choices and Challenges: A Qualitative Exploration of Professional Women's Career Patterns. *The Career Development Quarterly, 55*(3), 225–236.

Wieand, P. (2002). Drucker's Challenge: Communication and the Emotional Glass Ceiling. *Ivey Business Journal, 66*(5), 32–37.

Williams, M. T., Skinta, M. D., & Martin-Willett, R. (2021). After Pierce and Sue: A Revised Racial Microaggressions Taxonomy. *Perspectives on Psychological Science, 16*(5), 991–1007.

Williams, K. Y., & O'Reilly III, C. A. (1998). Demography and Diversity in Organizations: A Review of 40 Years of Research. *Research in Organizational Behavior, 20,* 77–140.

Wilson, B. L., Diedrich, A., Phelps, C. L., & Choi, M. (2011). Bullies at Work: The Impact of Horizontal Hostility in the Hospital Setting and Intent to Leave. *Journal of Nursing Administration, 41*(11), 453–458.

Winnubst, S. (2004). Is the Mirror Racist? Interrogating the Space of Whiteness. *Philosophy & Social Criticism, 30*(1), 25–50.

Wittrock, M. C. (1978). The Cognitive Movement in Instruction. *Educational Psychologist, 13*(1), 15–29.

Wlodkowski, R. J., & Ginsberg, M. B. (1995). *Diversity & Motivation: Culturally Responsive Teaching. Jossey-Bass Higher and Adult Education Series. Jossey-Bass Education Series, Jossey-Bass Social and Behavioral Science Series.* Jossey-Bass.

Woehr, D. J., & Huffcutt, A. I. (1994). Rater Training for Performance Appraisal: A Quantitative Review. *Journal of Occupational and Organizational Psychology, 67*(3), 189–205.

Wolfgruber, D., Einwiller, S., & Wloka, M. (2022). *Tackling the Backlash: Dealing with Internal and External Criticism of D&I Initiatives* (No. 16). Communication Insights.

Wolley, M. (2021). Making Diversity and Equity Bad Words Is Problematic. *Indianapolis Business Journal, 42*(21).

Womack, J. P., & Jones, D. T. (1996). *Lean Thinking: Banish Waste and Create Wealth in Your Corporation.* Simon & Schuster.

Women in the Workplace: A Research Roundup. (Cover story). (2013). *Harvard Business Review, 91*(9), 86–89.

Wonacott, M. E. (2001). *Leadership Development in Career and Technical Education* (Eric Digest No. 225). ERIC Clearinghouse on Adult, Career and Vocational Education.

Wonderlic, E. F., & Associates. (1983). *Wonderlic Personnel Test Manual.* Author.

Wong, C.-S., & Law, K. S. (2002). The Effects of Leader and Follower Emotional Intelligence on Performance and Attitude: An Exploratory Study. *The Leadership Quarterly, 13*(3), 243–274.

Wong, G., Derthick, A. O., David, E. J. R., Saw, A., & Okazaki, S. (2014). The What, the Why, and the How: A Review of Racial Microaggressions Research in Psychology. *Race and Social Problems, 6*, 181–200.

Woodcock, A., Hernandez, P. R., Estrada, M., & Schultz, P. (2012). The Consequences of Chronic Stereotype Threat: Domain Disidentification and Abandonment. *Journal of Personality and Social Psychology, 103*(4), 635.

Woodard, C. (2011). *American Nations: A History of the Eleven Rival Regional Cultures of North America.* Penguin.

Woodard, C. (2013). Up in Arms: The Battle Lines of Today's Debates over Gun Control, Stand-Your-Ground Laws, and Other Violence-Related Issues Were Drawn Centuries Ago by America's Early Settlers. *Tufts University Alumni Magazine*, A91.

Woody, B. (1992). *Black Women in the Workplace: Impacts on Structural Change in the Economy.* Greenwood.

Wright, P. M., & McMahan, G. C. (1992). Theoretical Perspectives for Strategic Human Resource Management. *Journal of Management, 18*(2), 295–320.

Wulf, W. A. (1999). Diversity in Engineering. In *Moving Beyond Individual Programs to Systemic Change, WEPAN Annual Conference Proceedings* (pp. 9–16). WEPAN Member Services, West Lafayette, IN.

Yadav, S., & Lenka, U. (2020). Diversity management: A systematic review. *Equality, Diversity and Inclusion: An International Journal, 39*(8), 901–929.

Yang, J. R., & Liu, J. (2021, January 19). *Strengthening accountability for discrimination: Confronting Fundamental Power Imbalances in the employment relationship*. Economic Policy Institute. https://www.epi.org/unequalpower/publications/strengthening-accountability-for-discrimination-confronting-fundamental-power-imbalances-in-the-employment-relationship/

Yoder, J. D., & Aniakudo, P. (1997). "Outsider Within" the Firehouse: Subordination and Difference in the Social Interactions of African American Women Firefighters. *Gender & Society, 11*(3), 324–341.

Yoshino, K., & Smith, C. (2013). *Uncovering Talent: A New Model of Inclusion*. Deloitte University, The Leadership Center for Inclusion.

Yukl, G. (1989). Managerial Leadership: A Review of Theory and Research. *Journal of Management, 15*(2), 251–289. https://doi.org/10.1177/014920638901500207

Zavattaro, S. M., & Bearfield, D. (2022). Weaponization of Wokeness: The Theater of Management and Implications for Public Administration. *Public Administration Review, 82*(3), 585–593. https://doi.org/10.1111/puar.13484

Zenger, J., & Folkman, J. (2012). *A Study in Leadership—Women Do It Better Than Men*. Zenger Folkman.

Zenger, J., Ulrich, D., & Smallwood, N. (2000, March). The New Leadership Development. *Training and Development, 54*(3), 22–27.

Zhu, J., & Kleiner, B. (2000a). The Value of Training Changing Discriminatory Behavior at Work. *Equal Opportunities International, 19*(6/7), 5–10.

Zhu, J., & Kleiner, B. (2000b). The Failure of Diversity Training. *Nonprofit World, 18*(3), 12–14.

Zietsman, D., & April, K. (2021). Homosocial Reproduction: The Lived Workplace Experiences of Diverse Millennial Women—Part II. *Effective Executive, 24*(4)(12), 37–61. https://www.proquest.com/scholarly-journals/homosocial-reproduction-lived-workplace/docview/2622691488/se-2

Zigarmi, D., Nimon, K., Houson, D., Witt, D., & Diehl, J. (2009). Beyond Engagement: Toward a Framework and Operational Definition for Employee Work Passion. *Human Resource Development Review, 8*(3), 300–326. https://doi.org/10.1177/1534484309338171

INDEX

A
Accountability, 98
Affirmative Action (AA), 7
Allyship, 83, 85, 100
American Black women, 13, 46, 79, 117, 118, 121, 124, 138, 140, 141, 158
American Exceptionalism, 8
Anti-racism, 83, 84, 135, 144

B
behavioral channels, 74
bias, 117

C
Career development in practice, 112
career development plans, 57, 87, 114
Career development theories, 111
Career management systems, 122
Cognitive-based Theory, 18
Cognitive diversity hypothesis, 40
concrete ceiling, 121

Conditions in the Workplace Environment and Career Advancement, 115
Cultural appropriation, 54
Cultural Intelligence (CQ), 54

D
Detriment of inclusive language, 83
Digital and virtual work, 107, 108
Diversity and career development, 109
Diversity change, 73
Diversity expertise, 145, 166
Diversity history, 6
Diversity in practice, 45
Diversity intelligence® (DQ), 1, 3, 20, 87
definition, 11
diversity management, 1, 7, 24, 39, 45, 59, 166
Diversity management in practice, 55
diversity movement, 8
diversity-prediction, 39
Diversity terms, 35
Diversity theories, 38

Diversity training, 60
diversity-trumps-ability theorems, 39
DQ and leadership responsibility, 19
DQ and leadership strategy, 78
DQ leaders, 20
DQ model development, 22
DQ theory, 10

E
Eight Drivers of Execution and DQ
    Implications, 81
Emotional intelligence (EQ), 50
employee creativity, viii
Equal Employment Opportunity
    Commission (EEOC), 16, 17,
    20, 21, 25, 35, 46–48, 118, 136,
    137, 162
Equity theory, 18
Executive Order 11246 (affirmative
    action or AA), 61
External obstacles, 80

F
Floyd, George, 25, 83, 84, 119, 135,
    144
formative evaluations, 98
Futile Efforts and Exhaustion, 135

G
glass ceiling, 122

H
High EQ versus DQ Implications and
    Propositions, 90
Holland's theory, 111
homophily, 115, 116
Homosocial reproduction, 116
Hughes' Diversity Intelligence (DQ)
    Conceptual Model, 23

Hughes's *Human Resource
    Development (HRD) Value
    Creation Model*, 2
Hughes and Liang DQ scale© 2020,
    46
Hughes five values, 2, 4, 5, 59, 123
Hughes, Langston, 7

I
Inaccurate performance ratings, 89
Inclusive language, 83
intellectual/mental intelligence (IQ),
    8
Intelligent quotient (IQ), 50
Intentional behaviors, 11
inter-personnel diversity, 4
intersectionality, 16, 79

L
Leadership-related intelligence
    assessments, 86
Leadership styles, 53
Leaders' lack of interpersonal skills, 12
Leaders' need for DQ, 14
Leaders Words Diminish Black
    Females as Human Beings, 14
Location value, 5

M
Maintenance value, 5
Manifest destiny, 8, 9
Manmade Designation of Diverse
    Peoples, 9
marginalized, 7
microaggression, 37, 38
Modification value, 6

N
National HRD (NHRD), 25

definition, 25
Negative intentional behaviors, 11

O
Occupational segregation, 116
Organizational mindsets, 139
organization development (OD)
    initiatives, 4
organization management, 99
Organization management of
    intelligences, 89

P
Passive aggressive behavior and
    microaggressions, 85
patriarchy, vii
people and technology, 1
People as Technology (PT) conceptual
    model, 2
Personal Obstacles and Career
    Advancement, 118
philosophical perspective, 4
Power of position, 56
protected class, 1, 13, 16, 25, 26, 40,
    47, 48, 55, 59, 81, 84, 98, 108,
    154, 156, 165
Protected class employees, 47
Protected class employee voice and
    career advancement, 119
protected class groups, 10

R
Racism, 8
Relationship management, 13
Resistance to DQ, 17

S
Self-management of intelligences, 86
Social capital theory, 52
Social segregation, 116

Spatial segregation, 116
Stereotype threat, 116
Stereotyping, 137
Structural segregation, 116
Subtle forms of racism, 116

T
Talent development strategies, 108
Team player and career advancement,
    120
The DQ paradigm, 45
The model minority viewpoint, 36
theory, 38
theory of diversity management, 39
Theory of successful intelligence, 139
theory of work adjustment (TWA),
    113
The Power of Language and the
    Impact of Labels, 83
The seven points, 2
Time value, 6

U
Unfair workplace environment, 115
UN sustainable development goal,
    156, 157
Use value, 5

V
value-in-diversity hypothesis, 38
valuing people and technology, 1
Visibility of protected class employees,
    57
Voice of protected class employees, 85

W
Within group diversity, 142
workforce inter-personnel diversity
    talent management system, 4
workplace environment, 115

Printed in the USA
CPSIA information can be obtained
at www.ICGtesting.com
LVHW080146221123
764347LV00056B/792

9 783031 332494